HOW POEMS THINK

AP   RHYMES   Gibbons '03

HOW POEMS THINK

Reginald Gibbons

The University of Chicago Press   Chicago and London

REGINALD GIBBONS is the Frances Hooper Professor of Arts
and Humanities at Northwestern University. His most recent poetry
collections are *Creatures of a Day*, a finalist for the National Book Award;
and *Slow Trains Overhead: Chicago Poems and Stories.*

The University of Chicago Press, Chicago 60637
The University of Chicago Press, Ltd., London
© 2015 by The University of Chicago
All rights reserved. Published 2015.
Printed in the United States of America

24 23 22 21 20 19 18 17 16 15   1 2 3 4 5

ISBN-13: 978-0-226-27795-0 (cloth)
ISBN-13: 978-0-226-27800-1 (paper)
ISBN-13: 978-0-226-27814-8 (e-book)
DOI: 10.7208/chicago/9780226278148.001.0001

Frontispiece: Reginald Gibbons, "Rhymes" (2013). Courtesy of the author.

Library of Congress Cataloging-in-Publication Data

Gibbons, Reginald, author.
How poems think / Reginald Gibbons.
pages ; cm
Includes bibliographical references and index.
ISBN 978-0-226-27795-0 (cloth : alk. paper) —
ISBN 978-0-226-27800-1 (pbk. : alk. paper) —
ISBN 978-0-226-27814-8 (e-book)
1. Poetry. 2. Poetry—Authorship. 3. Poetics. I. Title.
PN1031.G47 2015
808.1—dc23
2014043339

Contents

Introduction

HOW POEMS THINK

In this book, I explore a few of the many modes and devices of poetic thinking. I do so not comprehensively but illustratively. I don't propose a general theory of poetry, nor do I attempt a broad description of poetic thinking. Instead, I offer a gallery exhibition of some lesser-known exemplars of poetry's variety and of poetic difference and poetic continuity. Poetic thinking has technical, structural, and psychical aspects, and these encompass both the poet's process of composition and the reader's responsive process of understanding and experiencing the movement of a poem. How a poem thinks is the result of the poet's choices, the poetic mentality and poetic conventions shared with others, and the range of poetic possibilities overall. My exploration isn't about the uses of poetry, or its function or lack thereof in a society, or its alignment with ideals of one class or another either of society or of readers and listeners — whether elite or popular, independent minded or group identified, wealthy or poor, quietist or activist. Rather, I explore possibilities within language, poetic technique, and the poet's or writer's stance toward language and psyche. I explore what the poet understands poetry to be and to have been, and also some choices made by a poetic culture itself, as a historical continuum.

The stances that poets take toward everything *outside* poetry inevitably give particular leanings to what poetry *does*. The stances of a culture or mix of cultures, beyond readers and writers of poetry, both constrain and invite the individual imagination, offering some paths and avoiding others. Thus some portion of poetic thinking necessarily depends on thinking *outside* poetry. For example, some portion of religious thinking has not only been articulated, exemplified, and even created poetically but has also enabled and supported techniques of poetry. And vice versa.

The Latin *vice* means "instead of"; much of how poetry thinks is about an "instead of"—a "troping," a turning, an inversion, an inside-outing. (An "inside outing"—in the sense of an excursion—might be a way of characterizing the reading of a poem. Putting words on paper, or projecting them audibly into the air, is an "outing" of what is "inside" the poet. I come back to this in chapter 2.) Poetry plays on every element of language that we don't even notice when we are speaking. Rhythm, for example: When I was an undergraduate, I knew Clarence Brown, the scholar and translator of Osip Mandelshtam, who was supremely attentive to the fine points of language both literary and everyday. (Nadezhda Mandelshtam's *Hope Against Hope*, the first volume of her memoir of her husband, came out in English in 1970, and Brown urged me to read it; his own book on Mandelshtam came out in 1973, and I needed no urging. I read it greedily, because I wanted to know what in those Russian poems was so different from what I had understood poetry to be.) I recall Brown saying, with a smile, "Paronomasia and I'll tell you no lies." Brown's joke is based on a rhythmic figure, a few of which I describe later. The rhythm of "paronomasia" is the same as that of the words for which it has been substituted, "ask me no questions"; "paronomasia" is no verb, but it does have the word "no" inside it. (Very Russian.) Brown's joke means something like "Don't ask me for puns, and I'll tell you no lies," or "I'll give you no puns, and (thus) will tell you no lies." The joke creates two thoughts at once: the *rhythmic* pun on "paronomasia" (instead of a phonetic pun, the usual sort) requires us to think of and substitute not the similar-sounding words on which a pun plays but instead the rhythm of the words we have to recall from the full commonplace saying that is completed by "and I'll tell you no lies." The joke, by this rhythmic device, leaps past the phonetic resemblance that punning uses.

"This is all so poetic!" I might say, meaning by "poetic" what nobody usually means by this word. But it's what I'm after, in this book—a little of what nobody usually means by "poetic" but rather what the poets in my gallery *tend* to mean. A little poem by Walt Whitman comes to mind: "My Picture-Gallery." It was Donald Davie who first pointed this poem out to me, and, as poems will do when associated with a moment of learning, this one has stayed with me. Whitman wrote:

> In a little house keep I pictures suspended, it is not a fix'd house,
> It is round, it is only a few inches from one side to the other;
> Yet behold, it has room for all the shows of the world, all memories!
> Here the tableaus of life, and here the groupings of death;
> Here, do you know this? this is cicerone himself,
> With finger rais'd he points to the prodigal pictures.
>
> (Whitman 1982, 524)

If we were to recast Whitman's poem slightly for the sake of including the voice orchestrated by a poem, and the modes of poetic thinking of which a poem is capable, we might write (without any elegance of expression whatsoever), "In a little house keep I poems read and heard, it is not a fix'd house." The image-metaphor immediately begins to escape the poem's first use of it, for because it is in a poem, it calls to other poems and literary works. It is, as a metaphor, also Russian, it turns out, and allusions to it, and to many other such instances of this metaphor, buzz like cicadas, as Mandelshtam himself famously wrote. It's a figure used by Mandelshtam himself (to whom I will turn later): "Through life the skull develops / In all its forehead-breadth, from temple to temple; / It amuses itself with its immaculate sutures; / Its omniscient cupola gleams; / It foams with thought; it dreams of itself" (unpublished translation by Kutik and Gibbons). And a figure by William Goyen (to whom I turn in chapter 2): "Yet on the walls of my brain, frescoes [...] and over the dome of my brain Creations and Damnations, Judgments, Hells and Paradises (we are carriers of lives and legends—who knows the unseen frescoes on the private walls of the skull?)" (2000, 3).

We might continue our rephrasing of Whitman: "Yet behold, it has room for all the poems of the world! Here the crisscrossing thought and feeling, and here the ultimate language of meaning-making." I intend the chapters that follow as in part a poem gallery, and in part an exploration of how the poems say what they say, rather than an argument in favor of one interpretation or another of each one. Our full universal poem gallery exhibits a plenitude: on paper and on-screen and in voice recordings we possess an imaginary poetry anthology without end, like André Malraux's "museum without walls," or, as

Donald Davie rephrased it, "imaginary museum." But the poetry anthology without end is better than the universal art museum in that in one's own language the works are always originals, no matter where one finds them reproduced. The meaning-making of the original is undimmed, except by such loss of linguistic practice and cultural referents as the passage of time may have imposed. A poem re-creates its "aura" of human use each time it is spoken or typed or hand-inscribed or published again. Translations are indeed imperfect reproductions in the sense of their being only approximate to the original—damaged by their transit even though made by hand, so to speak. But when translations represent not only a poem but also some of its poetics, they can bring over something of poetry's powers that the target language does not have, or does not see, and thus does not *use*.

Poetry is almost always communicative in principle and in purpose (and when it is *not* so, our perception of its refusal arises from our expectation that it will *be* so). This does not mean that it is always "true"—a topic that goes back to the very earliest poetry in the West. Although the earliest poetry we know made much of being a special kind of truth, even Hesiod, when he told how he got his gift from the Muses, said that the particularly wonderful way of using language that they taught him is a way of telling lies, also. (He, too, made the claim, however, that he was telling the truth.) Like fiction, poetry is a way of saying what is true in some ways and in other ways not, depending on what one means by "true." During the twentieth century and the beginning of the twenty-first, the truth of poetry has again been contested both on the grounds of its failure to articulate aspects of reality that exceed powers of articulation and on philosophical grounds, which question the ability of any mode of language to articulate *any* ultimate truths. In response to such dilemmas, poetry has made use of every communicative resource of everyday language of all sorts, and some poets have devised ways of *not* communicating, by means of poetic techniques, and, most recently, some have entirely rejected the use of poetic *technē* (the ancient Greek word for any art or craft, high or everyday) while nevertheless calling their compositions poems. And, meanwhile, language is always in the process of being reshaped by usage and by the media that saturate us linguistically, day and night, inside the nearly inescapable dome of commercial and political public spheres. Yet poetic *technē* persists, as if it were an impulse in language itself (as I believe it to be, if "in language itself" is understood to mean "in our thoroughly linguistic human mode of being"—that is, in the infinitely complex ways we use language).

So poetry no less than speech makes use of the continual changes in language. Some of these are new memes ("at the end of the day"); and many such phrases pop out of frauds, scandals, and crimes, and the display behavior of human life; and some, with humor or opposition irony, inventively redeem for a moment the teeming linguistic terrarium in which both eloquent and horrifying language live.

Consider that, from ancient times, poetry has made frequent use of the image-metaphor of the honeybee. For the ancient Greek poet Pindar, it was one of his metaphors for the way song thinks: "the finest of victory hymns / flit like a bee from one theme to another" (Pythian 10.53–54; Pindar 1997, 1:365). Ah, but now there's our use of the (formerly) innocent word *drone*. The first English-language attestation of this kind of bee was around the year 1000. In 1946, the word was militarized (as attested in the *Oxford English Dictionary*). The otherwise useless male bee, a few of whom will impregnate a queen (thanks to our bee-house terminology, we imagine an antiquated form of human governance), is "a non-worker." Figuratively, then, *drone* has been used to mean "a lazy idler, a sluggard." But events and mechanical, weaponized drones move fast, and poetry does too: I have seen good poems with military drones inside them, and in Los Angeles not long ago, according to an online newspaper report, a man was planning to solicit donations for a delivery via drone of "poem bombs" accompanied by wildflower seeds. (To me this recalls young women poking the stems of plucked dandelion flowers and other blooms into the barrels of the rifles of troops staring at nothing, standing stiffly, at the March on the Pentagon in 1967, and elsewhere; if I were to use such a historical layering in a poem, I'd be very Ezra-Poundian.) For millennia, bees were a widespread symbol of harmonious and productive collaboration; honey, one of the great goods of life, has long been an emblem of human delight, as when Pindar called song-poetry, melody, and singing "honey-sweet." (In chapter 7, I touch on his demilitarized arrows—another of his metaphors for songs.) There is a Proto-Indo-European root that means "bee," so we know that long before there was a Pindar, that prehistoric language, the great-grandmother many times over of our English, was spoken in climates where bees were present. In a hive in Troy, perhaps, there was a future queen-mating Paris-bee who shirked work, just as Paris half-avoided battle with the Achaeans in order to make love to Helen (*Iliad* 3.421–47). In one of the war zones of our time, not so far from Troy, American military drones are returning successfully to their bases with clean wings. I am just following the associations, thinking—although in prose, and stumblingly, and attentive to the cicadas—in one of the ways a poem can think.

Often in this book, I use translated poems and translated poetics. If the inadequacy of most poetry translation also raises in the reader the question of how I, who have no Russian, can present so much comment on Russian poetry, I must answer that, first, I have had a very patient, passionately engaged, completely undaunted, and learned guide in the Russian poet Ilya Kutik. In our many sessions working together over a number of years, he has explained, rephrased, and analogized lines and passages in Russian poems and offered many solutions of his own in our translation of them, as together we have led English along some unfamiliar paths and found some unexpected destinations. Kutik's learning is completely enmeshed in his practice. He is one of those who can remember and quote a multitude of poems not his own.

And, second, I've done some homework, and the process of translating Russian poems with Kutik has given me the opportunity to try out in English some new moves (for English and for me). One especially daunting example: Osip Mandelshtam anachronistically likened Dante's characteristic image-metaphor to an airplane, which, while flying, constructs and launches another airplane, and then the second airplane does the same (I return to this in chapter 3). That is, only by means of the first airplane (image and metaphor) can the poem attain the second one, and only from the second one can it create the third, and so on. Mandelshtam's metaphor for metaphor itself— a meta-metaphor—is more startling than an organic meta-metaphor might be, since what is organic already reproduces itself from itself. Air speed was a new reality of Mandelshtam's era. Speed of thought, speed of simultaneous paths of thought (as if through air), comes into my discussion later as one of the characteristic modes of poetic thinking, but such speed depended on no mechanical analogies until, in the modern world, mechanical inventions caught up partway to the speed of thought. ("Thoughts swift as the wind," Sophocles wrote in the "ode to man" in *Antigone* [Sophocles 2011, 71], and we read such a line only to realize that in our world the wind is as slow as a worm. Mandelshtam's poems enact this acceleration in the human experience of physical speed as an acceleration of the speed of thought, and when we look back at Dante, for whom Sophokles' comparison was still valid, we see Mandelshtam updated Sophokles' metaphor, anachronistically likening Dante's swiftness of poetic thought to the speed of an airplane.)

Like the small portion of ancient Greek poetry that I have studied, the Russian poems on which I have worked with Kutik use a language that is highly inflected grammatically, which allows for great flexibility of word order, and also philosophically and theologically inflected (respectively). Because of the history of Russian culture, the Russian language is linguistically, poetically, and theologically much closer to ancient Greek than is any other language except modern Greek itself. Russian does things that English seems to have chosen *not* to do, and in some important ways simply *can't* do. Much of this book, in fact, could not have been conceived except as the aftereffect of translating poetry from Greek and Russian, as well as a few other languages. I began my study of poetry long ago by reading, writing, and translating, and translation has given me access not only to more poems but also to other modes of poetic thinking.

I also saw that the thinking and writing of the English poet and critic Donald Davie, who was one of my early teachers, and the French writer Hélène Cixous, an acquaintance much later in my life—in both their "primary" and their "secondary" works—were a self-divided inner process of translation back and forth between opposed impulses. They both wrestled with and wrestled free of some portion of what was given in the temperament and linguistic formation of each, in a process of becoming. That thought leads me to a poetic line that we might read as merely a temporal exaggeration of the life-long development of the poet's *technē* and thinking, which becomes itself only through its changes. This is the first line of Stéphane Mallarmé's sonnet "The Tomb of Edgar Poe": "Tel qu'en Lui-même enfin l'éternité le change" (1959, 90; in my translation, "Such a one as eternity at last changes into himself"). If we can hope for a life of poetry as long as that of man, then poetry will continue to become more and more itself only if it continues to draw, as it has done, on all its resources from beginning to end.

I use Davie, Cixous, and the many other poets and writers whom I quote and ponder to find my way at least somewhat against the grain of some of our assumptions about poetry, about composition and the psychic processes involved in it, and about language. I invite the reader to explore with me the implications of a few unfamiliar or persistent yet somewhat hidden aspects of poetics and to enter the push and pull of how poems think.

First, in chapter 1, I consider a personal, individual, aspect of writing poems: the poet's relationship to what seems to be in the way. I mean the grain of the poet's own linguistic and artistic being—mind, culture, and textures of writerly traditions. I draw on my own use, at different times in my life, of Davie and Cixous—the oddest literary couple ever, I concede. Both of them, in completely different ways and on different grounds, raise the question of how the poet, the writer, can gauge the honesty of his or her own efforts.

During the years when I was studying with Davie and for a few years afterward, he was seeking new poetic forms and shifting his poetic language somewhat away from abstraction and toward concreteness— and also a more spontaneous responsiveness. He was working his way through an artistic transition that pulled him in opposite directions— toward Modernism (which English poets regarded as very American), especially the work of Ezra Pound, and yet also toward the attractiveness of the Englishness of language and affect represented by Thomas Hardy. Davie's *Essex Poems* (1969) implicitly acknowledged his study of Russian and particularly the late poems of Boris Pasternak; this artistic encounter opened Davie's poetry into a new intensity, as Angela Livingstone (2014) and others have suggested. (Pound, T. S. Eliot, and other English-language Modernists do not seem to have known anything about the poetic techniques of Pasternak, Mandelshtam, or Marina Tsvetaeva, so it remained for a few later poets to push English-language poetic thinking a little way toward that other modernist *technē*.) Davie showed me the virtue (and the discomfort) of intellectual and artistic restlessness. I could never match the English bluntness of his honesty as both poet and critic.

In Cixous's work, from among her various purposes, I was drawn to her sense that freedom of thought, intuition, and being may only be possible if it's put under ultimate strain. Her example of how to test one's own writing and thinking was to choose one's own small canon, one's core texts. These must be writers or specific works that really *do* shake one's sense of one's own abilities yet which appeal deeply, intuitively, to one's artistic impulses. (They don't have to agree with one another artistically, or even—so to speak—like each other, across the centuries. Each is a focus of the writer's attention, and at best they complement each other in this regard, each one urging and permitting some particular urgency belonging to him or her.) The writer uses his or her little canon as a self-chosen challenge rather than as a source of approval. Now, the life of American poetry in the last hundred years has been a contradiction—American poets have often chosen an artistic libertarianism, not unrelated to narcissistic individuality, and yet, simultaneously, they have heard the claims of group identity and fashion. Not everyone can be entirely comfortable with an artistic restlessness that they cannot *join*. But then, the trajectories of Cixous and Davie suggest in different ways that such comfort is a mistake. And I don't at all dismiss the urgency of "thinking through" (and what I might call "singing through") some of the most perplexing experiences of identity—artistic and social—in America. Readers too explore such possibilities and cross-tensions. For me, this book is itself an indirect record of some of my own choices—at least a few that I could think through, while others have remained opaque to me, as in all of us who, as both readers and writers, seek the modes and paces of the kind of thinking and feeling that poems do.

Second, in chapter 2, I look at what I see as the necessary and productive self-alienation of the poet, who must work in words so closely, and with such openness to language, that only by coming to see the words on the page, and to hear them in the ear, as belonging as much to themselves and to the language as to the poet who composes them, can the poet discover *how* to think *with* them and *through* them, beyond the artistic limits of the ingrained individual habits of language and poetic thinking, and beyond the limits imposed by the poet's self-positioning within culture. But to compose this way, and to take pleasure as a reader in poems composed this way, runs against the dominant *mode* (in many different *forms*) of modern and contemporary American poetry.

Third, in chapter 3, with a focus on rhyme, I move to poetic thinking, not in the sense of the individual poet's modes of thought, but rather in the sense in which language itself is freed to think in poetry. I have read through the *Oxford Book of English Verse* looking for examples of rhyme that leads the poetic thinking rather than solely ornamenting the poem, and there is very little; I have looked for examples of what Ilya Kutik calls "centrifugal" rhyme, and there isn't any. The purpose, the function, of rhyme in the work of some of the greatest modern Russian poets is to throw the poem off course with the unexpectedness of what the poet discovers when the second word in the rhyme-pair shows up — off course, not with a sense of alarm but with the opposite feeling: discovery. And not for the purpose of pleasures, such as they may be, of near randomness, but rather those of unforeseen rightness. The goal is what was *not* foreseen and is *therefore* more prized for its justness as a movement of poetic thinking. I'll paraphrase and put a few crutches (as Kutik calls them) under my English-language expansion of some famous lines by Marina Tsvetaeva: The (true) poet takes care to *begin* a poem at a point that is already distant, already beyond the sorts of places where she might have begun the poem — in thought, in language. And then — to go only *further*. Not to safety (linguistic, emotional, structural, social, etc.), and not to disclosure, but to something unprecedented as expression and as something *seen*.

Fourth, chapters 4 and 5 on apophatic thinking move pretty far beyond English-language poetic thinking and the English-language reader's repertoire of responses, as I try to cultivate, using examples both in English and in translation, an awareness of a negative mode of thought. Such thinking has been very difficult for me to naturalize for myself, so I do not underestimate its elusiveness at its most imaginative. I cannot help thinking and feeling with an ingrained English-language mind, so when I try to grasp what could be done in translating a particularly difficult figure or idea in, say Mandelshtam, I realize that I am learning to *imitate* apophatic thought without actually *practicing* it. So in these chapters I work my way from apophasis as a rhetorical device to apophasis as a mentality, by steps. (Well, steps are precisely what the apophatic does not do.) This mode of thinking seems to be an opportunity that only a few Western poets have taken; the concrete historical development of poetry in English is an avoid-

ance of it almost entirely, or simply a failure to register it at all. English
has something of a dislike for it. Why that should have been so, I can
roughly guess, but I don't try to work it out in this book. It's not about
neurolinguistics; it's about aspects of our language, about culture and
theology, about the evolution of everyday English and American prag-
matism, taxonomical enthusiasm, fine discrimination, and the sheer
massiveness of the lexicon we use. Not surprisingly in this regard,
English and American (English) share the cataphatic Western mentality, even though to most poets and readers of poetry, English and
American poetry can be very different from each other. We English-
language citizens—or perhaps only subjects—might have thought
that language acquisition is almost the same experience for everyone,
but it is not. We learn not only how to speak but also how to think with
speaking, and the latter is determined subtly by some of the qualities of English and more generally by families, generations, techno-
logical eras, degrees of saturation by media old and new, schools and
churches, and the ethos of different sorts of workplaces and different
social classes. My two chapters on apophatic thinking cannot show
why it is a more developed mode of thought within Russian cultural
history, but by contrast we can see that we too have a kind of theology
of language, even if we never think of it that way. In poetry, our unconscious beliefs about language become more accessible to us as readers
(if our poets wish to approach such beliefs). A language may have its
own way of making various kinds of belief possible, including assumptions and beliefs about, and degrees of faith in, language itself. Since
such beliefs are different in Russian and English, the poetry is different and cannot be *translated* into English, or productively brought *into*
poetic composition in English, without an attempt to translate or generate the way that belief works—the poetics of what Russian words
do, as well as what they *say*.

I don't think the English theology of language has much to do with
a sense of the divine. And yet I can't be sure of that, because even in
the two creation stories at the beginning of Genesis we hear, at least
in the King James Version, something going on about language and
reality that has been Englished persuasively, even if it came originally
from Hebrew oral traditions (and Babylonian ones before that) and
has been translated and retranslated. Whatever language theology English has—I'm not speaking of *religious* belief but of what the English

language "believes" *about itself* and makes possible with its powers and makes impossible with its lack of other powers—is the opposite of the theology of language that came into being with Neoplatonism in late antiquity, and which then passed into Slavic languages because of the proselytizing of the Eastern Church among Slavic peoples. Hellenized, Orthodox-inflected Russian has a capacity for a kind of poetic meaning-making that we speakers of (British and American) English have scarcely ever practiced.

The concreteness and practical utility of English are much more like the pre-Christian qualities of ancient Greek. Pindar is wildly metaphorical and perhaps even more metonymical, but not mystical; Sophokles could convey sparkling qualities of the physical world, as in these fragments from lost tragedies: "Down the steep hills a grazing / antlered deer would come slowly / Lifting its nose [...] / And the fine points / Of its wide rack, / easing itself down unnoticed"; "As in green pale leaves / Of a tall poplar— / Even if in no- / Thing else—at the top / The morning air moves, / Flutters one feather" (Sophocles 2008, 81). The concreteness of English is like that of ancient Greek, it seems to me; for its legal and organizational language (Greek gods help us!), which has had so instrumental a function, English has depended on Latin. This English, this Greek, and this Latin do not nurture an apophatic mentality—which may be of no use at all in practical life, and we Americans and English have spent centuries toiling for the four horse-mounted and then horsepower-mounted doom-makers of our secular apocalypse: Practicality, Effectiveness, Change, and Money. But on the other hand, English does not *prevent* apophatic thinking in anyone who learns how to see with words, even some English words, in that particular way. I don't say, and I don't mean, that the rarity of apophatic thinking in English-language poetry is a failure of imagination; it has resulted from cultural and religious history and from poetic choices accumulating for centuries.

In the last four chapters, I look at a number of smaller elements, devices, and moves of poetic thinking in the context of the long-term resources of poetry. These unfortunately have undergone a very parsimonious selection by the passage of time. Yet they remain available for rediscovery and reuse, and even, it seems, for unwitting reuse, which may be the most interesting case of all. I look at the surprising antiquity of some aspects of poetry that we might have thought could only be modern, and the surprising survival of some aspects of the poetry of antiquity that we seem not even to notice, even though poets have gotten them into poems (also without, it seems, fully knowing).

I am no connoisseur of poetry handbooks or guides, but in those I have read I have not noticed any substantial discussion of the elements of the art and craft of poetry considered as modes of thinking and feeling. My purpose in this book is to describe some of the elements of poetry as ways of thinking that are especially entwined with the nature of this art. I would be eager to read books that look for the ways of thinking that are specific to other arts—how string quartets think, how dance thinks, how sculpture thinks—and of course no such book, even if it were very large, could even outline such a topic fully, much less detail it.

In depending as I do on some structuralist methods of thinking about language, specifically Roman Jakobson, Calvert Watkins, and Gregory Nagy, I do not mean or wish to try to participate in debates over the validity of such methods. What I use I have found completely persuasive, and in any case I am not qualified to sort out a position in general on structuralist linguistics, nor would doing so be of interest to me. And when I use the words *evoke* and *evocation*, I am not alluding to Louis Althusser's "interpellation" because I am not writing about the individual poet or reader as a citizen in an ideologized world, responding to what his society has formed him to be compliantly responsive to. Rather, I am writing about a psychic resource that makes us as poets and readers available to ourselves, able to experience and to nuance our own inner lives through the activity of reading and writing poems (and other kinds of literary works, especially fiction). My guide here is the psychoanalyst Christopher Bollas, and my use of him is simple, and, again, not meant to be taken as a participation in a larger debate on psychoanalysis or philosophy.

My quotations from Shakespeare's sonnets are all from the edition by Katherine Duncan-Jones (Shakespeare 2005); in the text I refer to them simply by number. All quotations from Emily Dickinson's poetry are cited according to Franklin's numbering (Dickinson 1999). Most of the quotations from Ilya Kutik are from personal communications; exceptions are noted in the text. English translations of classical poetry are my own unless otherwise noted. All the word definitions I quote are from the online *Oxford English Dictionary*. The

Greek definitions are from the *Greek-English Lexicon* (Liddell and Scott 1996). Proto-Indo-European root words are from the *American Heritage Dictionary of Indo-European Roots* (2011) and from the online source built on Julius Pokorny's work (Pokorny 2014).

I mention Osip Mandelshtam often—and so do some of the poets and writers whom I quote—and I prefer, among the several possible transliterations of his Russian name into English, the choice that includes that *h* in *sh*, for the sake of the sound it makes. But sources from which I quote use the older transliteration, Mandelstam. Spelling Greek names in English is always a problem. I prefer transliteration from the Greek: Sophokles, Kirkē, Phaiakians, and so on. But to choose familiarity over accuracy seems all but inevitably forced by convention, at least with regard to the very most familiar names. So sometimes, as in quotations, Sophocles, Circe, and the Phaeacians will duly be summoned into the reader's imagination by their Latinized names—as pronounced not in Latin but in English Latin. These and other ancient Greek names recognize their Latinized versions but are annoyed by them.

1

This Working against the Grain

In California around 1970, when in my early twenties I was living about fifteen miles inland from the shore of that "peaceful ocean" that was both a body of water and an idea, I was often trying to imagine how to write a poem that would be better, more interesting, than what I had written so far. I can still remember—because I have experienced it since—the mental sensation of pushing against a transparent barrier. So I went naming things and sensations, and extending sentences out to greater length on the wave-beaten New World west coast, where syntax too seemed a wave to be caught, ridden, an "articulate energy," in the transatlantic world of Donald Davie, with whom I was studying at Stanford. I was reading Robert Duncan, Kenneth Rexroth, William Everson, and Theodore Roethke; Adrienne Rich, Robert Lowell, César Vallejo, Pablo Neruda, Arthur Rimbaud, Stéphane Mallarmé, and Antonio Machado; Wang Wei, Tu Fu, Ezra Pound, Allen Ginsberg, and other poets. Poetic culture on the Pacific Rim included American and Latin American and Chinese poets I hadn't yet encountered on the East Coast, where I had been an undergraduate, nor on the Gulf Coast, where I had been too young and too provincial to become aware of what I might read either in English or in the Spanish I had already learned well. At Stanford I would write about the Spanish poet Luis Cernuda and translate his poems, under Davie's demanding eye, as my PhD dissertation and then first book. Doing so, in that cultural moment, and under that eye, meant becoming keenly aware of a particular and defining aspect of writing poetry in English: "the literary conscience—exact fidelity in language to the recognizable contours and spatial dispositions of the physical world" (Davie [2004, 137] on Pound). My new exemplars were not only E.P. but also the Poundian of that very region, Gary Snyder, who had been remaking Pound's Euro-poetics by thinking along a time-line that went all the way back to cave paintings, and thinking into the western American wilderness, and further west into Asia. And I was reading Denise Levertov's 1960s poems of a sensuous apprehend-ing of the physical world and the body, W. S. Merwin's *The Lice* and *The Carrier of Ladders*, James Wright's *The Branch Will Not Break* and *Shall We Gather at the River*, and his translations with Robert Bly of Neruda and Vallejo, and Bly's image work in *Silence in the Snowy Fields*. In Adrienne Rich's *Poems: Selected and New, 1950–1974*, a reader could see how, over those years, the images in the poems floated free of the formality with which she had begun and the thinking speeded up. At the same time, I was reading translations of classical Chinese poetry and field guides to western birds and trees in the mild-clime splen-dor of the landscapes of coastal Northern California and the magnifi-cence of the mountains and the air in Sierra Nevada parks. For the first time, I was reading Aristotle's *Poetics* closely and the treatise on awe by Longinus, *On the Sublime*. Near the end of my road trip west to California, before the interstate highways had been completed, through and toward places I had never before seen, my meandering route had led down into Gilroy on Highway 152 — as it was then. From above, I had seen and then had begun to enter a valley of farm fields and orchards, old trucks carrying crates of picked fruit and vegetables, migrant workers standing and bending in the fields under a Pacific Helios: plenty, beauty, and hardship. That too had been an encounter with a kind of sublimity but not frightening or incomprehensible: the human scale of it would compel me to respond. I had entered land-scape with awareness for the first time; my medium of response would be language; I was twenty-two.

Meanwhile in that part of the world: protest (and many poems, good and bad) against the war; political fistfights among compet-ing radical proselytizers; revolutionaries unarmed and armed; a sur-rounding para-academic community that included dropouts, stoners and hippies, and unaffiliated poets and writers. A charming friend I had known in the East was already an ex-grad student; after a semes-ter he had dropped out of physics and was subsisting by making house calls on ailing Volkswagens. Among English and writing graduate stu-dents there were group dinners for appetites enhanced by the intensity of intellectual discovery, poems completed, or weed; ramblings and wanderings on hiking trails and in conversation; weekend games of volleyball and softball; and disputes about the war and resistance and demonstrations, about poetic meter and free verse, metaphor and style. Amid frustration with deaf officials and anxiety about the war, anger at police departments, and the laughable or threatening intensity of enthusiasm for Mao among a few in my generation, there would come the occasional exclamation of an old-time Californian, growing two kinds of figs on her grafted garden tree or offering flowers from her beds, "You should have seen all this even ten years ago, when there were still orchards on El Camino Real!"

In Berkeley, on weekends spent in a poetic culture of more obscure, looser, improvisational, consciousness-annotating poems, there were stands on streets against cops, and on hillsides there were fragrant stands of laurel; the temptations were used books and LPs, winery outlets to which you took your own bottles, odd and improbable dwelling places, curious (long before they were licensed and bureaucratized) vendors of the handmade sitting cross-legged on the sidewalks. In San Francisco: music and cheap good food, more bookstores, the Vedanta Temple, the long-running festival of heedlessness in the park and the streets, and hippies. Along unsettled roads above low-lying towns, invasive eucalyptus trees had long flourished, and forests of native trees were thick with shadow. An abandoned apricot orchard still occupied a slope not so far from Stanford. In Half Moon Bay, broad silent fields of glowing pumpkins lay in thin fog; herons nested in treetops; on empty beaches, avocets were striding slowly, beaking through each wave's last thin rushing, and terns repeatedly dove with tucked wings and spear-point plunge. Sea otters lay in kelp beds close to shore, and dolphins arced across Monterey Bay. In the university library's copy of the *Hypnerotomachia Poliphili* (1499), shown to one of my classes by a professor, the printer's colophon was the image of a dolphin curved around the stem of a massive anchor. Even though poetry's powers of making meaning fully can be turned to any purpose, those powers seemed in that time inherently and sometimes courageously opposed, simply because of their complexity and subtlety and the sheer pleasures of them, to the realities of insistent war making and the continuing opposition to civil rights. Yet those same powers were seen as superfluous by makers of war and some activist poets, too.

There was more than sufficient blossoming in yards, woods, fields, flower gardens, bedrooms, minds, and poems, and also misery and unheard despair of many kinds, in many kinds of people; trash-fire smoke and shouting in some streets blended with incense and singing. Some of the PhD students were especially hungry for careers and competitive; many of the poets had no idea what might come next. A usually barefoot fellow graduate student in a seminar on poetry translation led by Davie had checked out the library's copy of Nicanor Parra's *Antipoems*, and when I asked him if he would give it to me when he was finished so I could take it to the library and check it out in my own name, he said he'd only taken Parra at his printed word, in the poem "I Take Back Everything I've Said," and had done what the poem said: to burn the book. He had thrown it into the easygoing fireplace of the house he rented with several other students. Two or three students concealed themselves in the university library one night and then came out of hiding in the empty building and with lucid wrongheadedness poured honey into the card catalogue drawers to protest the war machine. It was hard to draw clear lines concerning persons and issues, but it was easy to draw hard ones. Sitting at the head of the seminar table was the English poet who wanted stability and order in society and orderly imaginative accomplishment in poems; around the table, some of the student poets wanted to disrupt our society but were not very imaginative. It was a supremely interesting, dire, baffling time.

What is the grain of such thick, crowding experience as it grows and hardens in one's being?

The moment was one of reckoning for me. I was restless, hopeful, but anxious that I would not find my way, writing poems. With its permissions and prohibitions, the intricate weave of the times wove me into itself. Fortunately so, and perhaps not. Call no poet's work happy until it is completed (whenever that may be).

I don't mean I wished to improve myself. And I don't mean that a moment of self-reckoning as a writer brings with it any question of salvation — secular, artistic, or religious — as it did so famously for Dante, who made it the occasion not only of astonishing artistic will and mastery but also of spiritual resolve and change. (And made one of the greatest poetic structures—and with some of the most beautiful music of words—that has ever been created.) I still find myself reckoning with how to situate poetry among artistic alternatives, among poetic and human wrongs and rights. How to write. The decisions poets make may seem to be about the craft of writing—whether to solve an artistic problem this way or that. But there's existential work going on within the very craft of the poem, too. In the conscious and unconscious working out, say, of a line. Was Keats's poetic line simply a technical achievement? William Carlos Williams' earliest poems include many awkwardly Keatsian lines without Keatsian fusion of sound and sense, without existential weight in the luxuriousness of the language—and without much luxuriousness of language, either. Was Williams' new poetic line only a technical innovation? Didn't he have to go against the grain of that early work in order to mature into a different personal ethos in response to ordinary, everyday people and language? Artistic and personal permission to make such a change is itself a late benefit of Romantic ideas about poetry. To judge from the sequencing of Williams' *Collected Poems*, his shift was accomplished with suddenness and poetic certainty, even though for decades afterward he himself still felt uncertain about his work.

My geographic restlessness belongs to my late teens and my twenties: eagerly I left Texas for summer study of math in Flagstaff, Arizona, then again to attend Princeton, about which I knew nothing; and then I drove from New Jersey back through Texas on the way to Northern California, where, in the midst of graduate school, I had a Fulbright grant and for more than a year was abroad—a month in Turkey and an academic year in Spain—my first experience outside the USA, and decisive in many ways for me, although it was not the only experience that was so altering. However, in the years since those travels, since the view from a height above Gilroy, also, my artistic restlessness has only increased. For a long while I have been thinking about how it is that we evoke (from Latin *vocāre*, "to call") in ourselves a new artistic impulse, in order to begin again. Where does it come from? Do we indeed call it into us as something truly new? Do we know somehow that it's there already as a possibility and we give ourselves the permission we need in order to become the writer who will pursue it? How often is it the result of chance experience and encounter with a place, a person, a book? How much power of will must

be summoned in order to carry intuition—which is already the out-
come of unconscious trains of thought colliding on our inner tracks—
further, to at least a provisional artistic fruition? The struggle can be
between forcefully opposed aspects of one's self. In the short story
"The Horse and the Day Moth," William Goyen wrote, "There is the
constant, gentle and steadfast urging of the small, loyal friendliness,
the pure benevolence of some little Beginningness that lies waiting in
us all to be taken up like a rescued lover and lead us to a human courage and a human meaning. The rest is death: murder (self or other),
betrayal, violence and cruelty, vengeance and crimes of fear. But the
little Beginningness is in all of us, waiting" (1975, 212). Yet in the experience of some, such Beginningness may itself be more difficult
than friendly, more dangerous than benevolent.

Reading poems, we seek at least sometimes to be led through
the inner experience of a sequence of stages of feeling, new trains of
thought. We read in order to enact within ourselves a new articulation given to us on the page, to follow a movement of mind through
which we are led by the poem. Many writers and artists have said in
different ways (especially since the beginning of what we call—and
the poets themselves did not call—the Romantic era) that they have
tried to renovate or sweep away old habits of perception, thinking,
and feeling; old language; old poetics. The evidence is in many books
of poems. We seek reinvention of the art and at least in some sense,
even if not wholly, reinvention of ourselves as users of poetry. (Yeats:
"Whenever I remake a song / [. . .] It is myself that I remake" [1997,
557].) As readers and as poets we seek techniques for "defamiliarizing"
in poetry, which can become techniques of making our own thinking-
with-poetry fruitfully unfamiliar, even *productively* alien (from Latin
alius, "other"). One artistic goal I inherited from the poetic generations before me, going all the way back to Rimbaud and before him
to Coleridge and Wordsworth and Blake, was to make apparent in its
real strangeness all that is.

We do all our perceiving and saying and self-scrutinizing at the site
of our own psychic intensifyings and occultings. Outside us, the public sphere of image, sound, and thought is always changing and forever
adding to our collective mental landfill. It is the inescapable American
environment of what is said and shown and also of the perceptible
absence of what is neither shown nor said. Our inner mental environ-

ment, no less than the outer one, contains, however much we might like to avoid acknowledging it, lots of garbage. Some of it is neither biodegradable nor psychically reducible. There is tangible trash at the top of the highest peaks on the planet—no surprise—and in the remotest waters of the Pacific, and intangible trash in our own heights and depths. ("Intensidad y altura" [Intensity and heights] a sonnet by César Vallejo, I first encountered in my early twenties; I translated it several times over the years. It begins: "Quiero escribir, pero me sale espuma, / quiero decir muchísimo y me atollo; / no hay cifra habalda que no sea suma, / no hay pirámide escrita, sin cogollo" [Vallejo 1988, 400; I want to write, but only a frothing comes out, / I have so much to say, and I'm stuck in mud; / there is no spoken number that's not supreme, / and without some core, no written pyramid].)

Near the force field of Donald Davie's demanding certainties and uncertainties, I studied how to read and how to write from 1969 to 1974. He did not teach one how to do this; he lived out his way of doing it. The difficulty of pleasing Davie with a poem or a translation was the tonic I needed. I had studied the piano; I had listened to my teacher's recordings of my imperfect performances in her studio, sitting side by side with her and reading along in the score, marking it. Davie's responses to the readings in poetry that he assigned to us, or that we discussed with him outside the syllabus, were not always so easy to grasp. The range of his sympathies as a reader of poetry was greater than that of his affinities as a writer of poems. He seemed to contradict himself; I was young and wanted clarity. I have never forgotten reading an endnote to his *Collected Poems, 1950–1970*. It's not that I have remembered it word for word, and in fact, without my awareness, its thrust has been somewhat transmuted in memory, I am sure, to conform to what I want that note to say because of my own needs emotional and literary. I felt it was the gesture of a poet who worked very hard to open up his own work to himself, or to try to know capabilities in himself that he didn't feel were the most natural to him but which he wanted to have and to use.

In California, Davie was an anomaly. He was born and grew up in a small town, Barnsley, in Yorkshire, a rural but also coal-mining shire with two cities like opposing myths of the human — the industrial center, Leeds, and the medieval cathedral city, York. Stanford looked in those days like it had been monumentalized in vacant fields not so long ago from movie-set Mediterranean models; within its precinct, it still had much empty land on which nothing had yet been constructed. York within its medieval walls has the architectural atmosphere of long-lost proportions of human gathering in which every individual could be perceived; it was built on a huge scale of the divine and a cozy scale of the shop, the market, the human being. The last echo of clopping hooves can be heard in narrow passageways. I think it must have been York that first gave Davie a sense of the great value of the spaces of architecture in stone on a human scale.

He studied at Cambridge; then during World War II, he enlisted in the British Navy and was sent through the North Sea to serve at stations in Russia; some years later he helped found a new English university at Essex, where he devised an innovative curriculum for the study of literature, but then, embittered by the particular qualities of England's economic decline and the helter-skelter qualities of the rebellions of the young in the 1960s, he left England for Palo Alto. This was shortly after the death of Yvor Winters; Davie had been chosen — he admired Winters — to succeed this eccentric, conservative, crotchety critic and poet as the poet-scholar of the Stanford English Department. Winters had had a Modernist episode of luminous small imagist poems but had repudiated that early work. For decades he had set the poetic culture of the place, prizing reason, clear metrical practice, and morality, and some of his former students were (and are) among the most impressive American poets. Their work was not like that of Winters, nor anything alike among themselves, but I would say that something admirable in the seriousness of their poetic practice had been secured when they were Winters' students, either thinking with him or against him or both.

The English Davie might have seemed a surprising choice to replace the American Winters, and yet he was not. Except for his foray into Russian, his formation as a poet and thinker about poetry was deeply English, albeit dappled with his genuine curiosity and respect for some of the American Modernist experiments (and Russian ones) that almost all English poets had kept away from. He was politically conservative; he had been raised a conservative "dissenter" in religion

(Baptist), and in his own contradictory ways, he was a literary dissenter as well—the most conservative English poet to favor Modernist poets, and the most open-minded English poet, regarding American poetry, to admire the eighteenth-century English "Augustan" poets and also to champion the traditional English poetics and existential sobriety of Thomas Hardy. And Davie also cut against his own somewhat Augustan poetic use of the abstract and devised irregularities of form that owed a debt to both pluricultural, international Modernism *and* (again) its opposite, the English regionalism of Hardy. To his office, to the chair opposite his desk, I brought myself and my poems and translations, and trailing in with me came the war in Vietnam, and my experience during two summers working in Houston among the minor institutional initiatives against poverty, funded by the same Lyndon B. Johnson who was pursuing that war; my believer's leftism; my fondness for the conceptual tool I had found in Herbert Marcuse, "repressive tolerance"; and my provincialism.

Davie was an acutely responsive reader of Pound, but this artistic relationship had a lot of push and pull in it. It was characteristic of him that he could, and often did, both praise and doubt a poet or book, taking a principled stance that encompassed virtues and defects in relation to each other, and also sorting out the bad from the evil. "Pound *is* maddening," he wrote, "Pound is (a lot of the time) inexcusable. He is also, however, not always but often enough, a great and scrupulous poet" (2004, 202). Davie wrote forceful criticism—articulate, direct, side taking, and often moralistic—and he wrote a lot of it. At stake for him were values embodied in poetic choices and in language but also in life. This was an interlocutor to whom as a young man I brought only avidity for reading and writing, half-formed ideas, poems and translations that groped toward their realization; his challenge to my understanding of how much could be in the balance in a serious poem has been working on me ever since.

In his later years, he reacted against the English religious dissenting denominations in which he himself had been raised, and he joined the Church of England and edited *The New Oxford Book of Christian Verse.* By the time I last talked with him, on the occasion of a celebration of his career at Vanderbilt University in 1988, the year of his retirement and, at last, return to England, we had not seen each other for years, and in a letter he had sent me in 1986, he had expressed his hope that

I would never again write poems like those in my book of that year. Perhaps what had carried us rather far apart as friends was his aversion to my very American use of private life in my poems, and his yet more conservative politics and his theological shift to the established Church of England. (He wrote, "In lyric poetry—that's the clearest example, but to a degree in all sorts of writing—what you are doing is making the personal impersonal. This is different from making the private public" [Davie 1979, 29]. This conservative position follows from T. S. Eliot's, but also from Davie's temperament and literary positions.) At his retirement, though, he treated me warmly and I was glad to be able to express my admiration again.

The quick-witted Davie (he told us that in his university days he had been "an athlete of the examination room") had helped create a very notable poetic group, the English "Movement" poets, who had opposed the remnant stances and ideals of English Romanticism, poetic experiment, and emotional "slogging" (a word Davie found in a poem by Galway Kinnell and used against the latter's sentimentality and easy spirituality—as Davie saw it [1977, 275]). While Davie seemed to have only grudging respect for William Carlos Williams, he admired the Williamsesque book *American Scenes* (1966) by his compatriot Charles Tomlinson (to whom Davie himself had introduced Williams' work—a typical gesture). The Davie I knew, when I was his student, repeatedly surprised me by recommending poets to me whom he himself would not use as he thought I might. It was he who sent me to read Hugh MacDiarmid, Basil Bunting, Charles Olson, George Oppen, Ed Dorn, and others. (Not one of these, however, did he fail also to critique and even deplore, for one poetic fault or another.) He would tell one student to read Thom Gunn's *My Sad Captains* (1961) and *Moly* (1971) and the next to read Roy Fisher's *City* (1962). (These were recent books at that time.) The student would leave his office thinking that the poet whom Davie had mentioned was close to Davie's own heart and practice; and the student was not often entirely right. Davie's range was so great, and his half sympathies, at least, when teaching, so broad, that to each student who sought his counsel, he could offer a very different reading list. (Could the champion of Hardy and his descendants, including Philip Larkin, send me to read the unrepentant, and sometimes tedious, communist MacDiarmid? But he did, for the sake of the diction in MacDiarmid's magnificent "On a Raised Beach" and the inventive voicing of "A Drunk Man Looks at a Thistle.")

Davie's view of human mishap and human fate was Christian; he started from the premise of sin and the near impossibility of moral improvement. This jarred me. Repeatedly, from early childhood to the year of my flight from Houston, I had been told of all that by preachers and Bible teachers in the fundamentalist Methodist church my parents had helped found, out in the exurbs, where they moved when I was six. After inching silently further and further from such positions as a churchgoer, in college I dashed toward every idea and book that would overturn them. I was reading the canonical works assigned in a survey of English literature, and in a seminar on twentieth-century Spanish poets conducted entirely in Spanish, I was very tentatively beginning to learn how to think about such poetry—García Lorca, Rafael Alberti, Vicente Aleixandre. Nothing like this work existed in English, nor had I ever before tried to think about such poetry, or poetry in English. The poetics I encountered carried thought beyond where I had ever experienced it going; I had to learn how to think in new ways, to stretch myself upward or outward, mentally and in terms of poetic technique, for the poems were over my head and I was already standing on mental tiptoe. After my scattered reading, outside high school classes, of Plato, Dostoevsky, even Vedanta, I found intellectual heroes as I read, with voracious freshman appetite, Albert Camus and Thomas Mann, Eugène Ionesco and Antonin Artaud, and others. In my second year, I joined a very small once-a-week reading group led from ten till midnight on Wednesdays by the university's Methodist chaplain, one of the most important teachers for me in those first two years, after which he was sent elsewhere by his church. We read Dietrich Bonhoeffer, Paul Tillich, Martin Buber's *I and Thou*, Reinhold Niebuhr, and issues of the liberal Christian magazine *motive* (lowercase *m*), which was at the height of its persuasiveness with regard to war, sex, worship, and the nature of the deity. At the same time I was reading William James's *Varieties of Religious Experience*. Meanwhile fundamentalist fellow students—advised in advance, or forewarned, by an evangelical Princeton alumnus in Houston—had pulled me into their meetings, where for a year I dissembled and kept quiet, till I simply walked away from their abject yet grandiose submissiveness to the intense irrationality and dominating gaze of their brilliant leader, a thin, bent, elderly man with considerable physical strength and excellent Greek (neither of which I had). I needed to sort out, at least provisionally, where I could stand among eschatological and ethical dilemmas, especially the war. I enrolled in beginning ancient Greek—fascinated by the ancient world of the "historical Jesus" and by Plato. Greek was too much for me, however, costing me four hours of preparation for each of the four class hours each week, for I had no Latin in my mental back pocket. After the second semester, when we read Plato's *Crito*, I gave up and began to work harder at my major, Spanish and Portuguese. In my last year of college, I wrote a thesis—exhaustive and more than two hundred pages long—on the novel *El Señor Presidente* (completed 1939, published 1946), by the twentieth-century Guatemalan novelist Miguel Angel Asturias, the first of his two masterpieces, in which he employed surrealist treatment of language and scenes, and used an ethnographic attentiveness to indigenous and mestizo life. When I reached the door of Davie's classroom for the first time, I had also written youthful poems under the kind tutelage of Theodore Weiss, and with my undergraduate studies I had begun to create a personal history for myself as a reader, but I had not yet been able to imagine what such a history might be for me as a writer.

Davie's poems could be elusively oblique in an abstract way— "philosophical" in this sense—and many passages were difficult because of his poetic reticence about what was private, his way of generalizing and metaphorizing it. In "Cherry Ripe," from the 1970 collection *A Winter Talent and Other Poems*, he wrote, "Let orchards flourish in the poet's soul / And bear their feelings that are mastered by / Maturing rhythms, to compose a whole" (Davie 1972, 61). Thus, control over feeling; the importance of composing a poem as a whole, not a sequence of fragments: even after Modernism these may be unsurprising poetic ideals in the 1950s, but much more so in England than in the USA. The next poem in the collection is "Hearing Russian Spoken," in which Davie wrote of his attraction to what he also explicitly opposed in poetry, figuring the temptress as female and by implication not English speaking:

> Not just in Russian but in any tongue
> Abandonment, morality's soubrette

Of lyrical surrender and excess,
Knows the weak endings equal to the strong;
She trades on broken English with success
And, disenchanted, I'm enamoured yet.

(1972, 61–62)

Thus, his poems revealed and even commented on a contradiction of impulses. To give this story of a poet another turn—an extraordinary critic, perceptively writing from an unusually conscious position on the politics of poetic and social values, Davie was deeply engaged with what he saw as a kind of identity crisis in contemporary English poetry. He was also a learned author of studies of the work of the past. Whether in a book review or a study of the eighteenth century, he could be acerbic, even caustic, yet might also express his partial admiration for that which he attacked. In those years, his fruitful inconsistency somehow made sense. What was the *grain* of this writer, so to speak, when he seemed able to go against it in one way or another so productively? And yet at the same time this was very difficult.

Naturally, what he wanted first of all was to be acknowledged as a poet. And in retrospect, he seems to me to have been trying to find a way to derive more of his own poem making from a deeper stratum of thought that he acknowledged as self-contradictory. But I think that for him the self-opposing, the uncertainties and certainties, had to be understood not as primarily psychological—that is, unconscious— but somehow simply in the grain of one's personality, temperament, character. He had an anti-Freudian sense of inner life. Lifelong, his announced intention was to be reasoned and moral and accomplished and truly capable in many ways.

It wasn't easy for him. Here, from his *Collected Poems* of 1972, published when he was fifty, is the endnote I have kept in mind for many years. When he published a larger *Collected Poems* in 1990, this note, along with all others, was gone. The 1972 collection also had a brief foreword in which he wrote, "Some of the poems, especially the earlier ones, are a great deal more obscure than I meant them to be; and in those cases I've apologetically, if lamely, tried to clarify matters in some brief notes" (n.p.). In the 1990 collection, there is no foreword. The long 1972 note to his poem "With the Grain," originally published in his *New and Selected Poems* (1961), and a few other poems, begins this way: "The poem is obscure. Completed on 24 July 1957, it appears related to a note written three days before. Though this is a vulnerable piece of writing, I transcribe it here."

> It is true that I am not a poet by nature, only by inclination; for my mind moves most easily and happily among abstractions, it relates ideas far more readily than it relates experiences. I have little appetite, only profound admiration, for sensuous fullness and immediacy; I have not the poet's need of concreteness. I have resisted this admission for so long, chiefly because a natural poet was above all what I wanted to be, but partly because I mistook my English empiricism for the poet's concreteness, and so thought my mind was unphilosophical whereas it is philosophical but in a peculiarly English way.
>
> Most of the poems I have written are not natural poems, in one sense not truly poems, simply because the thought in them could have been expressed—at whatever cost in terseness and point—in a non-poetic way. This does not mean however that they are worthless, or that they are shams; for as much can be said of much of the poetry of the past that by common consent is worth reading and remembering. Nevertheless I have taken a decision to write no more poems of this kind, only poems which are, if not naturally, at all events truly poems throughout.
>
> For a true poem can be written by a mind not naturally poetic—though by the inhuman labor of thwarting at every point the natural grain and bent. This working against the grain does not damage the mind, nor is it foolish; on the contrary, only by doing this does each true poem as it is written become an authentic widening of experience—a truth won from life against all odds, because a truth in and about a mode of experience to which the mind is normally closed. [. . .] (Davie 1972, 301)

A nobly confessed self-doubt from an anticonfessional poet. An admission, in a book of his own poems, that he is "not a poet by nature." And also a self-defense, an assertion that his poems are worth no less on this account and are not fake. It is as though Davie had voluntarily offered to stand in the dock of some court of the poetry of his day (and not only of his day), self-accused.

❊

There is a larger grain than the poet's own, and that is the language the poet speaks. (I don't write for an audience, Marina Tsvetaeva says somewhere—I write for the Russian language.) A language has its particular nature. A comparison of two languages will help us see this. If, for example, we compare French to very distantly related Indo-European languages like ancient Greek or modern Bengali, then French seems extremely close to English. Yet the literary history of French, especially as regards poetry, is so different from that of English that much of what Davie takes for granted about poetry in English is not true of French poetry, as far as I can tell. In Davie's admission, "I have little appetite, only profound admiration, for sensuous fullness and immediacy," we hear what he appreciated in the work of Ezra Pound, whom he likened to a sculptor in language. Davie championed Pound's virtuoso use of the sensuous dimension of the rhythms of English, and the effectiveness of literature that

> create[s] the fantasy or the illusion of direct experience through the eye, the ear, the fingertips; and this means that the notion of a perception can be, thanks to the graces and powers of language, at least as powerful and convincing as the perception itself. This phenomenon [. . .] exposes the sterility of all those lines of argument [. . .] which start, as Plato did, from the supposition that through literature we experience actuality only "at one remove." The "remove" which language represents is so integral with human nature—the human creature being above all that creature who *speaks*—that to speak of it as "a remove" is already to betray our humanity. (Davie 1982, 102–3)

We might say of French poetry of the nineteenth and twentieth centuries—again, my example of contrast with English—that some of it is beautifully musical in its manipulation of sound and rhetoric, ideas and idealizations; vague and associative in its "logic"; and, in some poets, acutely ironic, as in those poems of Jules Laforgue from which T. S. Eliot drew a new mode of imagery. But most of that poetry—exempting the occasional poem like Arthur Rimbaud's vivid and earthy "Au cabaret-vert" ("At the Green Inn")—does not exemplify Davie's "sensuous fullness and immediacy" in the English-language sense. Davie himself contrasted Eliot and Pound by contrasting "musical time as opposed to pictorial or sculptural space," and preferred palpable, "sculptural" English to the French symbolist mode that moved a poem forward musically—that is, as an unfolding primarily of sound—in time; the symbolist poem did not move the reader's mind through stages of *seeing*. Eliot often composed as symbolist poets had done, "where words do not stand for events but are those events" (Davie 2004, 89–90). Davie wrote about Mallarmé and Paul Valéry from the specific, expected but somewhat narrow perspective of the English poetry of "logical, discursive" structure, poetic meaning in the sense of "a proposition in a treatise," the concurrence of syntax with argument, and descriptive specificity (85–87). Since the Modernists, especially, many English-language poets have tended to enact the physical sensuousness of reality by favoring—as I've already mentioned—a diction that is very precisely descriptive in visual terms, often musically thick with consonants, and tending toward delight in the particular thing (often using words of Anglo-Saxon origin) rather than in the generalized symbol. Davie's love of Samuel Johnson and the lofty generalities of Augustan poetry fit his own poetic impulse, which is certainly not French but does cut against or across the grain of the concreteness of much poetic language in both the Early Modern period and in and after the Romantic period that made use of the plenitude of the English lexicon, especially the specificity of English hyponyms. To us, Davie's "sensuous fullness and immediacy" of language would mean the similar effect of such diction in poets as different as Pound, William Carlos Williams, Basil Bunting, Mina Loy, Marianne Moore, Elizabeth Bishop, Seamus Heaney, and many others who in one way or another fill their poems with the particular. All along the way, Davie had written occasional lines of this kind, but in his 1972 note, he wrote that "by and large it is certainly true that the idea comes into my mind more readily than the sensuous experience which not only can stand, but must stand, as its symbol." I'll give an example: "Worry hedges my days / Like a roil of thick mist at the edge of a covert / Fringing a tufted meadow" (1972, 302). The mist and meadow are not the poetic site of thought, nor aspects of a physically imagined place, but rather, as he says, a symbol for the thought. And the poetic "hedge" is not a visual image of green but an abstract image made of mist.

By contrast to English, French poetry often creates a realm of symbols and idealized images, whether positive or negative. Even French surrealism does this, however absurd its images. As Yves Bonnefoy

so lucidly says, among his many comments about translating Shakespeare into French, the contrast of Shakespeare and Racine reveals
that

> opposing metaphysics [. . .] govern, and, sometimes, tyrannize the
> French and English languages. [. . .] English concerns itself naturally
> with tangible aspects. It accepts the reality of what can be observed
> and does not admit the possibility of any other order of reality; it has
> a natural affinity with the Aristotelean critique of Platonic Ideas. And
> if its words with Latin roots to some extent unsettle this intelligence
> shaped by this "devotion to the realm of things," they do not under-
> mine the natural realism of the language so much as simply make it
> easier to express those moments in life when we are guided by a sense
> of the ideal.

But in French,

> [t]he poet's statements do not set out to describe external reality but
> shut the poet in with certain selected precepts in a simplified, more
> circumscribed world. [. . .] Yet it is not an abstract world, for the Pla-
> tonic Idea is profoundly double-natured, in the sense of taking on the
> life of sensible appearance in its most intense and specific form. But
> this world is nonetheless a *place apart*, where the bewildering diver-
> sity of the real can be forgotten, and also the very existence of time,
> everyday life and death. Poetic creation, in short, is hieratic; it makes
> an inviolable place, and while the rite of reading continues, it draws
> the mind into this illusory communion. (2004, 217, 218)

Baudelaire, by contrast,

> is the most consistent and determined opponent of the Racinian
> theory. And yet this principle of exclusion I have referred to still gov-
> erns his poetry. Even though he is dealing with this particular swan
> or that particular woman rather than with swan or woman as such —
> with the idea, that is, of swan and woman — what these particular
> entities are like are [*sic*] not what matters to him. [. . .] Baudelaire is
> not trying, at any level of penetration, to describe things as they are:
> he is trying to convey the act of being, and the passion and moral feel-
> ing that can be based upon it. An intense, narrow aim that restored
> to poetry the almost obsessional detachment from the phenomenal

world that seems to be the fate of the main body of our work. It is as if words, in French, excluding instead of describing, always encourage the mind to shake off the disintegrating diversity of things; it is as if they always make the work of art a world of its own, a closed sphere. (Bonnefoy 2004, 219, 220)

I have quoted Bonnefoy at such length so that I could say that French abstraction is not like English abstraction, and that dismantling the authority of French abstraction, thinking outside Platonism, admitting rather than excluding the quiddities of the real world and of the body, and writing outside of the "closed sphere" of French poetry, is precisely what Hélène Cixous has done in much of her work, especially her fiction and her later autobiographical-theoretical works. By linguistic means very different from those with which English produces a sense of the material world, she has nevertheless brought a bodily specificity into her writing. It may seem comparatively abstract to the English-language reader, even though it contrasts with French poetic abstraction—while of course never failing to make use of some qualities of French, especially the rich possibilities of paronomasia, that display what is in fact similar in French and English: the plasticity, richness, and startling meaning-making possibilities of the sounds of language.

Bonnefoy writes that while English vocabulary (which we experience as a remarkable abundance) is in Shakespeare especially about "precision and enrichment," French poetry has mostly made use of "a vocabulary as reduced as possible, so as to protect a single essential experience. On the one hand, unlimited dissociation, receptiveness to every dialectical or technical possibility, so that an alert awareness can penetrate always further into the phenomenal world. On the other hand, all those evocations of sense entering into poetry as one enters into an order, to be completely transformed, dying to the world, becoming one with the Idea that is constantly being realized in the poem. English poetry is a mirror, French poetry a crystal sphere" (2004, 220).

Cixous, who after all began her critical work with Shakespeare and James Joyce, has especially emphasized the value of linguistic play, of yielding to the inventiveness of language itself in order to give not only language but also one's own psyche more freedom of discovery and articulation. I would not argue that she wants to create a palpability of language and of what language names and describes, a materialization of the physical world; it is evidently unusual to encounter work like that of Francis Ponge, which is minutely descriptive in his *Le Parti pris des choses* (published in 1942; this title can be translated as "On behalf of things"). The conceptual and phonetic play of Cixous's language, however, does disrupt the smoothness, the spherical idealization, that Bonnefoy describes, and that Cixous regards as an imprisoning of thought. But Cixous does not have to go against her own grain in order to champion and exemplify writing that opens a way for the language to play. She lifts into view an aspect of writing, or an experience of writing, and offers it in opposition to writing that is constrained by the typical use of rationality, by the limits imposed on women in patriarchic societies, and by the individual aversion to reading as an encounter with profound potential reversals of received ideas and received modes of articulation. For her, the writer begins from awareness of having committed a crime—like Augustine's childhood theft of pears—and writing is the exuberant, even if agonized (as in Kafka), fulfillment rather than redemption of that crime.

Why should language itself play? The reasons are not limited to psychoanalytical explanations for our saying (or hearing) the "wrong" thing (Freud's "parapraxis"—the English-language jargon for his German words *Versprechen* [verb] or *Fehlleistung* [noun], meaning to say something mistaken, or the thing said or done mistakenly). Language has a ceaseless impulse in itself to shift, change, morph, as we are using it—which also means when we are used by it. It's as if language looks for things to do within the rough boundaries of what someone says with it. Toddlers' language, amusing because it is not yet filled in as a complex and flexible system, becomes in adults a fully capable saying that is yet sometimes "mistaken" (from the psychoanalytic point of view) or simply playful as we speak. Cixous says that language, too, has an unconscious. The unconscious of language cannot be unique to any person, like the individual psychic unconscious in its idiosyncratic combinations of the genetic, the experiential, the familial, the social, and the historical. Cixous also sees an impulse in all language that insists on remembering, as she puts it, what we language users forget:

this linguistic remembering begins concretely with etymologies but also includes past usage, associative links by sound, and connotative links by concept and allusion. (*Etymon*, meaning an earlier form of a word, comes from ancient Greek *etumos*, "the true sense of a word.")

For us to be played, so to speak (so to speak) by language, is to find our way into the linguistically unfamiliar, into that which goes against our own grain, so as to think and to feel our way into a "mode of experience to which the mind is normally closed." By this, Davie meant a large shift of orientation—as when he acknowledged "How often I have said, / 'This will never do,' / Of ways of feeling that now / I trust in, and pursue!" (in his 1964 book *Events and Wisdoms*; Davie 1972, 135). Although Davie characterized this change as his individual and idiosyncratic experience, Cixous's work suggests that it is an experience we all might share, but which we might resist acknowledging, much less *using*. (Davie would be startled and unhappy to be linked with a writer like Cixous, much of whose work is Mallarméan in principle regarding language—in her wordplay based on sound and her embrace of language for its exceeding of its representational function. And she, I am certain, would only feel puzzlement at being linked with him in my exploration of the varieties of one sort of grain or another.)

I wonder how else a writer is to find a way to new work, and how else a reader is going to be able to hear what he or she is reading, if neither listens to what both know but which neither is aware of. Or, to return to my metaphor, if we writers and readers do not *allow* ourselves to go against the grain of what we expect ourselves to say and hear—in fiction, voices not heard before, and in poetry, small sprites of sometimes weighty unforeseeables. In fact, Davie seems to have been good at such creative listening, and he sometimes brought his awareness right up into the poems themselves. But awareness of impulses in different directions does not become resolution or synthesis. From Davie's later work, his "Mandelstam's Hope for the Best":

> Hope so abstracted as
> towards no temporal end
> but "a mode of address to facts,

to the world and to its persons,"
however it be attested
by every *grace* of behavior
sought for and found in language,
had better agree to be called
a living contradiction.
(Davie 1990, 358; my italics)

My purpose in contrasting Davie's stance with Cixous's is not to
advocate a theory but to come from different sides to describe aspects
of a process. I have described some aspects of Davie's poetry. What is
Cixous's writing like? She explores complicated structures of paradox
or contradiction, not simple binary oppositions. Her essays are often
autobiographical and her fiction includes accounts of reading and
trains of critical or theoretical thinking. Her prose devices are familiar to us from poetry. She sometimes compresses separate grammatical utterances into single, often unpunctuated ones, or on the contrary breaks utterances into fragments. She structures her writings by
association rather than by argument or narrative plot. She creates — or
offers to language itself the opportunities to create — plays on words
(paronomasia again) for the sake of the lines of thought and feeling
that such play opens. We who live inside the English language tend
to regard linguistic play on sound as *only* puns — a heavy sort of humor used by sportswriters — but puns in the resourceful language of
poetry and poetic prose proliferate meaning. Cixous also likes tropes
of doubleness, and thus of oscillation and substitution. To cite only a
few of the tropes that she herself explicitly has named: antonomasia
(which is a kind of weak metonymy using a phrase for a proper name:
"the author of *Rootprints*" instead of "Cixous"; more forceful is the
apotropaic usage in ancient Greece, such as "goddess of the cross-
roads" instead of "Hekatē" — let's not call out her name, for the indifference of a goddess is safer for us than her attention); amphibology
(ambiguity; but the etymology of amphibology suggests a throwing
of meaning on both sides of something, and so *both* meanings are in
play); and hypallage (shifting the application of an adjective from one
noun to another that is related — "the grateful shade," "the gloomy
night," yet it's the person who enjoys the shade or feels the gloom).
Cixous's work pivots on aspects of oneself as other, and one's language

as an "other." For the writer, language is an object in the psychoanalytical sense of an entity in which one has invested one's feeling— language not only represents what is outside language but also has its own nature. To write is to take a particular stance toward language, to be unable to think of it as if it were a transparent, unambiguous, easily effectual medium of communication. Its ambiguity and amphibology are part of its wealth, for expressive purposes. Of her poetics, Cixous has written: "It is in the poem, hybrid of music and language, that something of mysterious and unstoppable life can be produced, with subverted grammar, with liberties in the bosom of language, in the law of genders, in dance, the *dans*(in), the dancing of the poem, minimal world in movement, the poem speaking French, the tongue, very differently from prose, the poem playing with language more than it speaks, changed expression of drives—but here I am evoking only the poem that invents the other tongue within the tongue, the dreamtongue [...]" (1991, 148).

And even Davie, to whom this way of thinking would have been alien, might have added that the poem speaking English can do these things, too, albeit by different linguistic rules and literary histories. Although Cixous says she prizes "only the poem that invents the other tongue within the tongue," I am not certain that her poetics would require any specific poetic or stylistic practice. Her personal canon of writers exhibits no stylistic consistency (to mention only a few: James Joyce is no Thomas Bernhard, nor is Bernhard a Clarice Lispector or Jean Genet, nor Genet a Marina Tsvetaeva).

The art of writing and the art of reading, as I see them, are in part a dividing or perhaps a circulating of the psyche (by which I mean either soul or mind or both at once; each such term defers to some other, and there's no end to the deferring). It's a circulating of one's sense of language, too. It's a movement of our being in language—from observation and thought toward our objects (in that affective sense), and a returning again ceaselessly—a hermeneutics of emotional investment. Attentiveness in the writer—who is also a reader—brings the insight that what one thinks or feels unexpectedly is what one had already been expecting, whether in hope or apprehension, but had not foreseen. An intuition has come to consciousness from unconscious trains of thought that for a moment arrived or coincided somewhere in us. Christopher Bollas characterizes such thinking this way:

> Perhaps the sense of intuition is our preconscious experience of the ego's intelligent work, leading us to consciously authorize certain forms of investigation in thought which are not consciously logical but which may be unconsciously productive. [...] The fact that intuition seems to be an immediate knowing should not obscure the fact that it is the outcome of a sustained concentration of many types of unconscious and conscious thinking. [...] Intuition works as successfully as it does precisely because the subject thinking in this way does not see what he is working on and what he is working with. In this respect, its strength rests upon its hiddenness. It may be so successful, then, because the intuiting person is unconsciously able to explore lines of investigation that would meet with incredulous disapproval if he were fully conscious of what was being considered. (Bollas 2013, 90, 91, 92)

Thus a faith in spontaneity in writing can easily mistake words hurriedly written down as the beginning of new feeling, when in reality they may be the sudden availability of potent images or phrases, charged with feeling, from trains of thought already moving, as Bollas describes. And those words may also provoke us unknowingly to perform a "secondary revision," so that we can weaken their force and in that way their power to disrupt us, as Freud says we quickly do when "revising" our dreams. Dreams are halls of evasion as well as discovery, but the poem is not a dream, even though it can be like a dream. Thus in secondary stages of composition, the poet can retreat from psychic possibilities (these might be individual or social), or can entertain what might follow—by sound or other modes of association—from the unforeseen impulse that provided a phrase or an image. The movement of a poem is a collaboration with that intuition without which creativity is barren—it is the unconscious deliberateness of invention and insight. By this I only mean that the unconscious has its own deliberateness—as anyone in a deep reverie or a serious quarrel will have realized. And if it did not, then scarcely any art could be made or performed, and scarcely any difficult analytical problems could be solved, for in its meandering, multifarious way, the unconscious can think and feel and seek, and its discoveries are not accidental or random, even though they may be "wrong." This is precisely the thinking with a purpose that is not conscious, or the purposive yet not conscious attentiveness, that we call by the name "intuition." Curiously, the ancient Greeks had a word for thought, *dianoia*, that combines the preposition *dia*, "through," with the noun *nóos*, "mind." Gregory Nagy says Homer applies *dianoia* "primarily to Homer's train of thought, not to the rhapsode's" (2002, 29). And this suggests an unarticulated sense of artistic intuition — personified in ancient Greece as the Muse.

The Muse is for us moderns a metaphor. But it or she has been regarded as such, at least implicitly, since the very time of the Muses. In Greek, words for remembrance (*anamnesis*), divination (*manteia*), spirit (*menos*), the goddess of memory Mnemosyne, and other words associated with unusual mental activity, including madness (*mania*), derive ultimately from the same Proto-Indo-European root, **men-**, the same word root that eventually produced the Greek word for the Muse, *Mousa* (Pokorny 2014, root words 726–28). In *Cracking Up*, Christopher Bollas, discussing the activity of the unconscious during our waking hours, vividly illustrated the process of receiving an intuition or impulse from unknown unconscious thought, which brings with it something that can be known, if it can be admitted to language (2002, 9–29). The reader, in his or her own psyche, will ideally follow, in a poem, the movement of thought and feeling that has been discovered and crafted there by the poet, and will reproduce — albeit never exactly but rather in ways which at best will be fruitful — the moves, even the leaps, of discovery that the poet and language together have articulated, have seen with words. Something in such composing and active reading goes against the grain of easy expectation. It only works, however, if it works. If the movement plods, then there's little to care about except eloquence, which is enough sometimes. And at the other extreme, romping randomness can produce stylistic excitement, but can it produce anything of more moment? Or are we entering an age when randomness can be experienced as meaning? When meaning is thought to be only random? (The fault, dear Brutus, is not in our megabytes.)

By the early 1980s, it seems to me, Davie may have turned partly away, or may have been turned away, within himself, from the productive

going against the grain of himself. Did he experience less of his productive uncertainty? Or was there too much inner turbulence in this
effort? In his 1982 volume, *In the Stopping Train*, he included an "Ars
Poetica" in which he wrote: "Walk quietly around in / A space cleared
for the purpose. // Most poems, or the best, / Describe their own
birth, and this / Is what they are — a space / Cleared to walk around
in. // Their various symmetries are / guarantees that the space has /
Boundaries, and beyond them / The turbulence it was cleared from"
(1990, 284).

The etymology of the word *grain* throws a first link into view in the
Romance languages and then retreats back toward Latin. Its first
meaning seems always to have been "seed of cereal plants," starting
with wheat ("corn" in British usage). Many meanings followed, associated one way or another with those seeds, and then other particles
which like seeds are small and hard (sand, salt). I can never forget
the sensation in hot summer of plunging my hand and forearm into
an open wooden barrel of smooth oats in the hot, still, deep-scented
air of a tall one-room cabin — no interior walls, no finishing or fur-
nishings — raised above the ground on concrete footings, that my
father paid workmen from his weekend job to build next to his own
crude, small tin shed of a barn, where he kept alfalfa hay and where
his horse of one year or another could shelter out of storms, wind, and
sun. Behind our house and on the other side of a chain-link fence, the
cabin was a storage place holding horse feed, bridles, halters, and a
few saddles, rope, garden chemicals, horse medicine . . . Even in Texas
summer heat, the innumerable grains of the oats felt cool to the skin
and as slippery as if they were a dry water. Scrolling down through the
many groups of meanings, submeanings, and submeanings of those
submeanings in the entry for *grain* in the *Oxford English Dictionary*,
one arrives at last at "IV. Granular texture": "14. The texture of any
substance; the arrangement and size of its constituent particles, ap-
pearing in an exposed surface or in a cross-cut or fracture," and then
"b. in wood (cf. sense 15)," and finally: "15. The longitudinal arrangement of fibres or particles, in lines or veins more or less parallel along
which the material is more easily cloven or cut than in any other di-

rection: a. in wood, producing often the effect of a pattern." Curiously, the first two attestations are associated with liquid:

> 1565 T. Cooper Thesaurus, *Vndatim crispæ mensæ*. Plin. Tables hauynge grayne lyke waues of water.

> 1609 Shakespeare *Troilus & Cressida* i. iii. 7 Knots by the conflux of meeting sap, Infects the sound Pine, and diuerts his graine.

Simile: "grain like waves of water"; and metaphor: knots that "infect" the sound wood of the pine and "divert" the grain, as if, indeed, the grain could "flow." Here is the robust English vocabulary of the physical world, the metaphorical vividness, and some ideas that arise from categorizing the qualities of things by analogy.

I come to this corner of the OED thinking about the poet who writes against the grain—of temperament, of literary convention, of language. Definition 16. b: "Phr. *against* (also, *contrary to*) *the grain*: contrary to one's disposition or inclination; esp. in *to go against the grain*." I am probably giving myself too much credit when I imagine that I have gone against my own grain as I have groped for new ways of shaping a poem and of poetic thinking. Sometimes a new subject— but it is not so clearly defined as the word *subject* would suggest— simply can't be quite thought until there's a way to begin to find some form (traditional or "organic") or device or stance for it. For some poets, anyway, not all subjects can be fitted to the same form (even a poet's customary loose and "organic" form), although for other poets that seems to work. The grain of the poet might be in the voicing, not in the forming, or in the forming, not in the seeing-with-words, or in the seeing-with-words, not in the . . . With this phrase "seeing-with-words" I mean to suggest an integrative experience, not simply another instrumental use of language—a seeing with the mind what cannot be seen with the eye.

In any case, I do not think I have overestimated the very different ways in which Davie and Cixous have helped me to try to open up poetic thinking for myself. At any rate, I am in the grain of the English language, with its copious lexicon of words for the material, palpable, visible, audible, tasteable, world. And I am aware now that the knots in the wood that divert that grain, obstructing it and swirling it off this way and that, are themselves part of the grain. Not pine, perhaps, or spruce, which can run so clear, but oak, hardened into what seems gorgeously improvised movement, hard oak hard to saw and fiercely stubborn against the single-mindedness of the axe or the maul. In chapters 4 and 5, I explore poetry that thinks not with this particular kind of nomenclature for the material world but with another; and now that I have used the grain of French poetry as a first contrast to that of English, I won't dwell on it again—the opening of poetic thinking is not there, but in Russian, in another kind of *word*.

Fortunately, the Marks on the Page Are Alien

Exploring in the writer the complicated interactions of will, imagination, and the resistance and play of language, the unconscious and temperament versus artistic freedom, I cited a note by Donald Davie and some ideas articulated by Hélène Cixous—two strikingly different writers who from different points of view question what one writes "by nature." From Cixous, I took the urgent idea of listening to the language that we ourselves speak and that speaks through us and even at variance with us, of using what it invents and remembers apart from us. I also heard the urgency in her contention that the writer must stand where thought is more dangerous. Reading Davie, I have been especially jostled by the recognition of how hard it is for us (as it was for Davie himself) to reckon with what he confessed of himself and his own writing, as he sought to inhabit a new "mode of experience to which the mind is normally closed" (1972, 301). In 1972, when Davie published that note, even he, in his political and religious conservatism, courageously proposed this opening of one's being as the worthy aim of the imagination. And I'm sure he meant the reader's imagination just as much as the writer's.

In the first chapter I also mentioned briefly the way the human psyche circulates between one's sense of oneself and one's "objects"—those persons, places, things, attitudes, ideas, and so forth, to whom or to which one is emotionally attached, out of desire or anxiety, love or hate, fear or anger. Now I will explore this.

Now I explore the idea that the writer's experience of language is sometimes that of another. I continue to cite Cixous in this chapter. I use fiction more than poetry, in order to make my way toward more of what happens psychically when we read. Reading, and especially writing, can take one productively out of oneself or can invite one to work against one's own temperamental or psychic grain—and thereby to enter a fuller play of feeling, ideas, judgments. While the resources of fiction are different from those of poetry, they are analogous to those of poetry in how word by word, poetry thinks us forward and back in the text and in time, becoming for a moment (or much longer) a shaping of our inner life. Reading, we experience the sensation that a part of us, familiar or new, is imagined outside us on the page, evoking us; toward it we depart from ourselves for a moment.

In *Rootprints*, Cixous says that writing is not only a creating but also a recognizing of what is created as something apart from the one who writes it. She says one of her motives for writing is that she prefers "an intention which is not voluntary but is spread throughout me—this tendency to rehabilitate what is forgotten, subordinated. Or else it is an unconscious leitmotiv: When I speak it comes forth exterior to myself and I recognize it" (Cixous and Calle-Gruber 1997, 11). She speaks of the writing (part of the) self as an other in this way, too: "[A]t times, what writing does well is this meticulous work that one does not have the time to do, one does not take the time to do when one is not writing" (18–19).

In Cixous's practice of writing, an unforeseen, unanticipated, and even apparently mistaken articulation is the invaluable entrance to imaginative freedom. In Davie's note, he advocates, for himself at least, a resolve not to write in a way that is not a challenge to himself as he is. But neither Davie nor Cixous would ask anyone to write in the same manner or style as do they. So, writing fiction or poetry, I do not use Cixous's work or Davie's by imitating either of them stylistically. Instead, I want to seize whatever freedom of imagination I can—from what I had not foreseen in my writing (Cixous) or from what I have tried to accomplish by working beyond myself or against my own grain (Davie).

Even in using Davie's and Cixous's work in my thinking and practice as a writer, I am able to choose only a part of it. (I don't become fully aware of those parts of their works that I am not able to hear.)

In *Three Steps on the Ladder of Writing*, Cixous says: "When choosing a text I am called; I obey the call of certain texts or I am rejected by others" (1993a, 5). Our experience of being called by a person or a text is a recognition of what is other yet akin, and also an experience of what is already akin, despite being other. That is, creatively to "obey the call of certain texts," like obeying the call of certain persons, places, events, ideas, is to permit oneself an emblem of what one is already thinking and feeling unconsciously, and in so doing, to awaken one's own awareness of what one is already thinking and feeling, or might think and feel, and in that moment, to open up a new articulation. We use what we read in order to evoke something previously unarticulated or imagined only vaguely in ourselves; this being called in a writerly way can be a stylistic, libidinal, and paradoxical experience. The poem or novel that we read becomes for us an "evocative object" (Bollas 2011, 47–65) that restores to us some earlier emotional state and at the same time is available for us to use to think with in an intuitive way. We sustain aspects of ourselves by calling and being called by such objects in daily life, from the utilitarian (Bollas' example of this is a bank) to the familial to the artistic. As readers, we practice relating ourselves to ourselves and to others; as writers, we practice a relation to language, and through it, to everything else.

The last novel by the American writer William Maxwell is the seemingly autobiographical *So Long, See You Tomorrow* (1996). The novel is "lyric" in the way a first-person poem is "lyric," seeming to be the speech of the writer himself, rather than the compressed, inescapably somewhat self-alienated work that it is. The author-narrator describes a moment in his boyhood when, after having moved from a small Illinois town to Chicago, he saw, or thought he saw, to his great surprise, in the crowded hallway of his immense new high school, a boy he had known in his home town. But as they pass each other, he does not speak to this other boy, because the author-narrator's pained knowledge of the other boy's tragic childhood inhibits him from offering a greeting. No one else in that school knows what the narrator knows about the other boy. Somehow the weight of others' ignorance stops him from confronting his own pained knowledge; the crowd enforces, without any awareness that it is doing so, the silence of the individual. Somehow the author-narrator evidently senses that even to acknowledge the other boy is to unearth that boy's sorrow and shame, because this hello, unlike that of anyone else in the school, in which both boys are newcomers, would mean "I know you—I know what happened to you."

What makes this silence so moving may be the reader's knowledge that like the other boy, the author-narrator, too, has lived through an utterly disabling loss when he was a child. Narrating his own story many decades later, looking back at his memory of his own loss and of the other boy's loss, the author-narrator realizes with guilt that in fact he snubbed the other boy—who must have recognized him; so the author-narrator hurt the other boy even more than he would have done had he greeted him.

But there's another layer of back-and-forth. We may feel that the author-narrator snubs the other boy because by the other boy the author-narrator is unconsciously reminded of his own tragic childhood and continuing grief. To keep from feeling his own pain, he avoids empathy for the other boy's pain. But artistically I find it more productive to think of this moment the other way around—*because* of his own grief, ever present but unconscious, unacknowledged, even denied, the author-narrator is unable, among his welter of impressions in the school hallway, *not* to see the boy who is (or who only resembles?) someone he knew elsewhere, someone whose presence calls to him. He notices that other boy, in the crowded hallways, only because both of them have experienced great childhood grief. That is what each knows that the other knows. In the emotional structure of the novel, the other boy is a substitute, almost a metonym, for the author-narrator's own feelings. That is, the author-narrator already is emotionally prepared to recognize the other boy (who is also himself) and so is called by him. That other boy, despite the author-narrator's not speaking of it this way, is one of his objects.

As readers, we are unconsciously ready for certain poems, novels, stories, to evoke us; we are unconsciously ready for an awareness that our conscious minds might have resisted. We may duck the occasion, though, and continue down the hall, saying nothing, even to ourselves, not knowing why, or not even realizing that we have ducked.

As we read a text, we may be read by it. It might be a work that

can enable us to read consciously what we are now prepared unconsciously to read but have not yet read. This will probably be true even
if we have read that same work before, for we have all noticed on rereading fiction or poetry an ability to recognize and respond emotionally to elements we did not, could not, or would not hear before.

And a poem or a novel may finally be written out of such recognition of an object — sometimes, it's true, with a falsifying effect, but at
other times with the effect of occupying, or acquiring, something real
of selfhood. By an openness to a widening of inner life, the poet may
sometimes articulate "a truth won from life against all odds, because
a truth in and about a mode of experience to which the mind is normally closed," as Davie (1972, 301) put it.

This process is not merely self-reflexive, which could become self-
oppressive and may be insufficient for opening one's consciousness;
the process also brings to our awareness our unconscious understanding of words and the world, and this allows us to enlarge that understanding. Maxwell's novel is about grief and memory. Reading it, I
realize that it is partly from Cixous that I learned how to read it and
be read by it, how to be read, myself, as a being of grief and memory.
But to some extent I have had to go against my own grain to learn this.
And it seems I sought out Maxwell's novel to help me do this. It is
brief; over a ten-year period, some time ago, I read it three times; observing this of myself, I know that my motive was more than a liking
for it. (There were a few things about it that I did not like.) I used it —
not fully knowing that this was what I was doing — as a way of thinking something I had not managed to think before. This is how a work
of fiction made it possible for me to think.

Obliquely, Maxwell's novel is also about writing a novel. Reading it,
I am drawn into the imagining of writing it. Reading it with the conceptual tool I am calling Cixous, I am launched from reading into writing. So if as a writer I would like to use Cixous's work, I do not mean
that I will pick it up like a tool (i.e., that I will only address aspects of
the craft of writing). Rather, I would try to use it to understand my
own process of thinking while reading and while being read. In reading her work, I sometimes become conscious of what I had been pursuing unconsciously, of what I had wanted to know-by-writing, and
of how I had wanted to be-in-language. Even against my own grain.

To evoke within my own writing or writing-to-be what I intuit might be possible, I use Cixous or Davie, or another writer, sometimes as a kind of hovering presence, and even as an addressee. Cixous has said: "One also writes [. . .] for all the others one has read, that is to say in their honour." She goes further: "I write for the text. It is the text that is my first reader. My only reader, in effect" (Cixous and Calle-Gruber 1997, 101). This is a kind of dialectic of self-presentation to the self—the socially formed part of the self becomes visible to the more intimately formed part, and vice versa, for the two are not entirely the same.

My desire might include presenting, thinking about, myself, but this is my instrument, not my subject. I want to write further into the world—I'm thinking here of the phrase "writing into the world," which was used by Terrence des Pres as the title of what was for me his memorable book of essays about poets who undertook to write about the individual and history.

Yet in thinking about how and what we think, we are trapped by a kind of Zeno's paradox, in that even with some success at occasionally halving the distance between ourselves and the only partly accessible truths both inside and outside us, and becoming aware of why we think as we do, nevertheless at the same time we *are* acculturated and patterned and ingrained already; a tree may sense, in its way, many things, but can it sense its own grain? That seems to be the truth of our truth, our way of apprehending life and self.

Cixous has written, "I only copy the other, it is dictated; and I don't know who the other is" (1993a, 103). This reminds me of another articulation of the writer's relationship to an inner other—which we can call intuition, or the Muse (I return to her at later points). On a page of a small everyday notebook orphaned by his death, the American fiction writer William Goyen jotted down the following:

1. Writing is waiting (for)
2. Finding the Voice.

Hearing the Voice. Story is told to me, I tell it to you.
Otherwise I don't write — or can't write.

Inner others speak — and say what we did not expect, or had not even hoped to hear; or what we "ourselves" may not even have wished to say; or what we never expected to want to say. Their speaking made possible his writing, Goyen found. Their silence stopped his writing. He could not force them to tell him their tales, to let him hear the rhythms and intonations of their voices. You must write what nobody wants to hear, Grace Paley used to urge her writing students. Perhaps the instructor should say to the writing student, You should write what *you* don't want to hear. If my self-alienation is fruitful, then I discover how to accept and use the sense of an other within, whether I am, as a writer of fiction, creating a character, or, as a poet, creating a much more compact sequence of stages of inner life that the reader can for the moment experience as her own. I want to find a way to free myself to write what I hadn't entirely known how to wish to say.

To the writer, the relevance and value of self-alienation is something I first understood in a social sense when I discerned and pondered what Frederick Douglass, Emily Dickinson, and William Carlos Williams had experienced in common. In different ways, and for different reasons, these writers could not address in their writings the communities of those whose experience they shared and on whom they drew for the substance of their work, because those communities were cut off from — respectively — literacy, in the case of the American slaves, whose way of life Douglass had escaped; poetic innovation and mastery, to say nothing of unique metaphysical daring and religious doubt, in the case of Dickinson's backwater Amherst (and, as it turned out, sophisticated Boston as well); and again literacy, perhaps both functional and cultural, in the case of the immigrant families of New Jersey whom Williams treated as a physician, and about whom he sometimes wrote with intense acknowledgment of their fullness as human beings.

The 1845 autobiographical *Narrative of the Life of Frederick Douglass* combines the balance and contrast of eighteenth-century rhetorical eloquence with nineteenth-century specificity and historical urgency.

One of the most admired sentences in this work juxtaposes two incommensurable metonymic emblems—one an emblem of the illiterate slave's deprivation and suffering, the other an emblem of education and freedom, and perhaps also the literate man's obligation to write about and on behalf of the illiterate slave: "My feet have been so cracked with the frost, that the pen with which I am writing might be laid in the gashes" (Douglass 1982, 72). Dickinson's metaphors associated with consciousness and religious belief still astonish the imagination and affright conventional belief. Williams could neither write for his community of patients nor could he wholly please his Modernist, or later New Critical, contemporaries with his resolutely humble subjects, usually simple diction, lack of literary allusion, seemingly improvisational rhythms, and unpredictable poetic lines.

After I came to recognize the paradox of the separation of these writers from their own communities by their very purposes and practices of writing about, and on behalf of, but not to, and even against the grain of, those communities, I realized that Rimbaud's formulation of poetic liberation, *je est un autre*, might be not only a given or sought-for psychological state—as we all take it to be—but also a social effect of the very act of writing. "'I' is an other." Indeed, the poet's temptation to create the poem as a "consensual object," meeting an imagined audience halfway by rewarding already existing expectations regarding the manner and materials of the poem, is not only a social constraint but also a psychic one. ("Market" considerations do enter into the dissemination of poetry, but in a minor way compared to their power over prose.)

William Goyen used Rimbaud's sentence as one of the epigraphs to his novel *The House of Breath* (1950), where it has the effect of alerting the reader in advance to the multiplicity of selves who narrate the book, all of them also in some sense the author-narrator "Goyen." Christopher Bollas has written that in all of us the "containment of so many semi-autonomous [unconscious] psychic workings may be one of the reasons why writers or philosophers are disenchanted with the notion of a unified self." He has also quoted Fernando Pessoa's words (written in 1915): "I feel multiple. I am like a room with innumerable fantastic mirrors that distort by false reflection one single pre-existing reality which is not there in any of them and is there in them all" (2011, 70).

The act of writing, and the result of it, is to place something that was "inside" oneself outside oneself, where we are free to regard it as "alien" and then inquire of it what it is saying back to us — through our word choice, its evocation of our memories and states of feeling, its energy or inertness, its bluntness or subtleties, as language. Cixous says, "This is how I write: as if the secret that is in me were before me" (Cixous and Calle-Gruber 1997, 67).

And if, as Cixous also says, "the subject is only intersubjectivity" (77) — that is, the individual human being is in fact an interrelation with other persons, living and dead, known and read — it's also true that this intersubjectivity can be not only interpersonal (that is, social, as it must be if the writer is to have any understanding of life) but also intrapersonal or intrasubjective. What I mean is that, as far as I can tell, the word *intersubjectivity* must also mean a back-and-forth self-engagement within the writer between and among the different stances and the distinct experiences of different stages of life and our selfhood in different sorts of situations (even if not really different "selves"). What else is the fiction writer's creation of numerous "characters"? Intersubjectivity is also the back-and-forth between the writer and the writer's words on a sheet of paper — the "alienated" work that is external to the body of the writer. Might Freud's *fort/ da* game come into this somehow? If so, it would have something to do with the kinds of feelings the adult has in the midst of this internal back-and-forth, and in the midst of the back-and-forth of all the *objects* that approach one and depart, that one rejects and recalls (in both senses of the word) and reuses, psychically — including *home*: one's home in the world, if one has a home, and one's home within oneself. *Fort!* — "Gone!": out of the crib the small toddler tosses his toy, "a wooden reel with a piece of string tied round it," the symbolic mother. And then *Da!* — "There!": he pulls it — and her — back again. And again and again. Freud says that the child "compensated himself for [the mother's absence], as it were, by himself staging the disappearance and return of the objects within his reach" (1955, 14–15). We reassure ourselves, when we can, that we can survive the loss of our objects. Even more interesting: Do we throw *ourselves* out of the safe crib and pull ourselves back in, while making a poem? While reading one that matters deeply to us?

❄

We search for something, not knowing what it is, never having seen or heard it even when it was in the mind's eye and ear, or in the ears' and eyes' mind. We recall those experiences by which we have learned to perceive, to feel, to think outward along connections to larger realities—like a dirt path and an aunt's tobacco shop called The Two Worlds, in Oran, Algeria, or a street in Barnsley, Yorkshire; like a particular sea-green shirt of pale plaid, an episode of triumph or humiliation that could not be fully acknowledged or even disclosed to oneself, a song to which one danced at the age of fifteen or thirty-four or seventy, arms around another, or around an imagined someone who was absent, emotionally unattainable, or lost. Thrown out in rough word-shape onto paper or tried out viva voce . . . There it is . . . Where, with the practices of the art, it might be made at last into itself.

Czesław Miłosz wrote in his poem "Ars Poetica?" (which I first found in his *Selected Poems* of 1978):

> In the very essence of poetry there is something indecent:
> a thing is brought forth which we didn't know we had in us,
> so we blink our eyes, as if a tiger had sprung out
> and stood in the light, lashing his tail:
> [. . .]
> The purpose of poetry is to remind us
> how difficult it is to remain one person,
> for our house is open, there are no keys in the doors,
> and invisible guests come in and out at will.
>
> (Gibbons 1989, 4)

The keys Miłosz is imagining would lock, not unlock. We might call this the Theory of Miłosz's Tiger—the substantiation, by the bringing forth of the poem, of life within us, even of otherness within us, revealed by the act of writing. Or created by the act of writing. (His tiger has been created, in this sense, by the Muse-as-Magician.) Perhaps this-that-is-brought-forth can be considered animal in the sense of springing at least in part from the body and from the limbic portion of the brain.

The saying of poetry aloud is a way of enacting the essential role of the body in our use of language. The meter of ancient Greek choral odes is the rhythm of the steps of the chorus who danced and sang the ode in performance, and those dances may have been complex, for what characterizes the rhythms is the "wild diversification of meters" by the Greeks, compared to some other ancient languages (Herington 1985, 122). The three great tragedians were deeply ingrained with "the poetry of choral lyric; composing dances simply *was* the poetic act, as they would have met with it in their youth in the age of Pindar" (David 2006, 26–27). (The most ancient meter of all—which is unknown to us now, because it belonged to the prehistoric Proto-Indo-European language that is hypothesized as the origin of all the Indo-European languages—might have derived from weaving songs that encoded the patterns to be produced on the loom; I return to this idea later.)

Davie might not have credited our inner otherness, the portion of our nature that is bodily and animal, or the experience of being several; Cixous would not lament the difficulty described in Miłosz's second stanza, above, of remaining just one person; on the contrary, she has prized it. She might say that the purpose of poetry is to remind us not to want to keep our house closed and locked. Those who might enter are not all murderers and thieves. Well, perhaps some are. But there are intruders already hiding in our inner houses anyway—as Emily Dickinson acknowledged with ecstatic alarm: "Far safer, of a midnight meeting / External Ghost / Than it's [*sic*] interior confronting— / That cooler Host— // Far safer, through an Abbey gallop, / The Stones a'chase— / Than unarmed, one's a'self encounter— / In lonesome Place— // Ourself behind ourself, concealed— / Should startle most— / Assassin hid in our Apartment / Be Horror's least" (Dickinson 1999, Fr407). The conceptual pun on the self's "apartment" could not be more potent.

If the writing on the page is "alienated" from, "other" than, the self that created it, then when the tiger leaps out, the person who has written it should probably study the tiger. And listen to it. Cixous says that in any case "if one wants to be witness to human life," "there must be reading, one must be in a state of readingness [*lisance*], wide awake"-a "readingness" not only of books (Cixous and Calle-Gruber 1997, 67; brackets in original). Especially for the poet pondering the words, provisional and imperfect, on a sheet of paper—words not yet final, or beyond which the poem can't find any further way—the finished poem itself may be a gap, an aporia. Such words might even arouse fear if what they say, like a dangerous animal, has finally been freed from inner captivity. And Cixous adds, "To write is to have such pointy pricked-up ears that we hear what language says (to us) inside our own words at the very moment of enunciation" (85).

I'm trying to characterize the sense of being permitted and invited—perhaps suddenly, by some shift of internal authorities—that can arise when one becomes aware of being at an impasse. The ancient Greek poets regarded those internal authorities as external— the Muse or Muses—but asked of them not the craft of poetry, which the poets themselves had to spend years learning, but a prompting and reminding of what to sing, sometimes in great detail. The stimulus or—as it has often been described—visitation of an unexpected voice or even a phrase, within, permits something previously unimagined to be composed. In Allen Ginsberg's annotations to the facsimile edition of *Howl*, he mentions the moment in 1954 when, after having typed a line that was particularly scandalous in that time, he realized, reading it, that because it was unpublishable he was freed from constraints and could write anything he wanted. "This crucial verse [line 20 of the published text] militated against author's thinking of the writing draft as 'poetry' or 'publishable' in any way that would reach the eyes of his family, thus author was left free to write thenceforth what he actually thought, from his own experience." Ginsberg also reproduces Jack Kerouac's "List of Essentials," thirty rules for writing, which he had "tacked on wall above author's bedstead in North Beach Hotel a year before 'Howl' was written." From these rules or precepts: "1. Scribbled secret notebooks, and wild typewritten pages, for yr own joy[.] 2. Submissive to everything, open, listening" (1986, 126, 136–37).

"I only begin to become myself in writing," Cixous says (Cixous and Calle-Gruber 1997, 93). Writing poetry and fiction, writing anything of substance, can disturb those who do not write and choose not to read, those for whom the act of writing seems a falsification of the living voice. I recall the insistent demand to tell orally "in my own words" what *was* already in my own words but written down (and lying unread on the table), when during the Vietnam War I was given my "hearing" before a draft board in Houston. There I made my case for conscientious objector status. Words that I had put outside myself on the page were not, to the examiners of my patriotism and religious upbringing, authentically mine unless I could say them differently, spontaneously, on that very morning, when questioned. Yet it had been the months of thinking and writing, getting those words onto the page, that had led me to become the person who stood before those three seated men, requesting their permission not to be required to kill anyone.

For me their disturbance recalls a scene in Patrick White's novel *Voss* in which he portrays doomed European early explorers of the Australian interior. In some way this novel is also about the risk of exploring our own vast psychic interior, since we cannot help, complicated creatures that we are, sometimes feeling that our old selves, maybe our present self along with them, may be doomed, either because we cannot discover how to change them and escape being ruled by them, or because we do discover how. At a moment when the expedition led by Voss reaches the point of no return, White's explorers write letters that they think may be their last, they entrust the letters to their sole aboriginal guide, an old man whom they call by the name Dugald, and they send him back to deliver them, if he can, to the now very distant white settlements from which the explorers had set out. Wandering without haste, half-clothed in European garb that is a metonym for an unassimilable Western culture, Dugald encounters a group of fellow aborigines. They notice the flash of white in the pocket of his ragged coat, and they want to see what it is. Dugald takes out the letters:

> One young woman, of flashing teeth, had come very close, and was tasting a fragment of sealing-wax. She shrieked, and spat it out.
>
> With great dignity and some sadness, Dugald broke the remaining seals, and shook out the papers until the black writing was exposed. There were some who were disappointed to see but the pictures of fern roots. A warrior hit the paper with his spear. People were growing impatient and annoyed, as they waited for the old man to tell.
>
> These papers contained the thoughts of which the whites wished to be rid, explained the traveller, by inspiration: the sad thoughts, the

bad, the thoughts that were too heavy, or in any way hurtful. These came out through the white man's writing-stick, down upon the paper, and were sent away.

Away, away, the crowd began to menace and call.

The old man folded the papers. With the solemnity of one who has interpreted a mystery, he tore them into little pieces.

How they fluttered.

The women were screaming, and escaping from the white man's bad thoughts.

Some of the men were laughing.

Only Dugald was sad and still, as the pieces of paper fluttered round him and settled on the grass, like a mob of cockatoos. (1994, 209–10)

In this parable of oral versus writing culture, White portrays the exteriorizing of thought and feeling as the expulsion of "bad" thoughts in the act of writing. They are thus sent away. We Western readers see that this is true, in a not wholly mistaken way. Out come all the tigers of the poetic kind, lashing their image-striped narratives.

Since what one reads on one's own page is partly the unconscious content of both individual psyche and shared language, both individuated feelings and learned attitudes, "alienated" onto the page, one reads a text not only with the eyes but, as White has vividly illustrated, with one's whole culture, one's whole web of beliefs, even (and especially) with one's tongue (in both senses). As Cixous has put it, one reads with "the body. The entrails. Of the soul also" (Cixous and Calle-Gruber 1997, 90). Feeling, thought, and imagination begin in the body as well as in the mind. The ancient Greek word *phrēn* means the physical "midriff" of the body, also "heart" as "the seat of passion," and also "mind" as the "seat of the mental faculties, perception, thought." Cixous writes with the body, longhand; she cannot achieve her "interior voyage" with a machine. Writing longhand, she has said, "[I]t is as if I were writing on the inside of myself" (105). For her, one emblem of this quality of the act of writing is Stendhal's secret childhood writing on the inner waistband of his trousers (103).

For the writer, it's from one's own belly, from one's entrails, that one foretells one's own past feelings and thinking. The written page is the waistband around one's life. One must work to foretell not only the distant past but also the very moment before writing the words one is now reading. With one's own mortal entrails one reads word entrails which are one's own and did not require one's sacrificial dying in order to be brought out before the eyes and body, written or voiced aloud, and studied for what they portend, about the future or the past or the confluence of the two. Or maybe this foretelling of one's own past being (that is, this act of writing) did require one's death. As Cixous has said, "The relationship to death is fundamental. It's the cause. We live, we start writing from death. [. . .] But: for me, death is past. It has already taken place. My own. It was at the beginning" (82). In *Three Steps on the Ladder of Writing*, Cixous sends writers first of all to her "School of the Dead." If we want to write at all truthfully—

> (I hope you will forgive me if I use the word "truth." The moment I say "truth" I expect people to ask: "What is truth?" "Does truth exist?" Let us imagine that it exists. The word exists, therefore the feeling exists.) (1993a, 36)

—then we must at least "try to unlie" (36). And "writing or saying the truth is equivalent to death, since we cannot tell the truth" (37). To try to tell it, we try to write as if we were and were not ourselves. As if we were departing from ourselves by dying for a little while.

So let us consider the idea of departure as another sort of "de-family-arizing," not unrelated to the poetic and linguistic kind. Again I think of William Goyen, who seems to me to have been one of the greatest American practitioners of Cixous's *écriture féminine*; in an interview that he gave to a French literary magazine, *Masques*, in the year before he died, he said:

> Despite their [his parents'] disapproval, I applied myself to writing in order to liberate myself. [. . .] I was close enough to my family, but also very alone. I didn't understand anything about the pursuits and interests of children my own age. What they did didn't appeal to me. I was alone and remained alone, with one wish: to leave. I would remain sitting in a corner for hours. This would greatly annoy my friends. It was always like this. Next, I set myself to using anything

that allowed me some form of escape (sex, pills, alcohol, etc.). And now, regardless of where I find myself (at a concert, a restaurant . . .), I always sit where it will be possible for me to leave, because in my head, it is possible that I'll be inclined to do just that. (2007, 106–7)

Cixous: "Writing has been for me, since my childhood, the place of independence and escape" (1993b, 215). Earlier, I mentioned the back-and-forth between the writer and the work, between the writer and the other(s) within the writer, between home and away. Many of Goyen's short stories are about longing to go home, about going home and yet about feeling an urgent need to leave home, and about departing with both relief and regret. Goyen's several uses of a narrative of bodily geographical leaving and returning is also in effect a way to imagine a movement within one's own feelings.

There is a broader sense of it in the French aphorism of Samuel Beckett that Goyen liked to quote — "L'artiste qui joue son être est de nulle part. Il n'a pas de pays. Et il n'a pas des frères." As Goyen himself paraphrased it: "The artist who uses his life completely, throws it full into the tide, is of no place. And he has no country, he has no kin" (2007, 63). And yet Goyen the wanderer was a writer utterly grounded in, fascinated by, a captive of, his local place — both culturally and linguistically — in his portrayal of small-town East Texas in the first half of the twentieth century. Perhaps Beckett's aphorism is also about standing apart existentially from ourselves and others. It is about an imaginative death of oneself and of those to whom one is close, in love or anger, desire or hatred; or about an absence from them that can make it possible to write beyond the limitations of the psychologically consensual. Cixous has said: "Writing is first of all a departure" (1998, 139). This is a hard truth.

⊙ 3 ⊙

On Rhyme

A song is a form of linguistic disobedience.

JOSEPH BRODSKY (1986, 136)

Brodsky's apothegm is about Osip Mandelshtam, who himself wrote, "Poetic speech [...] is never sufficiently 'pacified' [...]. It is amber in which a fly buzzes, embedded ages ago in resin, the living alien body continuing to live even in its petrification" (1977, 80). In Brodsky's essays, collected in two volumes (*Less Than One* and *On Grief and Reason*), there are many passing comments about how poetry is written in Russian. Collecting these has given me a sense of rhyme that I had not gained from my lifelong reading of poetry in English, and now I think I can see in English, here and there, something like the most idiomatically Russian way of using rhyme — even though I don't know Russian. Brodsky says that the Russian poet wants a rhyme that is unforeseen, that counters expectation, that is a gesture of "linguistic disobedience." Yet in English, end-rhyme itself has been felt, especially by those poets who have avoided it, to be inherently a form of obedience. In the minds of most American poets, perhaps including many who choose to rhyme, rhyming is merely conforming to already existing poetic practices. And of course it's *very* difficult to do well — not to find the right sounds, but to find the right ideas in the right sounds. How might we see rhyme more as Russian poets do? The crux is surely in the relationship of rhyme to poetic thinking.

There are so many varieties of poetic thinking: from the narrative to the discursive; from the presentation of psychic and structural unities to the shattering of the links between images, feelings, ideas, and even words; from the staging of paratactic imagistic sequences to the syntactic interrelation of complex parts; from dreamlike free association that moves with an emotional progress across primary-process gaps, to meditations with brief, intense, singular focus; from a concentration of meaning so as to produce a sense of the unity of a poem, to a profligate proliferation of meanings so as to produce a sense of openness and indeterminate multiplicity; from the confession—narrative or meditative or imagistic—of inner life or outward acts to a rather impersonal presentation of aspects of the world; from the belief that language can reveal what it cannot name directly, to the argument that language can never represent adequately even what it can name, describe, and narrate, and can only generate more of itself in a self-reflexive recursion. (I have only begun to inventory the possibilities.) And there are so many devices and techniques of poetic thinking. Brodsky says that ideas and themes in poems are typically generated not by how Russian poets and poetry use language but by how the Russian language uses poets and poetry (1986, 124–25, 127). (He considers Thomas Hardy an example of what seems to him the less interesting—but in Hardy's case very impressive—example of how poetry can sometimes be made first from insight, and only secondarily from the sounds of words [1995, 312–375].)

Since the origins of poetry were in ancient oral culture, we might assume that oral poetry used end-rhyme, perhaps as a mnemonic device. But the oldest Western works (like the Homeric poems created in an oral tradition over hundreds of years) use end-rhyme in only a few lines. Likewise, the later imitations of and responses to the Homeric poems, including Vergil's *Aeneid* and the *Argonautica* of Apollonius of Rhodes, have few examples of end-rhyme. (And scarcely any work by ancient Greek and Latin poets uses end-rhyme.) In fact, "most of the world's 4,000 languages lack or avoid rhyme in their poetries altogether" (*Princeton Encyclopedia of Poetry & Poetics* 2012, 1182). It may be that rhyme is an advanced poetic technology that has only occasionally been used in an advanced way.

In our individual origins—our childhood—rhyme is present in the naturalness of our play with language. Iona and Peter Opie, in *The Lore and Language of Children* (1959) and other works, have provided innumerable instances of the pleasures and inventiveness of rhyming. It may be that rhyme is one of our adult ways of recurring pleasurably to our Edenic language days, if we were lucky enough to have them. But rhyme goes much further than pleasure.

Literary rhyme, simple or sophisticated, is first of all a way of marking individual verses as poetic. It is a structural device, whether to create snugness or pleasing complexity. And it thinks.

Whatever else all the devices of poetic language do, we can argue that all of them are for the basic purpose of marking poetic language as such; that is, they signal the difference between the special potency of language in a poem and the language used for other purposes that are less engaged with special knowledge, emotional intensity, portent, or the sacred. This is true even when the language of the poem is of an everyday kind, because meaning-making powers of language become intensified in poetry even when the diction is simple. The marked language of poetry effects the poetic stance toward language. And whatever poetry may be used for, it is first of all a particular stance toward language itself.

All poetic devices have an "indexical function," as Calvert Watkins shows in his formidably wide-ranging collection of studies of ancient and even prehistoric poetics *How to Kill a Dragon*. In a poem, each poetic device or effect is like an index finger of the poem itself with which the poem points to the "message"—that is, to itself—calling attention to itself as an occasion of language with a purpose beyond everyday functionality (1995, 29). Marked language *indicates*: "I am a poem (or prayer, hymn, curse, blessing, etc.)." (This idea of a metaphorical linguistic pointing is well established in language; a number of English words for forms of communication that at first glance no longer look related to each other ultimately derive, in fact, from the same word, the Proto-Indo-European root *deik-, including *digit, diction, predict, preach, betoken,* and dozens more.)

In modern English, rhyme at its most conventional and least interesting has been a pleasing ornament at the end of the line of a song or poem—when it was not dulling and, in the last one hundred years, associated with outdated poetic fashion. (Although there can be a historical or conventional association between any given poetic device and an attitude—like the prevalent American attitude today toward rhyme—I doubt there can be any innate connection, since every conceivable attitude has been expressed by poets in one place or another in every conceivable poetic mode and with the use of every poetic device.)

For artistic constraints, of which rhyme is one, to be productive, they must be turned into a mode of producing discovery, improvisation, liberation, ideas, and otherwise unattainable articulation. (This use of constraint to produce invention is the basis of the works of the twentieth-century French writers of the group that called itself a "workshop of potential literature," *Ouvroir de literature potentielle,* "Oulipo," including Italo Calvino, Raymond Queneau, and Georges Perec.) And the paradox of artistic constraint is what led Paul Valéry to say that poets are those to whom the difficulty of writing verse *gives* ideas, not those from whom it takes them away. There's no doubt that rhyme at its most meaningful and phonetically inventive — even when it is used for comic effect — is or can be a powerful cognitive device. It is part of how poetry thinks, how it makes its own sort of "logic" — that is, how it engages us with its own way of enchanting, informing, enlivening, persuading, and moving us.

There would have been magical thinking in the earliest use of repeated word-sounds in poetry — as would have been true of all the poetic devices used by rhapsodes, bards, priests, oracles, scops, imbongis, shamans, and others. Repeated sounds (and other devices) made poetic language more powerful in its effects than ordinary language as used by people without poetic skills. The special language of singers and chanters had powers of en*chant*ment and also efficacy in appealing to the divine, while the commands of kings exemplified a linguistic power over others. Ordinary people too might memorize a spell for healing or for troubling someone, if they could. (While end-rhyme is used in the magic spells, curses, prayers, and hymns of some languages, it isn't necessarily missed in those same sorts of magical utterances in other languages in which rhyme isn't used, because other indexical features — including subtler phonetic repetitions — are present, such as the use of special words, rhythm, symbols, metaphors, and also allusions to and invocations of divine powers.)

No surprise, then, that in the remote past rhyming has also created anxiety about its magical power — for example, among the English with regard to the Irish, whom the English conquered, ruled, starved, and contemned. The Celtic poetic traditions of the Irish preserved ancient poetic practices that English no longer had. Given the impressive intricacy of word sounds and poetic form in Gaelic and Welsh, so unlike those of English, and also the whole history of English political domination, it is no surprise that some of the English maligned or joked about pagan poetic powers. Brewer's *Dictionary of Phrase and*

Fable (1898, n.p.), an English work, preserves some of these prejudices in its entry on "Rhyming to Death":

> The Irish at one time believed that their children and cattle could be "eybitten," that is, bewitched by an evil eye, and that the "eybitter," or "witch," could "rime" them to death.

That is, it was a belief in both an evil eye and an evil mouth. And also in the subentry on "Irish rats rhymed to death":

> It was once a prevalent opinion that rats in pasturages could be extirpated by anathematising them in rhyming verse or by metrical charms. This notion is frequently alluded to by ancient authors. Thus, Ben Jonson says: "Rhyme them to death, as they do Irish rats" (*Poetaster*); Sir Philip Sidney says: "Though I will not wish unto you . . . to be rimed to death, as is said to be done in Ireland"(*Defence of Poesie*); and Shakespeare makes Rosalind say: "I was never so berhymed since . . . I was an Irish rat," alluding to the Pythagorean doctrine of the transmigration of souls (*As You Like It*, iii. 2).

Now, we understand that we do experience — we *are* — a continuous streaming of unconscious mental activity; we know that what we say and write, what we hear and read, can reveal to one person meanings beyond what is apparent to someone else, and we also know that mere words, with tremendous effect, can wound or bless, condemn or rescue. We can still feel a sensation of the inexplicable in language, even as the discipline of neurolinguistics is hovering over MRI machines to biologize it (which will then make some of what's potent available as mere method for inducing us to believe or buy something). We understand in a modern way, just as much as preliterate peoples did and do in their way, that the effect of words can be outsized.

There is another sense, too, in which language can still be thought of as magical, without our believing in magic. That is the somewhat "mystical" view of language that it has the capacity to listen to itself, and to respond to itself — that is, a capacity to rhyme itself.

❋

How then might rhyme think? What kind of cognition can rhyme achieve? When we read or hear a poem, a potent rhyme-pair sets us thinking and feeling on a short path that creates a conceptual and even an implied syntactic relationship between the two words, apart from the phrases and sentences of the poem. The thought created by the rhyme accompanies and supplements for just a moment what the poem articulates. That is, the rhyme may give us supplementary meanings and even phantom statements that the poem does not present explicitly. Despite its infrequent showing in English-language poetry, or because of it, it's this use of rhyme that I used to think was most important.

But most of the rhyming in any anthology of canonical poetry in English is ornamental. With an intricate weaving of repeated sounds all through the lines, so that the end-rhymes do not need to think very much, George Herbert could exceed the merely ornamental while using it. He begins his "Virtue" thus:

> Sweet day, so cool, so calm, so bright,
> The bridal of the earth and sky:
> The dew shall weep thy fall tonight,
> For thou must die.

(2004, 80)

We hear the dense indexical repetition of phonemes marking this utterance as poetic. Herbert not only end-rhymes "bright" and "tonight" but also rhymes "bright" with the first syllable of "bridal" in the second line; he half-rhymes "cool" with "calm," "bridal," and "fall"; he echoes the vowel in "cool" with that in "dew" with a precise aptness (dew is cool); he adds to the rhyme on the open vowels of "sky" and "die" the internal rhyme on "thy." Meanwhile there's the vowel echo of "sweet" in "weep," and more repetition of sounds. At the very least, all this gives us pleasures of the ear. And Herbert does add ideas by means of the acoustic equivalency of "bright" and "tonight" (this phantom statement is of a sharp contradiction) and the acoustic equivalency of "sky" and "die" (that is, in the paradoxical idea of the death of something that does not, cannot, die). The added meaning falls short of a discovery of a new *image* by means of rhyme; nor is anything visual created in the mind's eye by the way the word "sky" invites and finds the word "die" phonetically. (But with the advantages of our belatedness, reading Herbert almost four hundred years after his death, I do think of Osip Mandelshtam's image of a grave in the air, in his 1937 lines to the unknown soldier in what we know as the "Voronezh Note-books" [1996, 82].)

Herbert's density of repeated phonemes reminds us that the English language is an excellent medium for sound repetition that is short of full rhyme, and we hear this marker (in the basic indexical sense) of poetic language in poetry without end-rhyme, too. There is a lot of it in any poet with a great ear. Consider the opening lines of Thomas McGrath's poetic account (in Part One, section III, of his *Letter to an Imaginary Friend*) of the threshing during his childhood on an early twentieth-century farm in North Dakota:

> Out of the whirring lamp-hung dusk my mother calls.
> From the lank pastures of my sleep I turn and climb,
> From the leathery dark where the bats work, from the coasting
> High all-winter all-weather Christmas hills of my sleep.
> And there is my grandfather chewing his goatee,
> Prancing about like a horse. And the drone and whir from the fields
> Where the thresher mourns and showers on the morning stillness
> A bright fistful of whistles.
>
> (1997, 14)

Certain vowels and consonants are sounded again and again without being brought into full rhyme: wh**irr**ing, t**ur**n, leath**er**y, w**or**k, wint**er**, weath**er**, th**er**e, grandfath**er**, h**or**se, wh**ir**, thresh**er**, show**er**s, morn-ing; da**rk**, wo**rk**; stil**l**ness, fistf**ul**, whist**l**es; **la**mp-hung, **la**nk, **lea**th-ery; **leather**y, **all-weather**; **coa**sting, **goa**tee; and other repeated pho-nemes. Such rich sound used for such rich description has something to do with what McGrath, speaking about *Letter*, called "bringing [people] into the light of *speech*" itself, the light of language (Gibbons and Des Pres 1992, 91).

In such a passage there is a poetic "acoustic inevitability"—Brodsky used this phrase to describe the effect of the repetition of the vowel *a* in Anna Akhmatova's pen name (she was born Anna Go-renko; Brodsky 1986, 35). But in McGrath there is only the faintest, uncertain sense, although I think it may be there, although too subtly for me to analyze, that the sounds of the words might be generating ideas. Yet the variety and concreteness of McGrath's diction in this passage—like that of other poets who enjoy the chewy consonantal pleasure of *naming* in English—may be precisely what "acoustic in-evitability" in Russian is *not* like. Mandelshtam wrote, "No language resists more strongly than Russian the tendency toward naming and utilitarian application" (Mandelstam 1979, 121). And, by contrast: "Having expended its philological reserves brought over from Europe, America began to act like someone now crazed, now thoughtful; then all of a sudden, she initiated her own particular philology from which Whitman emerged; and he, like the new Adam, began giving names, began behaving like Homer himself, a model for a primitive American poetry of nomenclature" (125). Perhaps Mandelshtam would have agreed that for the ancient choral poets "to name something is not simply to employ its sign, but also to sing its melody" (David 2006, 47).

"Acoustic inevitability" can be illustrated more definitively when a rhyme word pulls the poem forward in a way that is both surprising and convincing—when, that is, the rhyme creates and justifies the movement of the thought. The sound leads the thinking. Keats's richly orchestrated odes to the nightingale, the Grecian urn, Psyche, and the divine personification Autumn, as lovely as these poems sound, only rarely seem to me to do this, but for a moment the ode to Melancholy is rich with it. While the second and third stanzas of this poem seem to rhyme only in an ornamental way, the first stanza's phonemic equivalencies speed the poem to thought and feeling beyond what it *says*:

No, no, go not to Lethe, neither twist
    Wolf's-bane, tight-rooted, for its poisonous wine;
Nor suffer thy pale forehead to be kiss'd
    By nightshade, ruby grape of Proserpine;
Make not your rosary of yew-berries,
    Nor let the beetle, nor the death-moth be
        Your mournful Psyche, nor the downy owl
A partner in your sorrow's mysteries;
    For shade to shade will come too drowsily,
        And drown the wakeful anguish of the soul.
                      (1995, 197)

Paradoxically, Keats's evocation of the ominous menagerie and poisonous garden of what we call depression gives his diction sensuous pleasures of sound and striking concreteness (which of course the English language loves and for which it rewards poets): wolf's-bane, nightshade, yew-berries, beetle, death-moth, owl. The repetitions of sounds—phonetic figures—lead the poem forward: the *w* and *n* of "**wolf's-bane**" are *compressed* (as are grapes!) into "**wine**," then the berries of the "nightshade" *become* the "grape" (i.e., the source of a second "poisonous wine") of Proserpine (whose name as Keats used it rhymes with "wine"). The "yew-b**erries**" become "myst**eries**" (!), for "Lethe" has led us by association to the cemetery "yew-berries" and the corpse beetle. The full rhyme of "twist" and "kist" makes of a tender, intimate gesture a violent torqueing—violence not explicitly stated amid the emotional languishing and decline of these lines. Note that the rhythm of the three-syllable dactylic rhymes, somewhat unusual in English in a somber poem, seems to enact descent, decline: "yew-berries" and "mysteries," and then "drowsily."

Most striking, one train of thought led by the sounds of the words goes from an *owl* to the melancholy *soul* at risk of self-destruction, and leaves the owl presiding, whether in type or in handwritten words, in a line-final position, *over* the rhyme-word and idea "soul." The owl, a denizen of darkness both literal and figurative, threatens to rule the soul.

The limitations of typography prevent me from indicating all the phonetic figures without a diagram. A double melody of *o* goes from "N**o**, n**o**, g**o**" to "D**o**wny **owl**" to "sorr**ow**" to "**Drow**sily" to "**Drow**n" to "**soul**." (Perhaps Keats's pronunciation made "owl" and "soul" a full rhyme; in both hostile and friendly ways, he was ridiculed for his Cockney accent.) This phonetic thread links together the owl, the cry of pain in the repeated "ow" of "downy," "drowsily," and "drown" (!), and the sensations and state of melancholy or depression. The thought moves inevitably, yet at the same time surprisingly, from toxic herbs to creatures of death and to the threat (or promise) of unconsciousness that would "drown the wakeful anguish of the soul." Each repeated phoneme discovers echoes of itself in other words, and these bring with them images of the bird, weeping, sleep, threatening water, and then, at last, what cannot be visually imagined, the soul. The end-rhymes and other phonetic figures do much more than ornament the poem and mark it with repetition of sounds and bound it with resonant line endings; they lead the thinking from idea to idea.

Brodsky writes:

Poetry is not "the best words in the best order"; for language it is the highest form of existence. In purely technical terms, of course, poetry amounts to arranging words with the greatest specific gravity in the

most effective and *externally inevitable* sequence. Ideally, however, it
is language negating its own mass and the laws of gravity; it is language's striving upward—or sideways—to that beginning where the
Word was. (1986, 186; my italics)

In his essays—published in English for English-language readers—
when Brodsky happens to speak of how poetry makes meaning, he
gives only passing mention to elements of poetic technique that are
not at the center of most poetry in English, in either the reading or
the writing of it. But he says enough to give us important information about Russian poetic technique. He mentions Marina Tsvetaeva's "word-root dialectics" (186), her "specifically poetic technology:
sound association, root rhyme, semantic enjambment, etc." (179),
and her thinking with a "pianistic rather than a standard grammatical logic," in which "each successive exclamation, as when keys are
pressed, starts up when the sound of the previous one dies out" (207).
(By this he means, I think, that the sound of a substantive word arises,
like a note in a melodic sequence, from a previous note or chord; the
poem like a musical composition is thinking by means of sound.)
Speaking of a poem by Tsvetaeva, he says that "a poet is someone
for whom every word is not the end but the beginning of a thought;
someone who, having uttered *rai* ('paradise') or *tot svet* ('next world'),
must mentally take the subsequent step of finding a rhyme for it. Thus
krai ('edge/realm') and *otsvet* ('reflection') emerge" (265).

Of the sound of Mandelshtam's poetry, Brodsky says, "[I]t became
more a song than ever before, not bardlike but a birdlike song, with
its sharp, unpredictable turns and pitches, something like a goldfinch
tremolo" (134). Clarence Brown wrote in his book on Mandelshtam
about this poet's "gaiety of language" even when his subject, his materials, are most somber and tragic, and the "boisterous joviality and
jangling" of the language of some of his poems (1978, 195, 227).

❋

Commenting on a few poems by the early nineteenth-century Russian poet Evgeny Baratynsky, Ilya Kutik has written:

Rhyme in Russian poetry is indeed a factor in the production of
meaning, rather than a mere phonetic embellishment, an extra flourish at the end of the line. The syntactical and grammatical possibilities

of Russian are inexhaustible, since we have genders, tenses, declensions and an extensive range of subordinates; in the absence of a fixed word order, a sentence can begin with any element. Rhyme, partaking of the "elasticity" of Russian grammar (a Greek freedom, according to the great eighteenth-century poet Mikhail Lomonosov), is consequently unpredictable and gives rise to unexpected images.

Kutik describes the poet's process of rhyming in Russian:

> [T]he poet concludes his/her first line with the most important word in the line, for which he/she then tries to find an unexpected, "distant" rhyme. The more unexpected (or unprecedented) it is, the more the meaning that emerges in the poem is surprising—and therefore profound. I should add that the tradition of Russian poetry is "vertical" and not "horizontal" (as is English-language poetry, among other traditions). By this I mean that almost every Russian poet, whether in the nineteenth century or the twenty-first, has a complete and profound awareness of his or her poetic tradition, a tradition that precedes the [poet's] very first poem and [includes] all previously known rhymes and word combinations. The "trick" consists in seeing the whole poetic map (or pack of cards), but not repeating oneself in cases where any particular rhyme has a pre-existent meaning.

Kutik uses the metaphor of "centrifugal" to describe the difference between such rhyme in Russian and rhyme elsewhere:

> [R]hyme is the primary centrifugal factor in our poetry, and not centripetal as in the poetry of many European poetic traditions. In French, for instance, the only fixed stress is on the final syllable, and unpredictability [of rhyme] is virtually impossible, as is compound rhyme (where the rhyme extends over several syllables). In English too it is well-nigh impossible since only the rhyming syllables are *heard* and not the complete rhyme-words. (One can see why free verse finally triumphed in French and English poetry, since it offers a liberation from the limitations and set patterns of the language, which in Russian do not exist.) In Russian, where words are "heard" in their entirety, with all their prefixes and suffixes, and not just the endings, *the creation of meaning through rhyme is the most vital justification of the poetic image*, since it is rhyme that prevents it from becoming what one might call "irresponsibly surrealist," in other words *unjustified,*

however unexpected and surprising it may be. It is as if the Russian poet was throwing a word into the linguistic abyss and waiting to see what other word it will return to. That is why Baratynsky [in his poem "Rhyme"] compares rhyme to the dove in the ark, which returned to Noah with a branch in its beak, a "message" from an unknown land. [. . .] [R]hyme is for the poet above all a searching device that animates the language. (2007, 565–67; my italics)

To give an example of how rhyme works at its strongest, I will use an example from Russian. I must repeat my earlier disclaimer that I know no Russian, but working for several years with Kutik on translations of his own poems and those of Boris Pasternak, Osip Mandelshtam, Marina Tsvetaeva, Gennadiy Aigi, Bella Akhmadulina, Alexei Parshchikov, and others, I have become acquainted with a kind of poetic thinking, based partly on rhyme, that few poets writing in English have pursued, and I begin to understand why translations of Russian poems do not show us what is marvelous about *how* thought and feeling, eye and ear, move in the originals. English does not have the resources for this that Russian does; nevertheless, I find myself wondering what English might be capable of if such a rhyming were pursued. Or if, as a Russian poet might say, English-language poets allowed English to listen to itself more. Brodsky put it this way: "[T]hrough self-audition language achieves self-cognition" (1986, 193).

And that cognition is not exactly what the English-language reader might expect. Hoping I have understood well the translation lessons I have received from Kutik, I will say that Russian poetry can think "synthetically" by *unifying* simultaneous *discrepant* connotations, gathering them together in the mind as one overall idea or impression from the simultaneous possibilities of, say, a poetic image. English, meanwhile, as we know, tends to think "analytically" by *discriminating* among the connotations of that image, ruling one or two in and all the others out. From my position of ignorance—although I think I have learned about as much concerning Russian poetry as anyone who doesn't speak Russian can learn, however little that may be—Russian makes it possible for poetry to think a meaning that includes, rather than chooses between, opposites, and also to apprehend a verbal negative space (analogous somehow to such space in sculpture) that is created by paradox, absence, negatives, and invisible qualities and entities rather than visible ones. Russian poems find vivid imaginary possibilities in what *is real* (or, to our English-language habits of thought, what *might* be real) but can't be verified by sight or touch; English does its imagining partly for the sake of the sheer linguistic vividness—sound, specificity, rhythm—of language that is "concrete." (We might think of Seamus Heaney's richly consonantal diction in his poems and in his translation of *Beowulf*—the English of Heaney's *Beowulf*, like the poem's original Old English, has a pagan palpability, if I may call it that, despite the poem's touches of Christian morality. Heaney's diction argues implicitly, in a way, for the rhythmic and phonetic qualities of Old English pagan mortality, and creates a felt contrast of *sound*, as do the most musical poems of Gerard Manley Hopkins, between the spiritual and the physical.) Russian poetry prizes making the absent, the spiritual, and the inconceivable seem palpable; English poetry mostly prizes making what is concrete and palpable and visible, thingy, touchable, seem present. To say this as Pindar might have said it (I come to him later), "Concreteness loves the English language."

In the following translation of Ilya Kutik's 1980 poem "Hunchback," which the poet and I have produced together, we approached the nature of Russian rhyming from several starting points, which I will take up in turn.

. . . and, like a cupola, the ceiling swelled up . . .

ANNA AKHMATOVA

He's ambassador and bishop of the twisted backbone;
Crazed as antique crockery; he's a bird-bud,
A flower-fledgling, a mum mediator between
This world and a miracle, swollen at their thoracic battle-line.

Hugging, so to speak, his own hump, he gusts across
An apocryphal Khazarian steppe in some Scyth-written Bible,
And maybe in that book he bends stoop-backed
Like a hump-beaked Judith over Holofernes' head.

Embracing his treasure-chest backpack of a hump,
Pursued by breast-thumping zealots who would exclude him,

Already he arrives, as foretold: a one-bag postman who
Amidst their two-humped desert dreams alone in his room.

(Kutik 2006, 26)

Thematically, Kutik's "Hunchback" links the swelling of a human hump to the development of an artistic gift, to the possibility of a miracle, of a roaming freedom (those Scythians), and even of triumph over what dominates us (the unhallowed unhollow dome of the hump; or the Biblical tyrant Holofernes). The hunchback carries, and is, the distortion of his own being. In the space-time continuum of relativity in matters poetic, through my English audio-telescope I see that it's not only the cluster of ideas brought together in the poem but also the poem's fast-moving train of association that is its subject (as well as its method). In the comments that follow, I am mostly transcribing and parsing what Kutik has told me about the poem and about the particular genealogy of one strain of contemporary Russian poetry that he and others have created since the early 1980s, usually called "Metarealism" (a name that the poets themselves did not choose). From within the limits of my understanding of the traditions and possibilities of the poetry even of my own language, I will have misunderstood some of Kutik's intentions and achievements, and in my account of the poem I will have unwittingly altered not only the poem but also some of Kutik's poetic thinking. But I hope to open up in English the possibility of a kind of poetic thinking that I did not even perceive before working at this translation and others.

Kutik argues that the differences between Russian and American poetry are really between two kinds of poetic speech in general, and two different poetic impulses. I take him to mean: two very different sets of permissions and prohibitions, goals and achievements, in our ways of writing—two different ways of poetic thinking, and of course two different linguistic and literary histories. In no way can we poets and readers, in English and in our historical moment, think by means of the same kinds of association that Kutik and his contemporaries perceive or achieve in Russian. This translation of "Hunchback" cannot readily be fitted into contemporary (or earlier) American poetry. The translation is a specific, detailed suggestion of what is missing in it.

Attracted by Kutik's use of metaphor—which seems to me just as unfamiliar, and therefore interesting, as, for example, the metaphors in the self-translated Zulu poet Mazisi Kunene, or those of Mahmoud Darwish (as we have them in English translation), and therefore exciting to ponder—I asked him directly what he was doing. He told me that for many modern and contemporary Russian poets, metaphor is inescapably intertwined with rhyme—especially for him and his fellow "Metarealists."

In looking back at earlier poetry and choosing (or being evoked by) their own poetic precursors, Kutik and the other Metarealists have prized poetry that reveals alternative worlds of the imagination. They regard metaphor as inadequate if it is only a vivid way of presenting or describing what is real and visible. And having begun as anti-Romantics and remaining so, the Metarealists dislike poems in which the poet's focus privileges his or her own experience or inner life.

No, they say: a poet is no Romantic hero, but is like everyone else . . . except that at certain moments he or she sort of swells (like the ceiling in the poem's epigraph from Akhmatova, or like the hump itself as the man matures). The hump is in a way an organ, for it is the capacity to see metaphorically what is *of the existing world but is hidden until words are found for it.* In fact, a poem is not about representing visible reality, but about attending to a "metareality." The hump is a kind of lucky deformity. It *attracts to itself* some image-rhymes which, without the hunchback, would not or could not be seen *as* "humps." They are not shaped as "humps" until in the poem they are *discovered* to be humps by means of language.

In another context, Kutik wrote to me that Metarealism "brings the thing over as such, as a whole, an invisible thing that the poet makes visible, convex, palpable—out of the blue (or rather, from the darkness of something that we don't penetrate)." That is, his metaphor for how poetry makes things visible to the imagination is that it makes them swell into perceptibility. They become "convex," as if palpable by the imagination, not one's fingers.

Metaphor itself goes through metamorphosis, Kutik told me. What came to mind when I heard this was the unforgettable passage in Mandelshtam's "Conversation about Dante" in which he explained that Dante *launches* into the air an image that is itself able to create, beyond the poet's own will. In Mandelshtam's own poems, the image is *not* a touch of detail for the sake of a vividness of description (as is typical in English-language poetry) but a metaphor. Here is Clarence Brown's translation of the passage:

As in all true poetry, Dante's thinking in images is accomplished with the help of a characteristic of poetic material which I propose to call its transformability or convertibility. It is only by convention that the development of an image can be called development. Indeed, imagine to yourself an airplane (forgetting the technical impossibility) which in full flight constructs and launches another machine. In just the same way, this second flying machine, completely absorbed in its own flight, still manages to assemble and launch a third. In order to make this suggestive and helpful comparison more precise, I will add that the assembly and launching of these technically unthinkable machines that are sent flying off in the midst of flight do not constitute a secondary or peripheral function of the plane that is in flight; they form a most essential attribute and part of the flight itself, and they contribute no less to its feasibility and safety than the proper functioning of the steering gear or the uninterrupted working of the engine. (Mandelstam 2004, 122–23)

The movement of a poem is by means of a series of images evoked by words whose similarity of sound (phonetic repetition alone or also morphological repetition, which is a drawing out of one word the next one) creates an image. Or rather: a word evokes another word through a similarity of sound, and this next word, chosen both *because* of its sound *and* for its availability as an *image*-word, takes the poem's next step of thought. Clarence Brown wrote of this mode of poetic thinking, "The idea of series, of one word-image being born out of another [. . . conveys] the essentially kinetic nature of this phenomenon. It is what Mandelstam himself repeatedly described as one of the most fundamental processes of poetry [. . .]. There is not necessarily any logical relationship between the terms of a series. If there were, its direction might be predictable and thus bereft of what is most basic to it: the surprise of perpetual discovery in unsuspected regions of the imagination" (1978, 285).

Mandelshtam's deep idea about poetic thinking is not idiosyncratic, for it can be seen in poems by his generational (in both senses of the word) contemporaries Marina Tsvetaeva and Boris Pasternak (poems that I know only through my cotranslating with Kutik and my reading of translations by others). And a flash of this kind of poetic thinking can occasionally be seen in poets who are not Russian in passages that almost leap into one's readerly awareness simply because

Mandelshtam's work has alerted one to a mode of poetic thinking which otherwise one might not even notice. Here are two examples of the *idea* of such image making—in that one image creates the next—albeit not of Dante's or Mandelshtam's full flight: from Mahmoud Darwish, "Mountain goats leap out of mountain goats onto the temples" (2003, 32), and Angela Jackson, "As if the house / built the house / and lived in it" (1998, 85). (In Kutik's own comments on his "Hunchback" below, he points out a few of the metamorphoses of his metaphors.)

Kutik has described to me how the anti-Romantic stream of Russian poetry flowed directly from the Baroque to the twentieth century without passing through the personal inner explorations begun during the nineteenth century. So we might mistake Kutik's hunchback for an unsurprising poetic descendant of the marginal figures—such as leech gatherer, beggar, discharged soldier, and others—brought so vividly into Romantic poetry by Wordsworth, or of various figures and scenes in the poems of John Clare. But of course there's no resemblance—Kutik's hunchback is a metaphor, and the poem has nothing from the everyday world in it. It is not a portrait but a feat of linked imagination and ear. Also, the late twentieth-century Russian Metarealists turned away, Kutik says, from the Romantic practice of making "their own lives (not only inner but also factual) the only subject worthy of being described." The English Romantics are not quite that slender, poetically!—but anyway Kutik's contrast with Romanticism in general is clear. Kutik's hunchback is not a metaphor for a poet who wants to claim unusual powers of feeling and sympathy for others and with nature, but rather a figure for the extraordinary but temporary powers of *transformation* of which the poet and language, together, are capable. The hunchback is an image of poetic imagination—no winged horse, no self-exalted hero of feeling, but a prophetic human aberration whose presence in the poem evokes startling metaphors for what can be seen not with eyes but only with imagination.

Human feeling may be paramount in almost all poetry, but what if it were *outside the self*, seen not lyrically but with what Kutik has called "epic sight"? He has explained to me, "Not 'I'm nervous' but 'My nerves are nervous.'" The artistic goal of Metarealism is to describe what cannot be seen—like the swelling of imaginative seeing-with-words, or the void inside a triumphal arch. Kutik has offered me some material examples—the inner functions of a tree, the microscopic wars of bacteria—but even his mentioning them felt like a simplification for my toddling poetry mind, for these clearly are not the real thing. These *can* be seen with the right instruments, including the microscope he himself mentioned. And Metarealists are not interested in showing the conflict between self and society, but rather a condition of otherness and of imagined possibility that can partly be known by what it is not. They want to apprehend other worlds within or beyond the social and political and psychological—not fantasize imaginary worlds but rather locate (meta)real ones, bringing them into visibility, in all their startling metaphoric specificity.

In English, the first word of a possible rhyme-pair is tested by the poet for the balance between the necessity it enforces that the second word have a certain sound and the opportunity it offers that the second word be different in other ways. Kutik's Russian version of this is that the first word invites another word with a similar sound, or attracts it by a kind of phonetic magnetism, or the first word discovers the second word for itself, out of love—almost without needing the poet. Even the new inventiveness of Russian rhyme in the early twentieth century (extended again late in the century by the Metarealists) seems to have been based on this word-love. In "Miscellanea" (1904–1918), which Kutik and I have translated in part into English, the poet Valery Bryusov quoted Pushkin: "'Rhymes live with me as a family: // two come on their own, and bring the third.' [. . . Pushkin means:] 'Two will come to me when they will. The third I will go and fetch, even if it doesn't want to come.'" Here the will attributed to the third rhyme word is negative—yet it is still its own will. And Bryusov commented that "all rhymes—whether they are 'uninvited' or 'brought back'—have the same characteristic peculiarity: they are *needed* because *speech* needs them, and not just as markers at the ends of verses. [. . .] The major purposes of rhyme are three: to create a new meaning, a new sound, a new image."

Moreover, when the second word has been evoked or attracted, the Russian rhyme also creates an image. Yet as important as it is for rhyme to do that, rhyming is justified because it does more: it is a searching for metaphor. The metaphor to which this Russian rhyming leads does provide an image, but to be worth putting into the poem, the image must be "meta." Kutik has told me, "'Meta' is what is after or behind or beyond the gap between one metaphor and the next. Metaphor, like a car with its lights on, starts seeing by itself through the darkness of the non-visible, the 'meta.' Visual metaphors, however striking they may be, are not 'meta' in themselves: they justify what we *already* know about the object or subject but haven't *noticed.* The 'meta' is not about what is possible in life, but about what happens in the realm of the imaginary, the nonmaterial." Let's say that metaphor vivifies visible things as they are, and that "meta" (the car seeing its own way in the dark) "thinks" about something that is real, some-where, somehow, but can only be "seen" if illuminated in and by the imagination.

And let's say that language thinks about *itself* in this way and makes its own discoveries, by means of sound. If Russian poetry at its high-est linguistic and artistic intensity works this way (Boris Pasternak, Marina Tsvetaeva, Osip Mandelshtam—these are the giants of the chosen tradition of the Metarealists), then we can understand how extremely difficult it has been to translate it into English, not only be-cause English can't do many of the things that the Russian *language* can do, but also because a translation of such a poem would have to give the reader the sense that each important and phonetically deci-sive word of the translation, too, was discovering the next, and finding it, as rhymes do in the original. And the reader would have to be able to think in a certain way in order to recognize an instance of that very thinking. This is a different poetic mentality from our own.

Russian rhyming, Kutik says, is about unpredictability, not secu-rity. In fact, he believes that this distinction defines the difference be-tween Russian and American poetry, in general. Or as Brodsky too said, American poetry "certainly keeps its eyes wide open, not so much in wonderment, or poised for a revelation, as on the lookout for danger" (1995, 204). Kutik adduces the famous—and often ad-duced—poetic motto of Tsvetaeva, the opening lines of her poem "The Poet," which I have already paraphrased. As I learned from his analysis of these lines for me, they cannot be adequately translated, because they do what they say, in the Russian way of doing it, and they connote far more than could any semantically equivalent words in English. However, paraphrased expansively (again) I believe they mean something like: "When beginning to speak in a poem, the poet is already very far away, and then this speaking itself leads, must lead, the poet much farther." Kutik says that to him it seems that we Americans, poets and readers alike, do not especially desire this linguistic "much farther," whereas on the contrary this "much farther" is just where Russian poets and readers feel a great poem in Russian must go. (The same key quotation is used by Michael Wachtel as the epigraph to the introduction to his *Cambridge Introduction to Russian Poetry*, translated—too simply, it seems to me—as: "The poet brings language from afar. / Language brings the poet far" [2004, 1]. Joseph Brodsky too quotes it, in his essay on Tsvetaeva's prose, as: "A poet starts his speaking from afar. / The speaking takes the poet far" [1986, 187–88].) In American use of rhyme, we evidently prefer to achieve security against danger, rather than unpredictability, wonder, and revelation. Even the exuberant offhandedness and unpredictability of some contemporary American poetry does not *sound* like this.

A poem by Tsvetaeva must go outward toward that which is not yet known by the poet or by the language, and not turn back to familiar ground. The poet should or must begin to speak not of and with what is nearby, already chosen or given, but with and from a place, an object, a feeling, an idea barely knowable yet. The poet must begin from words whose full meaning and connotations are not yet knowable in that moment of beginning but will be realized as the poem goes forward. It will *mean* (verb) its way. Brodsky puts it this way: "What has been uttered is never the end but the edge of speech, which—owing to the existence of time—is always followed by something" (1986, 186). And: "Language propels the poet into spheres he would not otherwise be able to approach, irrespective of the degree of psychic or mental concentration of which he might be capable beyond the writing of verse" (203).

Kutik has emphasized to me that this is more than the commonplace that a poet must make discoveries for himself as well as for the reader—because in this particular Russian way of poetic thinking, it is not the poet alone who makes the discoveries but poet and language together. Language is not solely the medium of poetry; the poet is the medium of language. Thinking and feeling accelerate: Brodsky called the *effect* of Mandelshtam's poem to an unknown soldier "a result of an incredible psychic acceleration" (1986, 139), and he said apropos of Marina Tsvetaeva that "poetic language possesses—as does any language in general—its own particular dynamics, which impart to psychic movement an acceleration that takes the poet much farther than he imagined when he began the poem" (1986, 202–3).

Or, Kutik has said to me, rhyme is a kind of edge or border that one listens past—not for the next word, but rather for the farthest word one can hear. And, he has said, rhyme is "centrifugal"—that is, when one word attracts the unexpected rhyme word for itself, this second word of the rhyme-pair throws the poem *outward* from itself as it exists so far, throws it off what had seemed its course. With this rhyme, the poem throws *itself* off a path that is safe, with a motion that is justified, created, vouched for, by the rhyme. The first rhyme/ image launches the second, and the second word changes the poem's direction, or "story" (to use an inexact shorthand word here). And new such words change it again and again as the poem proceeds, as each stage of feeling succeeds its predecessor—all within one poem. With the achieved rhyme, the poem has flung itself out of itself (to paraphrase a poem by Paul Celan, to which I will come in a moment). It has not pulled its own next move into a safe orbit, the way a "centripetal" word (and thus motion) in a lyrical, narrative, or rational cohesiveness abandons what does not seem likely to *become* relevant.

But centrifugal does not mean incoherent. Such motion achieves an authoritative coherence of sound and idea, feeling and image, that compels a reader's exhilarated trust—thus the thrilling "disobedience" (as Brodsky called it) "of a song." Centrifugal movement is outward toward that which almost cannot yet be imagined or grasped; centripetal movement keeps everything within the poem, closer to what is expected—emotionally or linguistically, by poet and by reader— and to what is knowable or already known, closer to ideas already shared by poet and reader, consensual.

For contrast, I will recall Wordsworth's comment about meter and rhyme in the 1802 version of his "Preface" to the *Lyrical Ballads*, the book that included poems by himself and by Coleridge. After the original 1798 edition had already announced a strong change—a centripetal one, in fact?—in English poetry, Wordsworth evidently felt an obligation to explain his own purposes. In this preface, his explanations, like most of his poems after the 1805 *Prelude*, pulled back some of what had been so effectively flung further. Rhyme, he explained, is a useful control, not—as Coleridge later recounted for himself—an opportunity for surprise. Wordsworth said that the purpose of poetry "is to produce excitement in coexistence with an overbalance of pleasure"; but if the poetry is very powerful, "there is some danger that the excitement may be carried beyond its proper bounds." Therefore the poem needs "the co-presence of something regular" (that is, steadily present) that will be effective in "tempering and restraining the passion by an intertexture of ordinary feeling." The "more pathetic situations and sentiments—that is, those which have a greater proportion of pain connected with them," which would be difficult to bear in prose, "may be endured in metrical composition, especially in rhyme" (1994, 262). Wordsworth's instance of the extreme is sorrow or horror. Not awe or wonder or exuberance of feeling or language—those feelings may be in the very grain of him, as some of his poems show, yet here he does not bring them to bear. Here he seems to want, and to want us, to pull the little toy back to us. *Fort!...Da!*

The creative process of going further by a centrifugal flinging or throwing—of imagination, of language, even of self, by means of language—ahead or outward and away makes me think also of something very ancient: the etymology of our word *symbol*, which the OED says derives ultimately from Greek *sumbolon*, "mark, token, ticket," related to *bolos*, "a throw." Similarity of morphology and other connotations or connections link *sumballō*, "to put together, unite," with the Greek verb *ballein*, "to throw." All this is in the *sym-* and the *-bol* of our *symbol*. The idea—which our language itself remembers, even if we do not—of a word that *throws* meaning or image does not seem out of place here. It is not an invention solely of Russian poets. In G. O. Hutchinson's commentary on a few of the large odes from ancient Greece, he mentions that the Athenian tragic odes—which were a form of performance adapted from choral odes of the earlier sort that Pindar composed—were made in such a way as to "enlarge the field of vision" beyond that of the characters in the tragedies; they carry the audience out of the immediate conflict into a related kind of thought in a different mode. Hutchinson writes that "the recurrent impulse to move away from the situation in hand comes from the lyric genre.... Sophocles and Euripides are particularly fond of beginning at a distance" (2001, 437–38). That is, the effect that those odes achieved on poetic thinking (and on an audience's feeling and thought) was centrifugal.

Centrifugal, flinging movement is the substance of this poem by Paul Celan (in my word-for-word decoding):

WURFSCHEIBE, mit	DISCUS, with
vorgesichten besternt,	foreseeings starred,
wurf dich	throw yourself
aus dir hinaus.	out of yourself.

(Celan 1975, 267)

In German, the last line of this poem (word for word, something like "out [to] your beyond/outward/outside") enacts with a repeated sound (phonetic figure) what it means: the small word is flung into the larger one, *aus . . . hinaus*. In line 1, the first syllable of the poem, *Wurf-*, and the last vowel sound, in *mit*, are compressed by line 3 into the repeated *wurf* and the vowel in *dich*, just as the poem's meaning is a tremendous compression of several ideas into its mere nine words: discus, person, poem, language. The poem tightens, tenses, in lines 1 through 3, then with a discharge of energy, of muscular language-imagination, in the last line it flings outward the thought, the feeling, the idea, of the self-sameness of (the person and) the discus throwing *itself*. Celan's poem, too, without end-rhyme proper or anything Russian about it, makes the sound of Brodsky's "acoustic inevitability."

Writing about Auden, Brodsky said that rhymes give the poet's ideas their "sense of inevitability," not the other way around (1995, 305). Otherwise, the flinging outward, the starting from afar and going farther, the seven-league strides between one word and its rhyme, would result (merely) in surrealism, which Kutik says the Metarealists disdain because it has no "meta." (Even Allen Ginsberg, rejecting the charge that *Howl* was a surrealist poem, wrote that his poem "is not surrealism—they made up an artificial literary imitation" [1986, 153].) While surrealism plays in this world or invents what cannot be, "meta" seeks to discover another dimension or world. The Metarealists are primarily concerned not with what is hidden *in the poet's unconscious*, but with what sort of poetic thinking can truly bring into visibility what is hidden *in the world*, while at the same time not robbing it of the aura it has by virtue of being invisible and mysterious.

Antonio Machado, in the age of surrealism, and responding to the French symbolism of Mallarmé, wrote: "Yes, one can manufacture mysterious trinkets, little dolls which have, hidden in their bellies, something which will rattle when they are shaken. But enigmas are not of human confection; reality imposes them, and it is there, where they are, that a reflective mind will seek them out in the desire to penetrate them, not to play at amusing itself with them. [. . .] Mallarmé also knew—and this was his strength—that there are profound realities which lack names" ([1964] 1989, 163).

Needless to say, the centrifugal qualities of the translation of "Hunchback" are not presented with sufficient poetic justification, and those centrifugal touches that we have achieved are not enough—even though, as Kutik has told me, his metaphors in this poem are comparatively "pure," "without much 'meta' beyond them," and thus should be somewhat easier for readers to grasp. The original poem rhymes *abab, cdcd, efef*; the translation does not rhyme, but it has as many phonetic figures as we could discover or produce, and at least some of the considerable metaphoric density of the original. For the discoveries of image and metaphor produced by rhyme in Russian, we tried to substitute a certain "boldness" of metaphor (as classicists sometimes call the more strenuous and mixed metaphors in ancient Greek poetry), by pushing the literal meaning of the Russian lines toward figures that leap a bit further because of what the particular English words make possible in sound and association. That is, our translation sometimes enacts the way in which the Russian poem moves rather than exactly what the Russian poem says. This is what I meant when earlier I mentioned translating poetics as well as the words of a poem, that is, their semantic content.

And it fell to me to make the translation somewhat interpretive of matters that would need no further hints for a Russian reader. Examples: Akhmatova had a famously hawkish nose, which she often showed in profile—hence Judith is a visual rhyme, with her "hump-beaked nose." The figure of a prophet is well known in Russian poetry, beginning with Pushkin (Kutik told me that he was not thinking of addressing this topos in a new way but was in the midst of this new way of writing when it happened to gather to itself a sort of figurative prophet). Kutik's prophet is different not in his spirituality or fanaticism but in his hump—it is meant to be visualized as physical and real, yet at the same time as metaphor it becomes *meta*real; it suggests powers as well as deformity. A Russian proverb says that the hunch-back or humpback—English has two words for this) can be "cured" (or "corrected") only by the grave. The Khazars (second to tenth century CE), nomadic Turkic peoples, shared the unsettled Russian steppes with the Scythians (nomadic, indigenous peoples of Russia's remote past; eighth to fourth century BCE), who of course had no *Bible*. In the Bible, or rather, outside it, the apocryphal book of Judith relates the story of this woman of violent heroism and her assassination of the invading, occupying military conquerer, Holofernes.

In Kutik's poem, these leaping associations, which are the forward and even centrifugal movement of the poetic thinking, are achieved by the echoed sounds of the Russian, so the rhymes make the resulting metaphors and meta seem very right while being also pleasurably zigzag. From what I have learned, in my Russian-deaf way, of how meaning moves in poems like those of Mandelshtam, Tsvetaeva, Pasternak, and here, Kutik, it seems to leap instantly from the completion of the phonetic figure, the achievement of the rhyme. And this instantaneity itself seems to me a contrast with English and other Western languages, in which, as Paul Valéry put it, poetry is a "*hesitation* between the sound and the sense" (quoted in Jakobson 1981, 38; my italics). Fast or hesitatingly, East and West, language listens to itself in poems and says something more of what *it* hears, and follows what it has heard itself say.

It seems a shame to provide portable bridges or flimsy crutches to the English version of the poem, but I too needed them and sought them from Kutik. So before Kutik and I show how the rhyming works in Russian, I will add a few more. The Russian word for *bud* can mean either a plant or an animal in its early stages. A backbone would be as white as china. The word *bishop* (or *missionary* or *preacher*) prepares for the *implied* metaphor of a Scythian "Bible" which, in their case, is the landscape they read, and thus its apocrypha would be places (steppes) not books. A single word in Russian means both to sleep and to dream. And there would be much more that I, reporting from Kutik, could add about this little world in a poem, but I don't want to spoil even the reduced pleasures of this translation, now that I have propped it up. The translation is probably wandering in a poetic landscape while unaware that the edge of the cliff of rhyme in English is actually rather far away and it needn't be so scared.

And how does the poem, or rather, how does rhyme itself, think? In

Russian, with multiple case endings and more elaborate conjugations than in English, to rhyme is comparatively easy phonetically, but it is difficult literarily—because of the convention that the poet will not rhyme identical parts of speech with each other nor use any rhyme that might already be familiar. We'll look at the second stanza again. The translation reads:

Hugging, so to speak, his own hump, he gusts across
The apocryphal Khazarian steppe of some Scyth-written Bible,
And maybe in that book he bends stoop-backed
Like a hump-beaked Judith over Holofernes' head.

Kutik wrote to me: "There are TOO many inner phonetic figures that lead to these particular rhymes. To show that, I would need to give the entire phonetic scheme of the poem, and then you would see, on your own, how each move leads where it leads." In Russian, the second stanza is:

V obnimku s **gorb**om, on na bibliiu **skif'iu**
khazarskim apokrifom **veet i, verno,**
sgibaetsia tam **gorbonosoi Judif'iu**
nad **golo**voi **Oloferna.**

The end-rhymes link the Scythians with Judith, and the word *verno* ("most probably") with Holofernes. Word for word (although not exactly in the same order), the Russian would read, as represented by Kutik in only the most skeletal way in English:

Embracing his hump, he on a bible of the Scythians
Hints (blows) with a Khazar's apocrypha, and, most probably,
Bends down in there [in the apocrypha] with [this *with* functions,
in English, as *like*, although not exactly so] hump-nosed Judith
Over the head of Holofernes.

Here is Kutik on what is "typical meta" here: that is, what produces image and metaphor through sound, while conveying what is not in fact visible in the real world:

First, a concept: *gorbonosyi* ("hawkish-nosed") is not associated (directly) with a hump, but only with a form of the nose, also with a special, Jewish nose, and yet *gorb*, which means "hump," is *inside* this word. Second, rhymes: *skif'iu-Judif'iu* is very *new* in Russian—it never existed, before! However, one doesn't come to such rhymes *from* the word *skif'iu*, but from the necessity to bring (to *show* visually) that *metaphysical* "hump" (which is not a *real* hump!) from as many angles as possible: stanza 2 is another angle. It shows the "hump" through Judith—her nose—and shows her bending over the head of Holofernes, which (the head) IS (as IF) that very hump, also. In order to say (in this stanza) that this hump is her nose, and is his head (i.e., that the situation *might be so*), I use a powerful sound-move: *veet i verno* (the first word is from one register of diction, the second from a very different one, very colloquial). Only such a move can justify the unheard-of rhyme *Judif'iu* (and bring the poem to it) through the *thing* (the hump) that is not yet visible but closer to visibility (*this* poetic state of visibility) in the next word, *sgibaetsia* ("bends over"; "Judith who bends down")—this is a very powerful and visual word in Russian. Thus, BEFORE we see (and hear) this word, *gorbonosy*, about Judith (*gorbonosoi Judif'iu . . .*) we actually don't know *who* is going to be bending over; when we find out this it is Judith, we are more than surprised, and even more surprised when we find out that she (Judith) bends over the head of Holofernes, because (A) the rhyme *verno-Oloferna* is just as unheard of in Russian (a pairing of the colloquial with the Biblical; the sudden concept of a head, a real one, which is at the same time yet another hump), and (B) despite the apparent unreality of the comparison or equivalence, the words convey something that seems very physically real, because the echoing sounds of the words seem to lead, on their own, to what the poem says.

Also, note that the short fourth line, "Over the head of Holofernes," *nad golovoi Oloferna*, becomes almost physical because of the way that "head" (*golova* is the Russian noun) becomes the *Olof-* in the Russian spelling of Holofernes. Also, the Russian for "circle," *kolo*, is evoked, too, by these sounds, and suggests the roundness of the decapitated tyrant's head. This is how language and the poet think together—one word was inside the other, but was *not*, until this line was written, because it was never before emphasized in this way. I put it in a rhythmically stressed position and the repetition became visible. Please note that the double *o*'s (which in this position sound almost like long *a*'s) are round shapes, like a head. But once I have cut Holofernes' head off, the reader can see that the head had been there, inside the name itself. And thus, in order to make *olov* and *olof* visible, to make the "head" visible inside the word *Holofernes*, by taking it off with a visible linguistic gesture (even phonetically, as "a-a" = "o"), this last line, like Holofernes, gets shorter.

I notice that Kutik does *not* say that *he* makes the fourth line shorter. Rather, "this is how language and the poet think together." In Russian, the words within words that hear each other, as Brodsky pointed out with regard to Tsvetaeva, are listening all the time. And words lead themselves to their several meanings — Mandelshtam even seems to say that (Russian) words choose the things to which they refer: "The word is a Psyche. The living word does not designate an object, but freely chooses, as though for a dwelling place, this or that objective significance, materiality, some beloved body" (1979, 115). This freedom of the word is also exercised in its seeking of its rhyme, as if with an instinct for liberation, not conformity. Or for disobedience, as Brodsky says. When Vladimir Mayakovsky describes rhyme in his essay "How to Make Verse," he says, "My rhyming is almost always unusual, or at any rate my rhymes have not been used before and are not in the rhyming dictionary" (Proffer 1976, 131). Kutik has told me that for Russian poets, Mayakovsky broke rhyme open in this way. He created a new way of listening to linguistic harmony. Brodsky calls it "the harmonic element of language, which is better known publicly as the Muse" (Proffer 1976, 7). "While identity of sounds describes so-called exact rhyme, much Russian rhyme," writes Barry Scherr, "especially in twentieth-century poems, is based more on similarity than on identity of sound. Second, the concept of what is and is not rhyme, and in particular the parameters of exact rhyme, may change from one era to the next. [...] Maiakovsky, whose innovations in rhyme were as striking as those of any modern poet, claimed that he began to create the line only after he had decided on the main word or rhyme. Furthermore, he believed there was a semantic affinity between rhyme words that served to link lines and hence the entire poem. Similarly, [D. S.] Samoilov talks of the 'associative power' of rhyme and how it serves both to organize the poem and underline its meaning" (1986, 193, 194). Scherr also writes that in the nineteenth century, the "enrichment" created by the "'leftness' of Pushkin's rhymes" (meaning the repetition of the sounds to the left of the stressed vowel on which Russian rhyme depends) was what the poet Valery Bryusov later regarded "as a key feature of twentieth-century poetry, which, [Bryusov] believed, had come to employ a whole new system of rhyming" (Scherr 1986, 193, 194, 200).

About the rhythms of his second stanza, Kutik told me: "The entire stanza gets metrically shorter, in its last line, just because of that cut-off head of Holofernes." (Here's a *thematic* instance of what the English terminology for poetic meter calls a prosodically "acephalous," or "headless" line!) Kutik added:

> The stanza seems to be cut off, as a physical gesture, too. Thus the stanza is *physical*, in the way it brings *palpability*—which is of great importance to the poets of Metarealism—into reality by means of language. It's not that the stanza *imitates* anything, but that what is happening in it *makes* the last line shorter. It needs to be shorter on its own, so to speak—by its own decision. What is heard is cut off— syllables cut themselves off. The thing *is* words, when it presents itself in this way. Especially important is that all of this is *not* a description of the hump itself but of what the hump is *not* (nose, head)—that is, the poem presents a metaphysical "hump" (a burden, a gift, etc.) by showing what it is not.

The poem shows what is around it—what Kutik has called the thing's peripheries—or hidden inside it. (This apophatic way of thinking is the subject of the next chapter.)

In the third stanza of "Hunchback," even we who can't read Russian would see from a transliteration and a word-for-word trot that the rhyme words link *torboi* ("with back-pack") to *dvugorboi* ("in the [desert] two-humped"), and *mire* ("in the world") with *kvartire* ("in the apartment"). The first pair is again very visual, showing the hump from two more angles, two more analogies: as if the hump were a pack (containing . . . ?—we are invited, no, we are required, if we are schooled in Russian poetry, to imagine for ourselves) and as if the *desert* itself, not the camels that cross it, had two humps (a use of hypallage). And the second rhyme-pair thinks its way from the largest physical scale to the smallest, as at the end the poem narrows its scene while exploding its vision. The foretold strange prophet arrives unheralded, and within his tiny room, within his being, within his hump, he carries a human reality as vast as the desert that he has not, in fact, crossed.

⊙ 4 ⊙

On Apophatic Poetics (I)

"TEACH ME THAT NOTHING"

Tonight as I walked I passed a little cottage on whose tiny porch two were in a very close embrace. The house was completely dark—as if it were there only to provide a front porch for the girl to stand upon and receive her lover. [1930s]

I am still trying to find my way; it is still dark, penumbrant, full of shadows . . . [1939]

I am living in complete darkness—this past year. [1939 or early 1940s]

How darkeningness may have a quality of light, and the light in the darkeningness— how so many of us do not see that, or how we forget that when light is seen from darkness we define darkness by the light. [1950s]

From the notebooks of WILLIAM GOYEN (2007, 145, 147, 160)

With an everyday sense of the apophatic, Verlyn Klinkenborg noticed that on a street corner in New York City his familiar Korean market had closed. He reported that in this store that no longer existed except as an empty space, he knew the exact location of everything he used to buy, everything that was no longer there. Klinkenborg wrote of how we retain "vanished places; apartments we moved out of years ago, dry cleaners that went out of business, restaurants that stopped serving, neighborhoods where only the street names remain the same [. . .] — places we knew almost by intuition until they vanished, leaving behind only the strange sense of knowing our way around a world that can no longer be found" (2007, n.p.). Apophatic rhetoric is a device, and the apophatic mentality is more like what Klinkenborg described, but it goes beyond the absence of what was, to what can only be known as absence, or what is inconceivable in the terms of our naming and knowing directly.

✿

Among the famously witty poems of Catullus, number 43 ("Salve, nec minimo puella naso") makes use of the rhetorical figure called apophasis, which is an "allusion to something by denying that it will be mentioned" (*American Heritage Dictionary*). This poem is very short, not to mention its being apophatic. (The sarcastic negatives are also a form of the rhetorical figure litotes.)

Ezra Pound's 1916 translation of the poem by Catullus is an exercise in apophatic rhetoric. "All Hail; young lady with a nose by no means too small, / With a foot unbeautiful, and with eyes that are not black, / With fingers that are not long, and with a mouth undry, / And with a tongue by no means too elegant," and so on (Pound 1963, 408). The young lady evidently has a big nose, ugly feet, pale eyes, stubby fingers, lips forever wet, and a habit of using crude language — none of which is said directly. Pound executes a pleasing poetic turn from the literal images of nose, foot, eyes, fingers, and mouth to the metonym of tongue, meaning not the literal tongue but her way of speaking. I won't mention the ugly glee of both Catullus and Pound memorializing a young woman by so exuberantly ridiculing her. That is the nature of satire.

In his sonnet 130, Shakespeare — somewhat like Catullus in his use of apophatic rhetoric, but with a warmer heart for ordinary looks that fall short of beauty — slyly composes his description of his lover out of the negative opposites of the terms he might have been expected to use in more conventional praise. "My mistress' eyes are nothing like the sun; / Coral is far more red than her lips' red," and so on, till we arrive at the couplet, Shakespeare's countermove that negatives all the previous negatives, and thus creates a positive: "And yet, by heaven, I think my love as rare / As any she belied with false compare."

Shakespeare plays several times in his sonnets against Horace's poem "Exegi monumentum" (3.30; I have erected a monument) by constructing verse "monuments" not to himself, as Horace did, but to love and lovers (for example, in sonnets 17, 18, 19, 55, 63, 65, 81, 101, 107). He ends the generously good-humored sonnet 18 with a well-known couplet about his own poem: "So long as men can breathe or eyes can see, / So long lives this, and this gives life to thee." In "Exegi monumentum," Horace's conceit is that an immaterial poem that lives in the memory, books, and voices of generations will outlive—and it has outlived—the stuff of tangible monuments. These, Shakespeare too evokes: "Not marble nor the gilded monuments / Of princes shall outlive this pow'rful rime" (sonnet 55). That is, the gesture of Shakespeare's poems is to evoke the stone and metal of great monuments by their absence (absence out there, where once they stood but now are fallen, and absence here, on the page where we see only the modest little ink marks of print). In place of those tangible monuments this poet offers the intangible poem that truly exists or "appears" only when someone recites, remembers, or reads it, yet which may endure longer than the durable, hard, cold monuments of metal and stone. The emphasis on the absence and transience of what is expected to be durable, as opposed to the survival of the near nothingness of human breath itself, invisible and fleeting, is a kind of apophatic conceptual play.

The Spanish poet San Juan de la Cruz (St. John of the Cross), who wrote much earlier than Shakespeare, made decisively religious use of the apophatic, beyond the rhetorical figure in my examples from Pound's Catullus and from Shakespeare. In his "Coplas hechas sobre un éxtasis de harta contemplación" (Verses written on an ecstasy of full contemplation [or meditation]), he unveils not the bride but the veiling. In Spanish the musical clarity of this poet's language creates a curious clarity of the unknowable, even in the first three lines: "Entréme donde no supe, / y quedéme no sabiendo, / toda ciencia trascendiendo" (Juan de la Cruz 1991, 1:70; my translation below). But rendered only by an unmusical word-for-word version, the poem begins this way:

> I went into a place where I did not know,
> and remained unknowing,
> transcending all knowledge.

> I knew not where I was,
> but when I saw myself there,
> without knowing where I was,
> I understood great things.
> I will not say what I felt,
> since I remained unknowing,
> transcending all knowledge.

Even to the point of not using visual imagery, this poem represents an apophatic state of mind, drawing no doubt on that mode of thought even within Catholic theology, as did Thomas Aquinas. As a refrain, Juan de la Cruz's poem uses variations on the last two lines translated above. It describes senses that do not register impressions, understanding that does not comprehend, darkness that is light, and an unknowing that defeats human knowledge as it approaches God.

Fulke Greville, a poet somewhat younger than Shakespeare, wrote a sonnet articulating a more conventionally Western sense of darkness as a negative space in the moral sense. In it, Greville fills darkness with the thronging fears and anxieties of what we call the unconscious: "in night, when colors all to black are cast," the mind brings not to light but rather to dark consciousness the inner troubles that sleeplessness or bad dreams allow or condemn us to apprehend. In dreams, the eye is "Not seeing, yet still having power of sight." And one's spirit, not seeing and yet seeing the demons that populate nightmares, "from this nothing seen, tells news of devils, / Which but expressions be of inward evils" (2009, 36).

The famous stanza of Andrew Marvell's "The Garden" that imagines "a green thought in a green shade" negates what is real in order to create an image of what can only be enclosed by thought; or perhaps it cannot be enclosed in thought, either (Fowler 1992, 603). More apophatic, though, is what some have called the most notable poem of the negative in English literature, the "Sonnet of Black Beauty" by Lord Edward Herbert (the brother of George). This poem reverses Greville's perspective (and probably that of most of us, to this day) on the opposites light and darkness, white and black (with philosophical, perceptual, and racial resonance). Black beauty is black whether in light or darkness, "unvary'd to the sight," unlike "that common light" whose colors can be cancelled by darkness; *black* beauty is a kind of "light inaccessible," and only our own "darkness" makes us think that it is extinguished by the dark (Gardner 1967, 95–96).

John Donne, too, although writing considerably earlier than Marvell, went beyond Marvell's rhetorical or conceptual play on the apophatic. In Donne's poem "Negative Love" (among manuscripts, also titled "The Nothing"), he depicts the most intense love as erotic—but this is a metaphorical enticement and true analogy for the love of God, a concupiscent reverence. Such love cannot be described by

what can be named, or rather, cannot be described because it cannot
be named:

> I never stooped so low, as they
> Which on an eye, cheek, lip, can prey,
> > Seldom to them, which soar no higher
> > Than virtue or the mind to admire,
> For sense, and understanding may
> > Know, what gives fuel to their fire:
> My love, though silly, is more brave,
> For may I miss, whene'er I crave,
> If I know yet what I would have.
>
> If that be simply perfectest
> Which can by no way be expressed
> > But negatives, my love is so.
> > To all, which all love; I say no.
> If any who deciphers best,
> > What we know not, ourselves, can know,
> Let him teach me that nothing; this
> As yet my ease, and comfort is,
> Though I speed not, I cannot miss.
>
> > > (2000, 133)

In love, Donne writes, "I never stooped so low" (we never get to
"high"—only to a level that's "higher" than low, which Donne also rejects) as to invest my belief in the physical body (lines 1–2: eye, cheek,
and lip suggest liveliness, beauty, and desire). And only seldom did I
even admire most the virtue and mind of the beloved—precisely because sensuality, on the one hand, and intellect (line 5), on the other,
already know what "gives fuel to their fire." These are "positives" to
the "negative" that cannot be known directly because it exceeds all
knowing. My love, even though it is feeble, trifling, ignorant (all of
these, older meanings of *silly*), is nevertheless braver than love that is
based on what the lover already knows of his beloved's physical, intellectual, and spiritual being. If I already know what it is in the beloved
that I most want, then let me miss my target (as if I were love's arrow)
when I love. For missing it, I attain the fullest not knowing, which is
what I am aiming at. To anyone who loves all that can be known, I say

no. If someone who is best at deciphering can know what we do not know—ourselves!—then let him teach me that unknown, that "nothing." So even though I cannot succeed (see "speed" in the *Oxford English Dictionary*) in aiming my love at what it wants, I am easy and comfortable and comforted because I cannot miss my target, since insofar as it is knowable, I do not desire it, and what I desire is what I cannot know, no thing known, "nothing." The most thingy and corporeal of human engagements, sexual intercourse, is the metaphor for what is most unknowable and impalpable—the divine.

Unlike Shakespeare, Donne does not catalogue negatives after the first four lines; his purpose is religious rather than amorous. What gives Shakespeare's sonnet 130 its humor is that rhetorically he does not achieve a negating of the lovely positives to which his mistress is lovably inferior, for by naming them he himself is evoking them in the reader's or listener's mind. Shakespeare assures us that the imperfect, which is to say, human, lover is beautiful. Donne says, on the other hand, that it's no good to name such qualities even to negate them, because the reality of the Beloved cannot be described. (To some readers, the eroticization of the divine will be familiar from sources as different as Santa Teresa de Avila and Ghalib.)

The structure of Donne's poem groups the lines into two sets of equal size, each set built on different rhymes sequenced in the same way. (In some editions, each of the two sets of lines is syntactically one sentence.) Each set of lines is a unit of thought. In the first, Donne names the positives that he does not seek, and asserts that he is happy to miss anything he can know. (I recall Randall Jarrell's "A Sick Child": "If I can think of it, it isn't what I want" [1969, 53].) In the second half, Donne is more discursive in presenting his paradox—he attains a discourse without visual images. Perfectly in keeping with this is Donne's decision *not* to phrase anything so that it can apply overtly to God.

Apophasis is an ancient Greek word that means a denial; the word combines a verb for "to say" (*phanai*) and a prefix (*apo*) which in this use means "away from, down from, far from," or in other words, "opposed to." The apophatic is not simply negation, however. When

Lincoln says with somber grandeur in his Gettysburg Address that "in a larger sense, we can not dedicate—we can not consecrate—we can not hallow—this ground," he means just that; his negatives are straightforward. Yet at the same time he brings into the minds of his listeners what he wishes *were* possible: the dedication, consecration, and hallowing of a field where so many soldiers had agonized and died. That is, Lincoln's apophatic rhetoric is a straightforward negative, but it implies something that is in fact present in mind, and perhaps in that occasion and in that place, despite the inadequacy (or even absence) of any name for it. What is present is an absence, like meaningful negative space in a sculpture. But in Lincoln's oratory or in poetry the negative space is linguistic.

The opposite of *apophatic* is *cataphatic*, which is a Christian theological term for what is more characteristic of philosophy and theology in the West. It too comes from a Greek word, in this case *kataphainô*, which means "to make visible." (The apophatic evokes instead the presence of what is inconceivable or invisible.) A cataphatic mentality names and even catalogues, whether its subject is things of this world, as for Aristotle and almost all English poetry, or its concern is in the theological sphere, as in the spiritual exercises of St. Ignatius of Loyola, which instruct the worshipper to approach God by meditative steps, each with a definable focus. We can see the implications for poetry in the contrast between an active, Adamic, cataphatic artistic impulse to evoke the visible world by naming it and a meditative, apophatic artistic impulse to evoke the invisible, the elusive, the absent, the not quite conceivable, the unnameable.

Apophasis as a negation that characterizes what cannot be stated in any positive terms comes especially from Eastern Christian (Neoplatonist; later Orthodox) theological ideas, above all from the fundamental idea of the inapprehensible nature of God. God must be conceived in terms of what God is not, which means that one cannot form a conception of God. The philosophical and theological scope of the apophatic is seldom encountered in the context of Western rationalism.

Perhaps the best-known nondefining of God was written by the Greek thinker whom we know only as Pseudo-Dionysius the Areopagite. One cannot exhaust a negative catalogue, but in his short work "Mystical Theology," this thinker covers compactly almost everything

which, by this definition of the divine, cannot be "covered." Here is
the whole of chapter 5:

> Once more, ascending yet higher we maintain that It is not soul, or
> mind, or endowed with the faculty of imagination, conjecture, reason,
> or understanding; nor is It any act or reason or understanding; nor
> can It be described by the reason of perceived by the understanding,
> since It is not number, or order, or greatness, or littleness, or equality,
> or inequality and since It is not immovable nor in motion, or at rest,
> and has no power, and is not power or light, and does not live, and
> is not life; nor is It personal essence, or eternity, or time; nor can It
> be grasped by the understanding, since It is not knowledge or truth;
> nor is It kingship or wisdom; nor is It one, nor is It unity, nor is It
> Godhead or Goodness; nor is It a Spirit, as we understand the term,
> since It is not Sonship or Fatherhood; nor is It any other thing such
> as we or any other being can have knowledge of; nor does It belong to
> the category of non-existence or to that of existence; nor do existent
> beings know It as it actually is, nor does It know them as they actually
> are; nor can the reason attain to It to name It or to know It; nor is it
> darkness, nor is It light, or error, or truth; nor can any affirmation or
> negation apply to it; for while applying affirmations or negations to
> those orders of being that come next to It, we apply not unto It either
> affirmation or negation, inasmuch as It transcends all affirmation by
> being the perfect and unique Cause of all things, and transcends all
> negation by the pre-eminence of Its simple and absolute nature —
> from every limitation and beyond them all. (1920, 200–201)

Whether in secular or religious terms, to articulate precisely that
which eludes articulation is a feat of imagination. And thus negative
or apophatic theology can speak of the divine even though it takes the
divine to be precisely that of which we cannot speak. Ludwig Wittgenstein's familiar maxim, which has been translated from German in
various ways — such as "Whereof one cannot speak, thereof one must
be silent" — is a kind of philosophical aside that we can take as secular and poetic. It has often been cited by poets and by antipoets. Yet
its truth value is dubious, since theology, philosophy, and poetry, in

opposition to the silence that Wittgenstein's maxim urges, have made from the very struggle to articulate "that of which one cannot speak" memorable attempts to speak at the limits of language, whether in passing or more ambitiously.

Throughout poetry in English, one encounters from time to time a passage like the following, from a poem by Linda McCarriston, "A Thousand Genuflections": "For something / of myself lives here, stripped of the knowing / that is not knowing" (2002, 56). An openness of not-knowing can invite into the intuition the unknowable. Yet we come to assume, without being aware of the assumption, that poetry in English, perhaps like poetry in general, can scarcely proceed without naming. Naming is part of the particular spirit of English. Naming is cataphatic, positive. It was not the task assigned to Eve (a point of legend and scripture that several women poets have played against) but was conferred on Adam. No matter how signifiers differ from language to language, naming often seems to add something to the being of what it names. Words and names distinguish this from that. They bring many pleasures of language and poetry, even as they may impose a categorization that not only fails to evoke by name what is real but also substitutes for the real thing merely a name. This might be called a kind of delusion of cataphasis (this word is not in the OED; perhaps it does not exist; I offer it as an opposite of *apophasis* meaning "explicit mention"). The delusion arises because ultimately naming can produce an emptiness, a word as a mere sound, or simply an idea that intervenes between the person and the thing, when what was wanted was the thinginess of the thing named; yet apophasis may produce a kind of *linguistic* palpability of what is unknowable directly.

When Wordsworth, who was born in 1770, completed the first version of *The Prelude* in 1799, he already had grasped the problem that when the poet experiences the natural world, especially, the Adamic impulse to name and categorize can occlude the apprehension of what is real. Half a century before there was a word for this way of treating the idea as if it were a real thing (*reification*, derived from Latin *res*, "thing"), Wordsworth wrote about "that false secondary power by which / In weakness we create distinctions, then / Believe our puny boundaries are things / Which we perceive, and not which we have made" (1979, lines 250–54).

The English language names with variety and gusto, inventiveness, fancifulness sometimes, having absorbed words from almost every-where, some of them rich with pleasing sound. English is omnivorous of nouns and has gobbled many good ones from other languages, like *rodeo, hashish, avocado, satori, raccoon, mantra, ukulele, et cetera*. Such words are among the innumerable traces of the imperial military and trading history of the English language. They have come to serve all speakers of English, and they have "homed" to English not only from conquered and explored places but also from the early invaders of Britain itself. They have come into English indirectly from the intel-lectual and artistic conquest and exploration in and of other imperial languages. (The now-English words in my brief list above come in fact from Spanish, Arabic, Nahuatl, Japanese, Algonkian, Sanskrit, Hawaiian, and Latin.) Observing from a great geographical, cultural, and linguistic distance, Osip Mandelshtam commented on the sheer appetite of English for words that name. He wrote that "Hellenistic" Russian, by contrast, does not have this trait. "No language resists more strongly than Russian the tendency toward naming and utili-tarian application," he said in his essay "On the Nature of the Word" (1979, 121).

Apophatic thinking might enter American poetry in three ways: as a mode of thought which, although rare, might be considered some-what present in English by around the Early Modern period (hence my examples from Shakespeare, Donne, Edward Herbert, and Mar-vell); as an import back into England and America of the work of some anglophone poets from cultures at the edge of the empire that England once ruled; and as an aspect of poetic thinking elsewhere that has been brought into English by translation.

I do not consider the rarity of apophatic poetic thinking in English a defect; it is simply a difference. As I hope I implied at the begin-ning, the interesting thing for any poet, it seems to me, is to open up one's own language to resources of poetic thinking from elsewhere. As Dick Davis (2002) argues in his essay "All My Soul Is There: Verse Translation and the Rhetoric of English Poetry," this very process has been decisive in most poetic innovation through the whole history of English poetry, and that history is not only literary but also linguistic.

In a poem that Ilya Kutik brought to my attention, "Ribh considers
Christian Love insufficient," William Butler Yeats—with all the fervor
of his own Platonism—fiercely articulates the negative space created
by the reversal of opposites. Ribh announces that what is "of God
[. . .] passes human wit," and therefore instead of seeking or studying love, Ribh studies its opposite, hate. Ribh says that the "light" of
hatred "can show at last / How soul may walk when all such things
[terror and deception, and perhaps love and hate, too] are past, / How
soul could walk before such things began" (Yeats 1997, 292)—that is,
somehow outside time itself, in another sort of "minus" space, as the
Russian poet Alexei Parshchikov called it (pers. comm.; see chap. 5).
Yeats continues in the voice of Ribh:

> Then my delivered soul herself shall learn
> A darker knowledge and in hatred turn
> From every thought of God mankind has had.
> Thought is a garment and the soul's a bride
> That cannot in that trash and tinsel hide.
> Hatred of God may bring the soul to God.
>
> (1997, 292)

Hatred of all that we think we know of God can bring us to love of
God as what we do not and cannot know. Thus words themselves
think and "see" (as the words of Yeats do here), in addition to listening to and even loving other words (as described in the previous
chapter).

Robert Duncan, another Platonist, wrote that "the word, its sounds
and meanings, may be 'recognized' by the poet, but the word itself
initiates all possibilities" ([1969] 1989, 261). But it's not clear to me
why, in Duncan's little catalogue of seven "kinds of form and their
associations with ideas of the universe," he used this formulation in
his description of projective verse (of Charles Olson and others) and
explicitly opposed it to "the Platonic form, where ultimate reality is
pre-existent in the ideal" (260, 261).

Endorsing Duncan specifically, Denise Levertov wrote of "the
poetry of linguistic impulse," describing how

> the absorption in language itself, the awareness of the world of mul-
> tiple meaning revealed in sound, word, syntax, and the entering into

this world in the poem, is as much an experience or *constellation* of perceptions as the instress of nonverbal sensuous and psychic events. What might make the poet of linguistic impetus appear to be on another tack entirely is that the demands of his realization may seem in opposition to truth as we think of it; that is, in terms of sensual logic. But the apparent distortion of experience in such a poem for the sake of verbal effects is actually a precise adherence to truth, since the experience itself was a verbal one. ([1965] 1989, 259; my italics)

The great American poet of apophatic thinking is Emily Dickinson, whose restless inquiry into the nature of consciousness and the divine often leads her to apophatic imagery, metaphor, and thought. What major poet has found his or her way more deeply into absence, emptiness, and ungraspable infinitude than Dickinson? Also, writing of despair or depression, she often works in negatives (see Dickinson 1999, Fr355). I am far from being the first to call her apophatic; and also, I mean only that this is one of the ways, not the only way, her poems think. But think this way, she does: "Prayer is the little implement / Through which Men reach / Where Presence—is denied them" (Fr623). She sometimes touches on absence and that which cannot be known when she evokes paradoxes of scale ("An hour is a Sea" [Fr897]; "Forever—is composed of Nows" [Fr690]) that bring into linguistic view, so to speak, what cannot be grasped through the senses—the mind or the coffin that contains infinity; the ocean that is smaller than the brain. (As Marvell wrote in "The Garden": "the mind, that ocean" [Fowler 1992, 603].)

That which is missing fills Dickinson's poems. At times it's with awe that she characterizes consciousness; at other moments she regards it as an affliction: "No Drug for Consciousness—can be—," she writes; the "Alternative," which is "to die[,] / Is Nature's only Pharmacy / For Being's Malady—" (Fr887). "I saw no Way" (Fr633). The soul is defined by "its Caverns and its Corridors" (Fr877)—that is, by its empty spaces—which she names cataphatically in "The Brain has Corridors" (Fr407); "The missing All, prevented Me / From missing minor things" (Fr995). Poem 1004 too is apophatic; the compressed lines—so characteristic of how she creates absences in her very syntax by such elision—can be read "as that endured, which, if it were uttered, would discourage [...]" or even "no Silence [...] so silent as that which *was* endured, which in its way *did* utter [...]":

> There is no Silence in the Earth — so silent
> As that endured
> Which uttered, would discourage Nature
> And haunt the World —

Dickinson describes how someone lost to us is perceived as greater, lost, than when present (Fr1045); she defines the pleasure of hearing music in terms of its marking the withdrawal of "Ecstasy's *impediment*" (Fr1511; my italics); and she writes, "I would not paint — a picture — / I'd rather be the One / It's [*sic*] bright impossibility / To dwell — delicious — on — " (Fr348). She calls God "Bright Absentee!" (Fr367).

And among a number of possible citations from the work of Wallace Stevens, the most familiar describes the "listener, who listens in the snow, / And, nothing himself, beholds / Nothing that is not there and the nothing that is" ("The Snow Man," in Stevens 1974, 10). This example can lead us to others that have little or nothing theological in them, as I pursue the secular apophatic.

Not surprisingly, the apophatic seems essential to the poetic thinking of a number of Greek poets. In Odysseus Elytis' prose piece "Open Papers" (translated by Jeffrey Carson and Nikos Sarris), he writes of strong opposites evoking and turning into each other (as what is present may evoke what is absent), or even fusing, while not ceasing to be opposites:

> Being in the least degree poetic, I loved to the greatest degree Poetry, in the same way that, being in the least degree "patriotic," I loved to the greatest degree Greece. [. . .] Contrary to those who try hard a whole life long to "construct" their literary likeness, I mean to destroy it at any time and at any moment. [. . .] Here's why I write. Because Poetry begins there where death has not the final word. It is the end of one life and the commencement of another the same as the first, except it goes very deep, to the extremest point that the soul can track, to the frontiers of the contraries where Helios and Hades touch. The endless course toward physical light which is the Word, and the Uncreated light which is God. Because it fascinates me to obey him I know not, who is my entire self, not a half-self that goes up and down the streets and "is registered in the records for males of Town Hall."

> It is right to give to the unknown the part that belongs to it; here's

why we must write. Because Poetry unteaches us the world, such as we found it: the world of deterioration, wherein a certain moment comes for us that is the only road surpassing deterioration, in the sense that death is the only road to Resurrection. (2004, 676, 677–78)

The whole self that one is and lives is the self that one does not know; "uncreated," "unknown," and "unteaches" seem active opposites, not mere negations of the word following the prefix un-. (Might "Uncreated light which is God" have been translated "not created"? There is a difference between "never having been created" and "outside the category of having been created.")

In "The Garden Sees," Elytis mentions a Byzantine icon-painter, "a Panselinos who paints as though God does not exist / and proves exactly the opposite." If the garden "hears the sounds, from the colors," then the perceived (garden) is now the perceiver, and it is perceiving (hearing) what cannot be perceived (colors as sounds). If "the writing stops // wants you to eat the fish bone and throw out the fish," then the new writing will begin with our perceiving of what we usually do not perceive, and doing what we usually do not do, till "your hand copies / the Inconceivable" (371, 372, 374, 379).

In "What One Loves," Elytis expands bounteously on the song by Sappho (frag. 16) in which she wants to see the absent young woman Anaktoria. In a note, Elytis' translators provide a close translation of the one stanza of his source text from which Elytis took the title of his poem:

> Some say a cavalry company, some
> name soldiers, some would call ships
> earth's fairest thing, but I say
> it is what one loves most.
>   (Elytis 2004, 440)

Here is a translation by Jim Powell of the surviving fragment of the poem:

> Some say thronging cavalry, some say foot soldiers,
> others call a fleet the most beautiful of
> sights the dark earth offers, but I say it's what-
>   ever you love best.

And it's easy to make this understood by
everyone, for she who surpassed all human
kind in beauty, Helen, abandoning her
husband—that best of

men—went sailing off to the shores of Troy and
never spent a thought on her child or loving
parents: when the goddess seduced her wits and
left her to wander,

she forgot them all, she could not remember
anything but longing, and lightly straying
aside, lost her way. But that reminds me
now: Anactória,

she's not here, and I'd rather see her lovely
step, her sparkling glance and her face than gaze on
all the troops in Lydia in their chariots and
glittering armor.

(Sappho 2007, 6–7)

To answer the question of what is most beautiful, Sappho's song first opposes to concrete things (soldiers on horse or on foot or on ships) an idea (what one loves most). Her own answer turns out to be . . . someone who is absent. Elytis' poem in response is a catalogue on this principle. He begins in prose, then under each heading he writes in lines what cannot in fact be put into his travel bag—because it is elsewhere, because it belongs to someone else, because it cannot be contained, because it cannot be transported, because it is lost in the past, because it cannot even be visualized (the line from Arkhilokhos). Here is a small portion of the poem:

I emptied and refilled my travel bag. "Only what's necessary," I said. And it was enough for this life—and for many others yet. So I set myself to listing them one by one:

CRETE
Sealstone with representation of chamois (Heracleion Museum).
The Prince of Lilies (Knossos).

THERA
Kore (fresco).

EGYPT
Portrait of a Woman (Ouserat, tomb no. 51).
Young Man with Antelope (Menna, tomb no. 69).

HOMER
dark water
gleaming entry wall
an endless bright aether burst forth

ARCHILOCHUS
with their souls in the arms of the waves

SAPPHO
long night

(Elytis 2004, 440)

Through many more objects, the cataphatic particulars are apophatic instances of what cannot be put into the travel bag. The poem moves from ancient Greece through the Italian Renaissance to more painters, classical and modern composers, and one or two lines each from poets of England, France, Spain, Greece, Ireland, Italy, and the United States. The bag (first emptied) will be packed only with what cannot be put inside it. For a sharp contrast, think of an autobiographical poem in English. To use Wordsworth's *Prelude* again as a contrasting example: Wordsworth and Elytis both write of inner and spiritual life by touching on outer things, but Wordsworth's reality is very present to him—visually, palpably, and as narrative; Elytis' apophasis is all absence and impossibility. A short autobiographical poem in English that collects fragments of memory, like part 2 of Gary Snyder's poem "The Elwha River," works just as Wordsworth's poem does; the last few lines are a list: "Swiss army knife stole [*sic*] from my pants / at Juhu Beach outside Bombay, / a fine italic pen, // Theodora, Kitty-chan, / bottle of wine got broke, / things left on the sand. / Lost things" (1965, 13). (Curiously, the second part of "The Elwha River," from which I quote, should be counted, too, among the lost things that the poem itself evokes, for it is not included in the poem as published later in the full text of *Mountains and Rivers without End* (1996). Perhaps Snyder inserted it into another poem or sequence, or gave it another title and preserved it separately, or left it behind in the realm of what one no longer has, with the fine italic pen and Theodora.)

By contrast, this is "A Wreath," by Yannis Ritsos (translated by Edmund Keeley):

Your face was hidden in the leaves.
I cut the leaves one by one to get near you.
When I cut the last leaf, you were gone. Then
out of the cut leaves I wove a wreath. I didn't have
anyone to give it to. I hung it on my forehead.

(1979, 95)

And these lines from his poem "Afternoon" (also translated by Keeley):

[...] Behind the windows
stand those who are missing, and the jug full of water they didn't
    drink.
And that star that fell at the edge of evening
is like the severed ear that doesn't hear the crickets,
doesn't hear our excuses [...]

(23)

An instance of the poetically apophatic brought into English from the ex-imperial anglophone realm can be found in the work of the Indian poet Arun Kolatkar. Kolatkar began to publish in the 1950s in both English and Marathi and continued to write poems in both languages for as long as he lived (Mehrota 2007, 50). In his "Heart of Ruin," a poem in his English-language sequence *Jejuri* (which reflects moments in a pilgrimage to the town of that name, and its cult of the god Khandoba) he evokes a ruined temple. Kolatkar makes no declarations of belief; indeed, he seems a skeptical participant in pilgrimage, one who notices paradox and social curiosities, but in "Heart of Ruin," after describing the fallen roof of the *ruined* temple of the god Maruti, and a stray dog and her puppies living within that ruin, Kolatkar concludes:

No more a place of worship this place
is nothing less than the house of god.

(Kolatkar 2005, 6)

Divine presence is in ruin and absence. Kolatkar does something similar in "Manohar," in which a friend looks inside a building he presumes is a temple only to discover it is a cowshed. "It isn't another temple," Manohar says in the poem; yet in the way the poem unfolds, his negation says that the cowshed is a temple. Another example is more gestural, when in "The Priest's Son," Kolatkar makes similar use of a humble "scanty patch of scruffy dry grass / burnt brown in the sun," a small site of empty ugliness. But then Kolatkar gives the reader an image of the positive opposite of the negative emptiness, a colorful opposite of the brown grass, an opposite in physical scale to the hills, and an opposite of death, a transience rather than a dead permanence. Here is the complete poem:

> these five hills
> are the five demons
> that khandoba killed
>
> says the priest's son
> a young boy
> who comes along as your guide
> as the schools have vacations
>
> do you really believe that story
> you ask him
>
> he doesn't reply
> but merely looks uncomfortable
> shrugs and looks away
>
> and happens to notice
> a quick wink of a movement
> in a scanty patch of scruffy dry grass
> burnt brown in the sun
> and says
>
> look
> there's a butterfly
> there

(20)

In Mahmoud Darwish's *If I Were Another* (translated by Fady Joudah), some passages seem to me to make much of the apophatic. For example: "They know the road is the arrival at the beginning of the impossible road"; "I have behind the sky a sky for my return, but I / am still polishing the metal of this place, and living / an hour that foresees the unknown"; "My privacy is what / doesn't lead to me" (2009, 45, 59, 150). In translations, at least, Darwish makes frequent use of metonyms: "The stranger passed carrying seven hundred years of horses" (59; that is, the "years" are substituted for the Arabic tradition of working with horses); and a much more complicated figure, "a bird pecks my language" (78). The "language" the bird pecks is a metonymic substitute for "mouth" or "poem"; or for words that are seeds or bugs or trash. In the first metonymic possibility, the effect is that speaking and listening are pecked—and the pecking bird is a metaphor for something inimical to both: impatient political readers, wanting poems more readily usable in the public sphere? In the second, the effect is that individual words are eaten. A bird does not speak, but perhaps sings. What is this bird? Are we not able to take apart the nesting (a curiously apt metaphor) of metaphor and metonym here? Is the effect one of unknowable complexity? It seems to me that metonymy and apophatic figures are somehow akin in thought (although I am well aware that Russian Metarealism, to which I turn again in the next chapter, is very much about metaphor, not metonym.)

The poet Adonis, in a preface and a concluding essay to his poetry collection *The Pages of Day and Night* (translated by Samuel Hazo), writes that the Islamicization of Arabic destroyed poetry in that language, and thus "the Arabic language has nothing more to tell us. Rather it has become a language of silence, or rather it tends to reduce expression to silence. Its orbit is muteness, not diction" (1994, xiv). This is not apophasis but suppression.

However, Adonis also writes that "the light [that poetic investigation] may cast on the unknown only enlarges the unknown's dimensions, announcing its depth and extremity as if the light were transforming itself into night" (1994, 105). Beyond my knowledge, there may be evidence that a philosophically Platonic or theologically Plotinian sense of the apophatic entered Arab culture through the preservation by the Arab philosophers of portions of Greek antiquity. Ilya Kutik views Adonis' sense of the apophatic as unsurprising in one who was formed in an area (now Syria) that willy-nilly inherited among its particular traditions, however faintly, traces of Byzantine culture.

Adonis has argued passionately for the beauty and freedom of mind of pre-Islamic poetry, and for the modern Arabic poet's need to recover some aspects of that ancient poetics. From his analysis of the influence of Islam on Arabic poetry in his *An Introduction to Arab Poetics* (1990), I infer that his apophaticism is not religious but existential.

In a poem that explores many dimensions of the apophatic, Zbigniew Herbert writes in "Study of the Object" that "the most beautiful is the object / which does not exist" (2007, 193).

⊙ 5 ⊙

On Apophatic Poetics (II)

VARIETIES OF ABSENCE

"Nothing, nothing is certain, except the insignificance of everything I can compre-
hend and the grandeur of something incomprehensible but most important!" [Prince
Andrei] . . . A Russian is self-assured precisely because he does not know anything
and does not want to know anything, because he does not believe it possible to know
anything fully . . . In church there were always few people; Natasha and Mrs. Belov
would stand in their usual place before the icon of the Mother of God, built into the
back of the left-hand choir, and a new feeling of humility would come over Natasha
before the great, the unknowable, when at this unaccustomed hour of the morning,
looking at the blackened face of the Mother of God lit by candles and the light of
morning coming from the windows, she listened to the words of the service, which
she tried to follow and understand. When she understood them, her personal feeling,
with its nuances, joined with her prayer; when she did not, the sweeter it was for her
to think that the wish to understand everything was pride, that it was impossible to
understand everything, that she only had to believe and give herself to God, who in
those moments—she felt—was guiding her soul.

TOLSTOY (2008, 293, 639, 659)

I'm going to put some crutches under another translation of a poem
and then offer it up. Since the extent to which this poem makes meaning out of the sounds of Russian cannot be reproduced in English,
only some analogous effects of sound remain, in the translation, and
a sequence of images.

In this elegy for Robert Lowell by Andrei Voznesensky (which
Ilya Kutik and I have translated), Lowell is brought onto the page
by means of several images that can be imagined in a visual or quasi-
visual way, such as a violin that does not exist but which is the one instrument, so Voznesensky feels, that plays the lost music of Lowell's

being, for it is a kind of imaginary way of accounting for Lowell's characteristic posture; it's also a distant metonym for Lowell's poems. And this nonexistent, *invisible* violin then *vanishes*! Double apophasis, one might say.

Then Lowell's stature (in both senses) is represented not by his standing *under* a "violent notch" in a wall to compare his own height against that of the very tall Peter the Great, but by his *entering*—this is the impossible part—that notch, that little "void." And then the notch-void makes a sound—it rings like a telephone vibrating with a call that no one can have made, and of course no one can answer. The English word *ringing* can't convey the distinction of telephone rather than bell, and the English-language mind wants to know which it is; but melding both possibilities is a Russian way of hearing the image. That "violent notch" is another instance of hypallage, and perhaps an apophatic one—the axe-blows to the wood were violent, not the notch they created. And the notch is called a "void," as if vast emptiness were in that small splintery space.

Lowell's cemetery is presented as an internal absence, since Voznesensky imagines it not only as a place of burial but also as a *buried place*. Voznesensky imagines Lowell's tombstone as a bookmark or "post-it" in a buried *cemetery* . . . that is a *book*; metaphorically that image would be an anthology of all the dead poets. But the poetic self in the poem says he cannot find Lowell, who would be the page of that book that the "post-it" representing him had marked, "for someone has pulled all the post-its" from the ground (the edge of the book). So these impossible post-its, like the violin, vanish too. All of these are apophatic images of that which is present and real to the poetic self in the poem but can only be apprehended through qualities that are impossible or absent.

A Graveyard Within: To the Memory of Robert Lowell

You came in through my Peredyélkyno gate
Tilting your head to the left a little—cheek to one shoulder—
As if holding a violin that's invisible.
Now the violin has vanished. But I've got to hear it!

Peering myopically, you stepped into Peter the Great's wood hut.
Inside's a notch two meters high hacked by an axe.

To measure your own height, you entered that notch —
The void left behind by the stature of Peter.

How this void, instead of the body it lacks, is ringing!
Under the violent notch stands a new shadow.
In the graveyard the maples have shed their leaves.
And the violin one can't get hold of is moaning.

Deep in the woods, an internal graveyard is itself interred.
Your mother and father — and where are you? . . .
From the ground someone has pulled all the post-its
And now it's impossible to find the right page.

How's it going, Robert, in your new nowhere?
We all carry our own graveyards within us.
Now what name do you have? — whistling through
The all-encompassing void, a pestle for crushing ennui.
Your former name lies flat on a gravestone.

At last you've booked your way out of our labyrinth.
What's up, shadow — you under the notch in the hut?
I'm bringing you some of Pasternak's rowan berries.
(But they won't help Robert.)

An absent presence addressed as the "shadow" of the last stanza, Lowell is absent to yet one more degree in the compressed ambiguity of the final play of pronouns in Russian; because of the way English handles pronouns, Kutik and I could only achieve some clarity by abandoning such compression and using the second-person "you" in the next-to-last line but the third-person proper name "Robert" in the last line, when the poem itself seems to utter an aside to the reader. The reason Voznesensky brings the rowan berries to the notch in the hut is that the notch, itself an absence of wood, "remembers" the man who stood in the place of the absent Peter the Great, and who had metaphorically "entered" the notch itself. Thus an apprehensible invisibility or negativity or absence. But wherever Lowell is, now that he is dead, is nowhere at all, and the berries can do nothing for him. Visible and tangible, these berries from Pasternak's bushes are only for the living.

✻

The modern literary-critical term often used for a gap in meaning or
the impossibility of discovering any "transcendental signifier," such as
"God," on which other words depend for meaning, is the Greek word
aporía that I used earlier. This is an alpha privative formation, in which
the initial *a-* is like our *non-* and *un-*. Since *poros* has multiple meanings
in its centuries of use in antiquity, from "a means of passing a river,
ferry, ford," to many figurative usages, *a-poros* in ancient Greek meant
"having no way in, or out, or through," or a difficulty, a perplexing (and
much else). So the "gap," the emptiness, between what is possible and
what is wanted becomes in itself real (thus, another instance of the
apophatic). Yet the "gap" or aporia is also an opening through which,
indeed, meaning can be pursued.

But the apophatic mode in poetry is not an attempt to prove that
language is wholly inadequate to represent anything in that gap or
anything that cannot be imagined cataphatically. It is a way of suc-
ceeding in imagining by means of the negative, a way in which language can enter into negative or empty or hidden or invisible spaces,
quiet or violent, or into paradoxically opposite points of thought and
feeling—as Greville, Donne, Edward Herbert, and a few others did
centuries ago.

I have not especially emphasized, so far, that apophatic thought is
mystical. I don't believe that every variety or degree of it necessarily is.
But to give just one very striking example of the mystical, I will quote
Pavel Florensky's study *Iconostasis*, in which he wrote that the iconostasis (the screen holding icons, which in a Russian Orthodox church
is interposed between the worshippers in the nave and the altar in
the sanctuary) makes it possible to *see mystery* by *blocking* the view
of the (entirely tangible) *altar*. He wrote, "[D]estroy the material
iconostasis and the altar itself will, *as such*, wholly vanish from our
consciousness as if covered over by an impenetrable wall." Thus "to
speak figuratively, then, a temple *without* a material iconostasis erects
a solid wall between altar and temple; [with its icons] the iconostasis
opens windows in this wall, through which we see (those of us who can
see) what is permanently occurring beyond: the living witnesses to
God. To *destroy* icons means to *block up* the windows" (1996, 63; my
italics).

Several years ago, in response to an e-mail I sent to him about Metarealism, the late Russian poet Alexei Parshchikov replied to me (in English) about the poetic stance of his work:

> [T]he apophatic disposition is no doubt very important for poetic images, as it marks places which exist neither materially nor virtually (i.e., in cyberspace). And it is hard to figure out a ground for such a framework in our psyche. Meanwhile we do know about it and are even ready to imagine such a minus place. We are aware somehow of the presence of these "negational" sites and use them as if they were conventional points of reference, even though they rest upon a different mental equilibrium. [...] We are looking for limits of language, where imagination just begins.

Associations between sound and sense—both the subtle meanings innate in some phonemes and those created by the use of particular words in a poem—produce an intensity of meaning beyond the semantic values of the words, and also create or make possible in some poets and readers a mystical sense of language itself, if we may call it that. For some, the realm of the divine is the ultimate hidden realm or "minus place" of meaning evoked by and in language. During our early years all of us have a gift for the play of linguistic sound and meaning which later, in some, leaves a residual ability that is called poetic. Each individual's use of language, as well as the language usage of groups, also creates in us intense emotional associations in the relation between word and referent. We know that language is largely— but not perfectly—an arbitrary sign system, yet Roman Jakobson, touching on this in his foundational essay, "Linguistics and Poetics," crucially qualified the supposedly pure arbitrariness of language as a system, which had been proposed by Saussure (1981, 44–45; and elsewhere in Jakobson's work). Linguists have qualified that arbitrariness considerably more, tracing the sounds, grammatical features, and connotations that link some signifiers to specific qualities of things in a nonarbitrary way. Because of some cultural and at least a few transcultural associations of meaning with phonemes, we can leap from word to word in ways both unexpected and meaningful. And in its form, any word may also carry a portion of its own history inside itself, and this portion too speaks in specific ways, as an etymological echo of a word's origins, sometimes deepening the meaning of a word as it is used at present, especially in a poem, where readers proceed word by word attentively, allowing the resuscitation of meanings that had been lost. A word's present meaning may also be extended in poetry by a gesture toward what it used to mean.

So perhaps it is not such a great stretch, if one could have practiced it for some time, even for a linguistic secularist, to understand the Metarealist technique of inviting a word to seek another that it — as Kutik says about Russian — "loves." If words themselves evoke other words in the process of composition, then the poet will be following not a visual but a verbal impulse, and the image that arises may enact a kind of freedom from the visual and the visible. (Such evocation must be poetic, that is, creative and free, rather than a routine association of one word with another because of the ready-made quality of that association.) Kutik's poetic word which itself seeks out, "loves," the second word that completes the rhyme, seems intimately linked in Russian to a mystical sense of language. And in a more general way, the poem itself as an object of love, and poetic language, too, is not a new idea, nor is it specific to an apophatic or even a mystical sense of language itself. Giorgio Agamben has written that the *body* of the troubadour song, and of medieval poetry in Italian as well (composed of course by men) was figured as female, with metrical "feet," a sometimes "limping" or "crippled" rhyme, a "face," and a "tail." Dante's Beatrice, as a metaphor, is one of the greatest realizations of this poetic device. Agamben says: "Behind the Provençal and Dolce Stil Novo theory of love stands a radical reflection on poetic language" which is expressed in the (male) poet's use of "the feminine name and figure. [. . .] For the Provençals as for the Dolce Stil Novo poets, the experience of love was the experience of the absolute primacy of the event of words over life and of *what is poeticized* [*il poetato*] over *what is lived* [*il vissuto*]. [. . .] Beatrice is the name of the amorous experience of the event of language at play in the poetic text itself" (1999, 28–29, 57, 58; the italics and bracketed Italian words are Agamben's).

❋

Recall Lord Edward Herbert's "Sonnet of Black Beauty," in which darkness quenches all colors, but darkness is itself an opposite kind of light. In Orthodoxy, "negative theology," the apophatic way of thought, is a "way towards mystical union with God, whose nature remains incomprehensible to us." For while "all knowledge has as its object that which is," apophatic theology holds that "God is beyond all that exists," and thus can be approached only by drawing "near to the Unknown in the darkness of absolute ignorance. [. . .] For even as light, and especially abundance of light, renders darkness invisible; even so the knowledge of created things, and especially excess of knowledge, destroys the ignorance which is the only way by which one can attain to God in Himself" (Lossky 1957, 28, 25). That is, a transcendent God is ultimately hidden from human understanding *by* his seemingly understandable or perceivable qualities. Analogously for poetry, even at its most secular, much of the world may be occluded by or within its own visible qualities and hidden by its own nameability.

The apophatic poetic impulse flies in the opposite direction from the Adamic desire to name what is apprehensible as actual, specific, particular, and present. The Adamic must eventually lead to aporia, but apophatic thought makes aporia its medium. (A line from Mahmoud Darwish: "He taught Adam all the names, so that the great mystery could reveal / our journey to the mysterious" [2009, 34].) The apophatic poetic impulse opposes the desire to name. It does not substitute instead an impulse to be abstract, but rather, in some other sense, it thinks toward a different kind of opposite to the Adamic. I think this opposite has to do, as Mandelshtam suggested, with a sense of the word that includes an awareness of a history that is still *alive* in it, going back (in Russian) to the Greek—hence Russian as a "Hellenistic" language. The word possesses, always *is*, a cluster or cloud (my own inadequate metaphor, not Mandelshtam's) of meanings and connotations apprehended simultaneously and held in mind, not sorted out as English does to attain a fairly clear, and at best, unambiguous meaning.

For poets writing in English, detailed descriptiveness is second nature, perhaps very literally ("a second nature"), because it is of the very nature of English—in both senses of that phrase: the qualities of English, and the way English names all that belongs to nature. To the extent that we imagine in language, "nature" in English is both the vastness of the world we did not ourselves build, and which we contrast too simplistically with "culture," "settlement," "farm," "city," and so forth, and also the sheer wealth of English nomenclature with which we speakers of English unwittingly may check off, categorize, and even conceal (an apophatic idea) with our language. Because we speakers of English have created over many centuries such a pleasing abundance of taxonomical terms, we name "nature" differently than how it is represented in, say, Spanish or—I am only guessing— in the Chinese-language mind. That English abundance is a linguistic treasure, and it is in our grain as our cultural heritage, as a cast of mind created by our formation in language. It is not the only sort of linguistic treasure, but tallied with such taxonomical profusion both formal and vernacular in English (and with regional variants—*redbird* versus *cardinal*, *cottonmouth* versus *water moccasin*), nature itself in English has a kind of word-thinginess, a particularity, almost a palpability, in the sounds of some words (the sibilants of *lady's slipper*, the emphatic double beat of the poisonous *wolfsbane*, the plosive *p* and sharp *k* phonemes in the name of the long, lithe, fast-swimming, quick-striking *pike*). Apophasis in such a thicket of thinginess will come with difficulty.

If, as Vladimir Lossky wrote, theological apophaticism "is, above all, an attitude of mind which refuses to form concepts about God" (1957, 38–39), then we might say that an apophatic poetics is a mentality that refuses to limit itself to existing articulations of what reality is. This is not skepticism merely; apophaticism is not about a distrust of language but, in its way, about a great trust in the plasticity with which language can evoke what cannot be described. We do not speak amid the ruins of language, even if we are sometimes speaking a "language of ruins" ("Farewell," in Adonis 2010, 54).

An apophatic poetics does not practice any one poetic style. It is not a style or method but a mentality, a mode of perceiving, a swerving mode of multiply imagining. Marina Tsvetaeva begins with that Russian idea of words which themselves find their way to other words. Here, from 1923, is the longer passage from which I have quoted several times already. It is for me the touchstone of these chapters on the apophatic. In this forever inadequate translation (as yet unpublished) that Kutik and I have made, we use enjambment to emphasize individual words typographically as a device analogous to, albeit weaker than, Tsvetaeva's phonetic and syntactical emphasis of them, her putting her poet-potter's hand on them, one at a time, and reshaping them:

> A poet—taking
> off far beyond himself
> utters words.
> The words lead far
> beyond what was meant by—
> the poet.
> By planet-
> ary ways and super-
> stition paths,
> Along the
> alleyways of alle-
> gories . . . Be-
> Tween "not" and "be";
> even heaving himself from
> a bell-tower he'll
> veer up in a de-
> tour . . . For the way of
> the comet
> Is the poet's way.
> Links that have been
> wrecked between
> Cause and effect—
> these are his links!

As Tsvetaeva says in this poem, poetry goes further than language can go, it exists in the gap between "not" and "be" or "being," it defies linguistic gravity, and in the most clearly apophatic image, the last in this series, those destroyed links between cause and effect are the very links by which (or through the absence of which) a poet moves from one word or image or idea to the next.

Lossky the theologian articulated "the perfect way" to God; but poetry is not religion any longer, and it seeks a human, imperfect way. (I think of a line by Adonis, "Even the stars dream of living in a hut of reeds" [2010, 225].) On our merely human path, too, we grasp for the seemingly ungraspable; we sense in our spirits the unsayable sensation and effect in us if not of the divine then of the uncanny, at the very least, and the joyous, and the exalting, and the unfathomably soul-wrecking. Even the utterly secular Russian writer Daniil Kharms found that in Stalin's Soviet Union there was ample call for the writer to imagine the invisible and the impossible because of the savage power of the state to *make* a person invisible, to make existence impossible, both bodily and in remembrance. Composed in 1937, what is now called "Blue Notebook, No. 10" implies in its last sentence, with still powerful fearfulness, why the earlier sentences are poetically necessary (translation by George Gibian):

> There was once a red-haired man who had no eyes and no ears. He also had no hair, so he was called red-haired only in a manner of speaking.
>
> He wasn't able to talk, because he didn't have a mouth. He had no nose, either.
>
> He didn't even have any arms or legs. He also didn't have a stomach, and he didn't have a back, and he didn't have a spine, and he also didn't have any other insides. He didn't have anything. So it's hard to understand whom we're talking about.
>
> So we'd better not talk about him any more. (Kharms and Vvedensky 1987, 57)

"No eyes and ears" is a metonymic way of saying that he made sure that he saw and heard nothing. Perhaps I'm mistaken that this use of opposites is metaphorically apophatic; it is at least rhetorically so, and Kharms made it larger than that. Not only is the man not a man — in his political context — but he is made never to have existed (from the moment he is arrested, his very being becomes a prohibited thought). Kharms articulated a description by negation, and the narrative implies — only implies — that the person has been negated by the state. Such a reality can require an apophatic gesture.

✻

As I notice something that to me seems apophatic in poets as different as Kolatkar, Ritsos, Donne, Dickinson, Voznesensky, Elytis, and Darwish, I feel the strain of discovering (dis-covering, making un-hidden) the apophatic. I am trying to recognize a way of thinking that is new to me. And by contrast I am sensing more deeply how my stance toward language itself, and toward poetic thinking, is certainly not innate in me as a language user generally. It's a lifetime's task to become able to attend to the grain or the song of one's language as fully as the mental sense of touch and the ear can. My new awareness of the apophatic has not given me the ability to *think* it deeply, to use it, although I now can, as poets have already done in English, recognize some of its aspects, metaphors, images, and episodes of absence, vacancy, invisibility, and an especially deep sort of paradox. But I know that that's not the same as apophatic thinking. Linguistically, conceptually, perceptually, philosophically, I have no agility at this.

In his "The Last Train Has Stopped," Mahmoud Darwish wrote, "Where can I free myself of the homeland of my body?" (2003, 15). But if the body of my language is also a kind of homeland, then I'm not trying to free myself from it but rather to enter (create?) spaces in it that I hadn't known could be inhabited. Or to dance with feet, and see with an "I," that are capable of moving and thinking differently. There is indeed a distinction between the dancer and the dance — and the dancer may be able, even if only just barely, to imagine and attempt a dancing that remains beyond his abilities.

In "Excerpts from the Byzantine Odes of Abu Firas," Darwish wrote, addressing an echo: "Take me with you to my language, I said" (2003, 87). I want to say to the poems in which I find an apophatic opening, "Take me with you to the thought I almost have." No, that's not it. Take me, in Tsvetaeva's way, *beyond* that "thought." Isn't this one of the great things that poetry is able to accomplish? "Take me with you to my language," I say to the poem I am reading, and to the poem that I myself am writing. In the poetic dance with language, it's not only the dancer but also the dancing that invents the steps. Here is the apophatic step.

❋

The closest approximation in contemporary American poetry to Russian apophaticism might be the work of the Russian poet who made for himself a second poetic home, however oddly constructed, in American English: Joseph Brodsky. The apophaticism of Russian Orthodox thinking that so saturates the Russian language is available as a poetic resource to a Jewish poet, too. Brodsky's poetry, including the poems he himself wrote in English or wrote in Russian and himself translated into English, can seem superficial, meandering, and linguistically rather awkward to native speakers of English. And in fact many American readers of poetry do not hear Brodsky's poems in English as fully idiomatic. But perhaps we can see the artistic impulse behind some of what he was doing—the play of the poetics of the poem rather than what seems the awkwardness of the wordplay. Now, although among Brodsky's many essays there is none on apophaticism, nevertheless he made comments like this: "Poetry has a certain appetite for emptiness, starting, say, with that of infinity" (1995, 198). American poetry, though, he said, is "rich and extremely lucid in detail," and "[t]o my eye as well as my ear, [it] is a relentless nonstop sermon on human autonomy; the song of the atom, if you will, defying the chain reaction" (204). (This is an image he used also in his late poem "Anthem," which he wrote in English.) The precise microcosmic individuality of the English-language word-atom, and the enormous wealth of vivid detail in the English-language lexicon, are both at an opposite extreme from the multifarious identity—composed of several or many atoms—of the Russian word-molecule and the resounding, synthesizing image-metaphor.

In his "Elegy: For Robert Lowell"—the first poem that Brodsky wrote in English, and perhaps the best of all those so written, he seems to be writing English with the poetics of Russian. For instance, he rhymes words that are not the same part of speech, as when in part 3 he half-rhymes the verb "graze" with the noun "grease," and reverse-rhymes the adjective "flat" with the noun "flag." But our ears haven't been trained by our own poetic tradition to hear the sameness of the initial fl in "flat" and "flag" as a phonetic chime that is as emphatic as rhyme, which convention has long defined for us as making a louder clunk than that; reverse rhyme belongs to the Russian way of hearing. Having offered the reader a porcupine in the first stanza—as if to hint at Lowell's skunk, which links poetically to Elizabeth Bishop's armadillo — Brodsky makes use of a number of end-words which in English are half rhymes or less; he thinks with them. When the first word finds the second and the (Russian) rhyme is achieved, the poem takes a slightly different, gently centrifugal, direction.

Brodsky uses the word "needles" at the end of line 4, then by adding only one more letter he (or the word "needles") finds the word "needless" for the end of line 6. The gleam of the porcupine's quills suddenly becomes "needless," a word that now contains and repeats the word "needles" inside it. In stanza 2, from the word "People's" (which with its vowels echoes "needles" and "needless") he finds his way — or English does, as it tries to learn new moves from this new master — to "pebbles." As Brodsky would have heard it, I believe, this move pleases by creating the surprising metaphoric link between the people and the pebbles, which the (Russian) rhyme "justifies" poetically. With this, the poem fulfills the possibilities of its earlier image (the weeping of mourners at Lowell's funeral as a metaphorical *wave* of persons that "breaks" on the altar) with the idea and image of a real tide rushing up over a pebble beach; and now the reader is on that beach, and the tears in the mourners' blind pebble eyes are wet with the tide of grief:

> In the autumnal blue
> of your church-hooded New
> England, the porcupine
> sharpens its golden needles
> against Bostonian bricks
> to a point of needless
> blinding shine.
>
> White foam kneels and breaks
> on the altar. People's
> eyes glitter inside
> the church like pebbles
> splashed by the tide.
>
> (2000, 147)

Then comes the apophatic opposition of "a lot, / a lot of Almighty Lord, / but not so much as a shred / of your flesh." And again, an apophatic absence: "When man dies / the wardrobe gapes instead" (147).

In the second part of the poem, Brodsky's images of language can't be visualized in the forms of anything that really exists, but it's not difficult to imagine them visually nevertheless:

> On the Charles's bank
> dark, crowding, printed letters
> surround their sealed tongue.
> A child, commalike, loiters
> among dresses and pants
> of vowels and consonants
>
> that don't make a word.
>
> (148)

The line "that don't make a word" is the negative that names what it says is not. Late in the poem Brodsky writes of death:

> It might feel like an old
> dark place with no match
> to strike, where each word
> is trying the latch.
>
> (149)

Again, the negative: "no match"; and the image of the immaterial and invisible—the (old) word—trying to become material (each word a hand trying to unlatch a door that does not exist). Brodsky then writes of "the invisibility of / lingering soul" (149).

Evidently from a perspective that is natural to speakers of Russian, Brodsky wrote poems that may remain elusive for speakers of English, not primarily because Brodsky's English can seem somewhat forced, I think, but because Brodsky was composing with a translated poetics. While his taste in American and English poetry was somewhat rearguard, in that he favored rhyme and metrical lines and he especially praised Hardy, Frost, and Auden, his taste in Russian poetry was for the (formerly but still formidably) avant-garde difficulty which in Marina Tsvetaeva and Osip Mandelshtam had to wait, in the Soviet Union, a few generations even to be known by many Russian readers, much less appreciated. But note that Boris Pasternak, Tsvetaeva, and Mandelshtam created an avant-garde in which meter and rhyme still structured a familiar sonic regularity by means of which, paradoxically, the thought moved in almost unprecedented ways.

Brodsky was at pains to try to characterize for the English-language readers of his essays Tsvetaeva's way of writing by ear—opening words up as if they themselves can speak to and hear each other, based on their own sounds and roots. And in Mandelshtam he described the "acceleration" of consciousness, image, and feeling produced by Mandelshtam's "oversaturated" poems, arising from a violently oversaturated existence in the midst of which Mandelshtam looked to the clarifying ideal of a world civilization (1986, 123–44, 176–94, 195–267).

A late poem by Brodsky, "In Memory of Clifford Brown," written in Russian then translated by the poet, is structured by the rhetoric of apophasis throughout:

> It's not the color blue, it's the color cold.
> It's the Atlantic color you've got no eyes for [. . .]
>
> It's not a regular ice floe, meltdown-prone. [. . .]
> It's not a guileless tune that chafes in the darkness [. . .]
> It's not a simple space, it's a nothing [. . .]
>
> (2000, 450)

When I asked Ilya Kutik about the apophatic in Brodsky, he told me that it "is mostly a way of speech from the vantage point of 'absence'—not 'presence.' He speaks from the 'point of view' of 'emptiness' all the time." I'll secularize a sentence in Lossky's *The Mystical Theology of the Eastern Church* (1957, 25): If in seeing an object—an inanimate thing, a place, a person, an event—one can know what one sees, then one has *not* seen it in itself but has seen instead what was too readily intelligible about it, an intelligibility of the object that is inferior to the thing itself. Or let's imagine what we do *not* even see in itself—neither the material object (the empty, gaping wardrobe that is now metonymically the absence of the person Robert Lowell) nor the immaterial image (alphabet letters gathering on the banks of the Charles River).

Since it is so important to our ability to survive, to attain some human freedom, and to help others to survive and be free, that the powers of reason, and the ability to understand what is, and to make it intelligible to ourselves, not be denied, even in poetry (Brodsky himself said this at different moments), what would be the role in human life of a kind of poetic thinking that did not accept entirely the apparent reality of what one sees and experiences? Or, to put this question more fairly, what would be the value of a poetic thinking that deliberately or temperamentally sought to articulate more (not less) than is intelligible in everyday perceptual terms? (I posit this without in the least meaning that the part that cannot be seen is in any way supernatural.) Brodsky himself showed that what he cherished in English poetry has to do with the English-language immersion in the material world, as in his substantial essay on Thomas Hardy's poem "The Darkling Thrush" (1995, 312–75). My point has not been to oppose poetically apophatic negative definitions and evocations to the expected particulars and positives of American poetry, and indeed of the English language, but to set them in relation to each other. They exist. With characteristically sunny confidence, Brodsky wrote that

> in the process of composition a poet employs—by and large unwittingly—the two main modes of cognition available to our species: Occidental and Oriental. (Of course both modes are available whenever you find frontal lobes, but different traditions have employed them with different degrees of prejudice.) The first puts a high premium on the rational, on analysis. In social terms, it is accompanied by man's self-assertion and generally is exemplified by Descartes's "Cogito ergo sum." The second relies mainly on intuitive synthesis, calls for self-negation, and is best represented by the Buddha. In other words, poetry offers you a sample of complete, not slanted, human intelligence at work. This is what constitutes the chief appeal of poetry, quite apart from its exploiting rhythmic and euphonic properties of the language which are in themselves quite revelatory. (1995, 206)

⊙ 6 ⊙

The Curious Persistence

TECHNĒ

[P]oetry as divination; poetry as revelation of the self to the self, as restoration of the culture to itself; poems as elements of continuity, with the aura and authenticity of archaeological finds, where the buried shard has an importance that is not obliterated by the buried city; poetry as a dig, a dig for finds that end up being plants.

SEAMUS HEANEY ([1979] 1989, 263)

In the *kitchen*, when I take *cumin* from among the little jars of herbs and spices, or pour something through a *sieve*, I'm also unwittingly sustaining words older than I can imagine, words that originated in languages that no longer exist and were spoken from the Mediterranean to India. The most ancient version of the word *cumin* was not very different in form and sound from our word. And the same is true of some other modern words, such as English *cow* and *breast* and both halves of *agriculture*. To cook with cumin is to savor a very ancient human taste. More amazing, I think, is that to use such very old words is also to bring into speech (and poetry), although not often into our awareness, the antiquity from which they came. I might also have made, in a different life, a little charm to ward off this or that, with cumin seeds in it, perhaps, or other aromatics. The spell I might have chanted while holding my little cumin-seed sack would have been a kind of verbal apotropaic amulet: by saying it or thinking it I can feel like I'm pushing *away*—the *apo-* part of this ancient Greek word—a disturbing or dispiriting thought, the visitation in my mind of an unwanted figure, or some danger or illness.

I am fascinated by the antiquity of poetry, or rather, of poetic thinking. I don't mean allusions to ancient poetry, although I will mention some, in passing; rather, I mean the present-day practice of devices and structures of poetic thinking that were used long ago—not used today as ornament or allusion, as in architecture, let's say, or painting, but as core elements in our contemporary practice of poetry.

No less than we do today, ancient poets, with forms and devices and tropes, intensified the meaningfulness of language and articulated ideas, feelings, beliefs, experiences, to exceed the meaning that could be conveyed and enacted in other modes of thought and discourse. Why, among other marvels of language, should some such ancient practices of poetry have survived to remain so available today? If it is interesting that cumin—the word as well as the spice—should still be in use, is it not even more interesting that such a simple device (and, at its most interesting, a mode of thought) as the use of repeated phonemes, from subtle to emphatic, should have originated so long ago and should also still be in use in most poetry?

Since very little—but more than most readers might suppose—is known about poetry that was composed, performed, and heard long before the invention of writing, we cannot go back to a poem in a prehistoric language to study directly the continuity of poetic composition, any more than we can recover from a tomb on the central Asian steppes the words of a recipe for horse and thistle stew. And although we should feel a reasonable skepticism about our ability to know the past, we are also unwittingly constrained in the opposite way by our ineradicable everyday modernity, which disables our interest in and alertness to the past.

Plenty of people would have sought some of the same engagements and pleasures in ancient Canaan and Cairo and Rome as seek them in present-day Chicago, Shanghai, and Sydney—and Rome. Of course we shouldn't minimize the discontinuities in historical changes and cultural differences in thought and human experience, but looking at the poetry of ancient Greece, we may appreciate that some of the ancient techniques of composing a poem are as familiar as those of uttering an apotropaic wish. Even though ancient ideas about how those techniques of poetry related to the very existence of the world and everything in it were quite different from our ideas about . . . well, perhaps most of us don't think very much about the relation of artistic techniques to the sheer existence of the world and everything in it, and to our ideas about all that.

❊

My curiosity about ancient poetics in the context of this book is not so much about "the function of the poet and of poetry" in the social realm as it is about "poetics" understood as "the technique of poetical composition" — I take the clear wording of that distinction from Ernst Robert Curtius (1963, 468).

The poet's traditional role regarding language itself is to make possible the full flowing and potency of meaning-making with words. Most poets today still subscribe to this relationship to language. We all use language meaningfully; the poet has and has always had techniques for concentrating that meaning-making. The fiction writer William Goyen, who called some of his stories "arias," said, "People in my life told me stories, and I sang. They had the speech, and I got the voice" (2007, 115).

For most of us, it is exhilarating and frightening at the same time to see all the stars on a clear night. We may also feel an awareness that what we see has been seen from the beginning of human time, and always as a contrast in scale — the frightening magnificence, the baffling incomprehensibility — to the human scale of life. Osip Mandelshtam put this into a memorable line in a poem written during the most barbaric years of Stalin's rule. In the scene, there must be a woodpile: implicit warmth — or immolation. Mandelshtam wrote: "Starlight like salt on the blade of an axe" (2004, 40). Such a fusion with or interpenetration of the immensity of the clear night sky and the minuteness of a crystal of salt and of the individual human being under the night sky, of the indifference of the universe and the malice of an axe, is not apotropaic but rather a gesture of acknowledging yet mastering with metaphor a nearly inexpressible sense of danger — existential and political — and doom. Are the stars transformed into a mere sparkling of winter salt rime on a galactic executioner's axe? Are the crystals or grains of the salt on the axe transformed into burning stars on a colossal weapon or tool held in human hands? Such a poetic line seems a self-fulfilling poetic gesture that makes real what it imagines, combining two images of the real into an unreal complex. Mandelshtam himself blurred the boundaries between poetry, the palpable, the imaginary, and the apophatic. He famously wrote that reciting Pasternak's poems aloud could help cure tuberculosis

(1977, 83). He was characterizing the poems' bodily rhythms, surely, in the chanting style of recitation of Russian poets. But I think he must also have meant that they had such intense movement of mind in words, of thought in repeated round trips between evoked presences and absences, that to recite them was to enact something restorative, not apotropaic, not fearful, in one's body *and* spirit. That which was human and remains human in our cognition itself, through prehistory and history, furnishes the space of poems more frequently than those of fiction, I think, although in only an implicit way.

Yet this is not really a surprise. If instead of noticing the curious persistence of ancient poetic technique I were thinking about narrative in the same way—on a continuum from Homer to some recent American novel—then it might seem merely obvious that human beings practice narrative, presumably in all cultures and times. We *like* narratives; narrative is one of the ways we think, and it has a (complex and varied) "logic" of its own. If my question were about narrative devices, I might be looking at ancient techniques that continue even today to create the experience and authority of literary narrative. (For example, some of the messenger speeches in Athenian tragedies shift from past tense to present tense at climactic moments to make the narrative more immediate—a technique amply and continuously exploited in the whole history of narrative since.)

Both narrative and poetry make use, as does all our language use, of the deeply cognitive tropes of metaphor and metonymy, and these tropes are evidently aspects, modes, of all human thinking. In such instances, what ancients did and what we do are within a historical continuum simply because they arise from our nature as thinking (and talking, singing, and listening, then writing and reading) beings of the same species, and poetry is a use of language that so concentrates thought as to make it move faster and more intensely. Some devices of language and cognition are (and always must have been) so intensified in poetry because they are integral to ways of imagining what cannot be imagined without them.

Many of the elements and devices of poetic craft that now fill the glossaries of poetry handbooks would have appeared in an ancient text of this sort (had there been any like our own) two and half millennia ago. (I quote the first Greek book on how to write, later.) They would have accompanied other ancient elements of poetry that have not survived because the function of poetry in private and social and civic occasions, and of poets, in societies, has changed repeatedly. Therefore some of the poetic devices of songs, epics, and the Athenian tragedies (the latter were the focus of Aristotle's analysis of poetics) have disappeared. And yet much of the ancient poetic technique and some of the occasions (such as elegy) and topics (such as the inexpressible) of ancient Greek poetry are still in use today. The surprise is their antiquity. The previous chapters have reached to this side or that to explore some devices, modes, and stances of poetic thinking and poetic mentalities, but now I will explore not what is unfamiliar but what we might have thought was only familiar to us moderns.

As we would expect, ancient poetry used a poetic language that was more consistently "marked" as poetic than what we hear in contemporary poetry — not only by traditions of poetic practice but also by the movement of thought and the stance of the poet toward language and poetry itself. Some of that is gone. Choral poetry no longer exists, because its occasions, its social function, and its ethos do not. But ancient poetic thinking by and large moves in ways familiar to us. To be sure, the variety of cultures, communities, material circumstances, everyday practices, and beliefs out of which the range of ancient poetry arose could not be more different from the formation of people in most present-day societies. Yet in the poetry of many ancient places and times we moderns can easily recognize how a poem is "poetic." I will confine myself to ancient Greek, because my knowledge is limited to that language, place, and time.

I'll give a brief example of how ancient Greek poets marked poetic language with a texture of sound — phonetic figures of the kind I have already highlighted in English and Russian poetry. The first stanza (strophe) of Sophokles' "ode to man" (this particular Greek word for "man" has the sense of mankind, but of course as a noun it is gendered male) makes clear that phonetic technique hasn't changed. There is no end-rhyme but instead a dense texture of repeated sounds. In my transliteration into our Roman alphabet, I mark most, but not quite all, of the phonetic figures using bold type, italics, and underlining to sort the repetitions:

Polla ta *deina* kouden anthrōpou *dei*noteron pelei.
Touto kai poliou peran
pontou *kh*eimeriōi notōi
*kh*ōrei, peribru*kh*ioisin
perōn hup' *oi*dmasin, *the*ōn
*te ta*n huper*ta*tan, Gan
aph*thi*ton, akama*ta*n apo*t*rue*t*ai,
illomenôn apotrōn *etos* eis *etos*,
hippeiōi genei poleuōn.
(Sophocles 1998, 34)

(At many things—wonders, terrors—we feel awe, but at nothing more than at man. This being sails the gray-white sea running before winter storm-winds, he scuds beneath high waves surging over him on each side; and Gaia, the Earth, forever undestroyed and unwearying, highest of all the gods, he wears away, year after year as his plows cross ceaselessly back and forth, turning her soil with the offspring of horses. [Sophocles 2011, 70])

Poetic devices, tropes, and other figures not only mark the language of a poem as poetic but also, as I have mentioned, achieve the mobility of thought and feeling in a poem. The marking and mobility are still the practice of almost all poetry in modern times, albeit more subtly when the poet is using everyday language.

In the modern world, the language of poetry, which descends ultimately from the language of ancient ritual and belief in many cultures, no longer includes very much of the lexicon of relations between the human and the divine. Yet through era after era, from the Middle Ages to the present, we see a sustaining of the poetics that began in ritual, a continuous practice in our own language that still, as it did long ago, leads or invites language from its posture on its routine paths into moving at an angle to everyday speech and writing. This can be evident even in poets whose diction seems offhand and veers from register to register, such as John Ashbery's. Many traditional elements of poetics are not rejected even by those who reject others.

The strong marking of poetic language in ancient Greek poetry (epic, lyric, dramatic; chanted, sung, or recited) includes special words used only in poetry, words for which there were everyday counterparts for the same thing—a "language of the gods" versus a "language of men." As Calvert Watkins has detailed, early Sanskrit literature uses different words for "horse": "as *háya* he carried the gods [. . .] as *áśva* men." Levels of poetic diction differentiated by their social and religious values scarcely survive in modern poetry in English, but Watkins points out the analogous "horse" of everyday language versus the "steed, mount, charger" (1994, 5); we might add at least a few more to the everyday level, such as *nag, oater, trotter, mustang, hack, cayuse, bronco,* and so forth, and one more elevated and obsolete term, *courser.* (This polarity is like that of *snake* versus *serpent.*)

Ancient poetic language might use euphemisms for things that had no elevated name, as when Sophokles, in the choral "ode to man" in *Antigone* that I quoted above, called mules—those laboring creatures without the physical grace and heroic associations of horses, despite their use in some eras and places as war animals—the "offspring of horses" (Sophocles 2008, 33). In my translation (with Charles Segal) of this ode, I would now change the word *horses* to *equines* to suggest more clearly how Sophokles, needing to mention plow mules, must get his *thought* as far as possible from the ignoble Greek mule *and* his diction as far as possible from the Greek *word* for "mule," because it simply isn't a word that can be put into the same stanza as the sacred name of Gaia. Change in what is judged as appropriate in poetic diction isn't a choice that language itself makes, or individual poets; a literary culture, within its larger society, decides.

Twentieth-century democratization of education, culture, and thus the language of poetry has maintained the *effect* of using different levels of diction, but now the standard English of mortals, not gods or God, is the high level, and the other level—sometimes low, sometimes merely specialized—includes jargon, slang, technical terms, and vocabularies associated with particular communities and forms of knowledge, from medicine to the theater, from musicians to drug dealers, from chiropractors to cops, from horse people to sales staff to sailors. Such vocabularies allow the poet to create sometimes sudden movement up and down, or near and far (a key "po-mo" gesture, long used elsewhere, too: among comics it's a familiar move for a laugh). Bilingual poets from outside the dominant culture in a multilingual society also use different registers of diction when they "code-switch" between the dominant and the subsidiary one. Víctor Hernández Cruz has written masterfully in English, Spanish, and both at once and has articulated this linguistic tension in two concise lines: "He says nada / yo digo something"—a chiasmus of English/Spanish/Spanish/English (2001, 79). Immigrants and their children, racial and ethnic communities in America, border dwellers of more than one ethnicity and tongue who share vocabularies from two different languages, and others introduce new words and revitalize the idea of contrasting vocabularies, and the use of such contrasts in poetry.

Pamela White Hadas' exultantly worded "Box-Car Bertha," presented as a rambling account to a "Professor Doctor Dear," spectacularly mixes diction that is recherché in an elevated way ("dromomaniac"), coined as mock slang with a poetic sense of etymology ("redemptioneering, "explaterations"), and drawn from hobo slang ("candy train," "gandy-dancer," "shimmy-de-fer") to create a tour de force of what Bertha herself, performing it, deprecates as "your all- / time word-fuck, if you please" (1998, 46–49). Implying a life of hard treatment and hard treating, the poem does not nod toward the divine and human levels, of course, and yet it establishes the mobility and energy of the hobo slang (which for its metaphorical vividness and speed is certainly divine—in our slang sense) as opposed to the implicitly inert diction of Bertha's silent interlocutor, the "Professor Doctor Dear." His words although absent are clearly on a contrasting level; presumably they would be abstract, monotonous, cold.

We don't use poetry for any of Pindar's purposes, by which I mean the purposes of Pindar and those who commissioned his public odes, those who performed them, and those who were present as spectators at those ancient Greek performances. We don't use poetry as a mnemonic guide to agriculture, or—except in mock performative or secretly wishful ways—as a charm against illness or to attract love.

We have no access to what it felt like, as lived experience, to *compose* poems like those of Hesiod, Sappho, Pindar, Bakkhylides, and other ancient Greek poets, or to perform as a rhapsode—that is, to compose from traditional materials, and in some circumstances to do so *while performing,* as when singing or chanting or reciting an episode of the *Iliad* or *Odyssey.* If we imagine Pindar composing his odes partly by voice and memory (as Mandelshtam did, and Robert Frost too), and partly in writing, we can believe that we share at least some understanding with him of the process of creating the poem. He certainly wrote his songs out to be sent to his commissioning patrons, and the very texture of them suggests that he intended them to be read closely in the years after they had been performed, for "while he often says essentially the same thing, he never says it precisely the same way" (Race 1990, 187). There are other hints at writing: Pindar exhausts the Greek category of words for light of all kinds, and as in the ninth Olympian ode, at some moments he "feigns to cast his script aside and invite us to imagine the existence of an original poem composed for the occasion but rejected in the course of its performance" (Gerber 2002, 31, 40).

We can't know what it was like for a rhapsode or chorus to perform poetic compositions in the midst of the complex social practices and contexts in which the performance was both a momentous and yet also a familiar event. We don't know what it felt like to *listen* to a recitation of a Homeric episode, or to a choral or solo song—listening as participants ourselves in the "song culture" of ancient Greece. In a tiny victory ode (16 lines) for a boy, Lachon, from the island of Keos (in modern times Tzia or Zea) who in 452 BCE won the sprint at the Olympic Games, Bakkhylides wrote: "[T]hanks to Victory, the hymn of song-ruling Urania [one of the Muses] gives [you] praise in an ode sung before your house" (Campbell 1992, poem 6.10–14).

In another ode Bakkhylides wrote that "the light of man's excellence does not diminish with his body; no, the Muse fosters it" (Campbell 1992, ode 3.90–91). That is, song itself fosters the excellence of which it tells. (This is not about magic but about the social function of poetry—what poetry was for, in a different time and place and language.) We cannot join the townspeople who watched and listened to the danced song and who experienced, after and far from the games, the excellence of which the chorus sang; we can't share their pride and exaltation when in the ritual performance the chorus danced and sang to the boy and his family the line of Bakkhylides' song which, composed in another place and earlier, also described what the chorus members themselves were presenting *at that very moment* as they sang it: "an ode sung before *your* house." And yet we recognize, perhaps with surprise, the metapoetic quality of this last moment as something that could also be found in poems and performances by our contemporaries.

And it seems very remarkable that portions, at least, of such compositions are artistically and psychologically legible to us—in the original Greek and even when translated into modern languages. Perhaps what remains in modern cultures from ancient cultures is the appetite for poetry and the capacity for poetic composition. And the continuity between the poetics of Pindar and Sylvia Plath, Sappho and Ezra Pound, Homer and Sterling Brown is apparent despite all the differences in the characteristics of languages, the social functions of poetry, and the historical and ecological circumstances in which poetry has a role. In ancient Greece, these might range from large, socially influential, and even decisive occasions—as when the lives of some of the Athenian soldiers defeated by the Spartans at Syracuse were spared because the Athenians could recite lines of Euripides, whose work the Spartans loved (Plutarch 1960, 242–43)—to small-scale and mostly psychological functions; from ritual to secular; from narrative and mnemonic to occasional and lyric. The poems of our day (short of poetic experiments in other media), even those that call language and meaning into question, and even every sort of bad poem, make use of many of the same elements we can see in Bakkhylides and Pindar, Homer and Sappho and Sophokles. Even among beginning undergraduate writing students, whose knowledge of poetry, past or present, is very small, I have always seen nascent abilities to produce and to learn how to produce, no matter how inexpertly, patterns of sound, rhythmic emphasis, structures of expressive shape, and other aspects of poetry that have been historically characteristic of poetry since very long ago.

My high-school Latin teacher got in touch with me and sent me some books on Latin prosody. Latin prosody has entered my work but in a secret way and I don't ever want to discuss it with anybody.

ALICE NOTLEY (2013, n.p.)

When occasionally I could stand a little further away from the sweet difficult work of translating Sophokles I could see how strange it was—even if I could do it only inadequately—to do it at all. The strangeness of being able to do it was what I liked best about it. Even as I was learning how to make out the Greek fully, translation also made possible—as it can always do—my noticing and pondering of aspects of English and English-language poetry that I had not previously thought very much about. One of those aspects was the way we notice mostly the historical changes in poetry and the interruptions of the continuity of poetry. Even though we may not like them all, those changes and interruptions are reassuring; they keep poetry alive. Poetry changes in manner: forms, rhetoric, preoccupations amid social life, and private musing. And it must change, as must language itself, over time, since the changes in poetry may have more to do with its function in human societies than with its craft as a heightened technology of language.

The continuities of poetry have included speaking to gods; entertaining guests; sustaining and widening the fame and glory of ancient Greek warrior-kings, heroes, and winners at Greek athletic games; preserving the memory of the ordinary individual person in elegy or funereal epigram; celebrating weddings and genealogies; cursing and praising; declaring love; thinking aloud, so to speak, about youth and age, love and exile, grief and joy; securing traditional knowledge and attitudes and also introducing new values, new ideas, new materials, newly articulated lived experience, new perceptions, new perceiving. No wonder then, that a scholar of the most ancient poetry who also looks at modern poetry would affirm that in his major work it is his goal "to emphasize the longevity and specificity of verbal [poetic] tradition and the persistence of specific verbal traditions" (Watkins 1995, 10).

About those gods: it might be poetry which in part has created and sustained not only rituals but also the very gods in whose honor or worship those rituals have been enacted. In ancient India the gods, no doubt with considerable appreciation, responded by sustaining poetry itself, while among the ancient Greeks, gods were patrons of poetry—Apollo and the Muses—who might choose to favor some poets over others. That is, priest-poets brought a sense of divine intent to human beings; and the interactive process between ritual and word, between action and expressive efficacy, between conscious linguistic intent and unconscious aspects and powers of language use, helped make gods and beliefs real to human beings. Herakleitos (frag. 93): "The lord whose oracle is in Delphi neither speaks out nor conceals, but gives a sign" (Kirk and Raven 1957, 211). The sign is tinged with wonder, and at the same time is "obscure." The human capacity to feel a transcendental wonder, and to interpret that which produces the wonder, could not, cannot, entirely be articulated in the ordinary shapes of discourse or in ordinary language. (Plato famously said that wonder was the origin of both poetry and philosophy.) But even if people believed that wonder of such a religious cast could be articulated in ordinary language (as in later times, including our own), ordinary language is weak in ritual, and ritual is felt as weak in ordinary language (hence the profound fidelity of many speakers of English to the King James Version of the Bible and to the Book of Common Prayer.)

Poetry predates philosophy simply because oral cultures predate writing. Poetry does reveal implicit philosophy in the beliefs it sustains with its special utterances. Later, philosophy inquired explicitly, analyzing rather than singing. Poetry could attain great length (such as epic poems) because of the mnemonic elements of formal composition and the memorization of narratives, but only the technology of writing made analytic thought possible. Poetry sustained reverence for gods, and gods themselves. But some gods have "died," as we say— a large number of them at the hands of ancient Greek and later philosophy—even as others were preserved by theology. The human trust in the reality and the will of some gods paled, was doubted; human beings noticed the failure of these gods as supernatural lords from whom mortal human beings had hoped for aid and meaning. (This is a worry in *Oedipus the King*.) Zeus, Baal, Thoth, Ishtar, and many others fell from the human grace that had sustained them. But poetry and poetics—so integrally and irreplaceably a part of now-dead worship, belief, and knowledge of the divine—have not yet died or failed. (That poetry occupies the tiniest proportion of human endeavor and attention, compared to its sway in the past, is a different matter.) The manner in which language is used for poetic thinking—the "poetic function," with its effects of rhythm, sound, trope, grammar, syntax, structure, citation, allusion, relation to ritual, and so on—did not end with the end of the religious practices and rituals out of which these effects grew, and which these effects sustained.

Formulaic language—using the *technē* of poetry—was used for calling to Marduk, Yahweh, Baal, Apollo, Aphrodite, Zeus, and all the other gods of ancient peoples. Yahweh created man in His own image; and the priest-poets who compiled Genesis and other ancient Hebrew books made God somewhat in their image: that is, the deity's language had the power to make material things happen with (immaterial) words. In his *doing* things with words, Yahweh used *syntax*; in the first account of creation in Genesis, the man and the woman do not speak, but in the second account of creation, Adam, who like Eve—later—has full linguistic fluency, including syntax, is at first restricted in his tiny Edenic role to *nouns* only, for his task is only the naming of the animals that Yahweh has created. In that second account of creation in Genesis, Yahweh, Adam, Eve, and the serpent all converse. Later, Yahweh's priests and prophets were able sometimes to make material things happen with immaterial words by communicating with their god—as in Elijah's contest with the priests of Baal (1 Kings 18)—but their success depended on appealing to Yahweh with righteousness of purpose and of language. It was not their words but Yahweh's power that intervened in the material world, yet clearly their words belonged to a genre of address some of which was poetic.

Yahweh's curse on man, woman, and serpent includes poetic lines that evidence the survival in the Hebrew prose of an older poetic tradition, and the presence of our whole repertoire of poetic devices evidences the survival of ancient poetics in modern poetry. Which is not to say that poetry is inherently religious but that particular kinds of religious utterance have a poetics. Hence the perceived efficacy of the especially intense language of a priestly or ritual prayer or an invocation. The special language required in ritual communication and performance (rhythm, phonetic figures, tropes, allusions, etc.) produced the special powers of poetic language, and the special powers of language, intensified by poetic *technē*, made ritual more meaningful (even if it could not make it effectual at changing reality). Poetic technique still makes some poetic language meaningful by organizing language for reading aloud, as if the tiny ceremoniality of an utterance could be a small ritual still. (Not necessarily religious. I remember a friend, a passionate although self-denying smoker of cigarettes, who would look lovingly at the glowing end of her occasional smoke and address it rhythmically, saying: "**Oh** my **little bonfire!**")

We can regard a ritual with smoke or a glass of beer or wine as a descendant of the soma cup of the *Rig-Veda*, the wine cup of the Greek drinking party (*symposion*), and other vessels of metaphorical significance in the faraway past. When a libation was poured from a ceremonial vessel, to the tune or chant of words with special qualities of traditional phrasing, rhythm, and the sounds of words, the occasion was an act of invoking, honoring, respecting, and communicating with the divine realm. We don't share such beliefs and traditions—which in their time seemed eternal—but the physiological effect of alcohol is not likely to have changed in human bodies, so we do share the same physical and mental effects of intoxication, although not the same cultural meanings of those effects. To us there's nothing sacred about being lit. Some surviving shamanistic religions in our own era still link—as many ancient peoples did—the *fluidity* of intensely emotional, visionary, and companionable states of mind with intoxication derived in the ancient ways from plants (mead, beer, wine, natural hallucinogens). Even in modern times, the sense of a visionary effect of intoxication is not entirely gone, and in the minds of some poets, the disinhibiting and thought-loosening effects of alcohol and some drugs have seemed a way of re-creating something ancient, and, by experience and association, authoritative. And through the whole course of human history, alcohol or drug intoxication has been praised and practiced for the sake of its disinhibition of creativity—especially, I would think, the movement of thought by association rather than in narrative or discursive modes. In honor of the poet Anakreon of Teos (who lived a very long life between the early sixth and early fifth centuries BCE) a statue was later erected in Athens. It was described by the second century CE Greek geographer, mythographer, historian, and tourist Pausanias, who wrote that Anakreon was "the first poet after Sappho of Lesbos to make love his main theme," and added that "the statue represents him as a man singing when he is drunk" (Campbell 1988, 31). (The translation of Pausanias by Peter Levi mentions that "there is a copy of the statue of Anakreon in the Carlsberg Glyptothek at Copenhagen" [Pausanias 1979, 1:70n145]. One can see him still, online.)

And it seems extremely unlikely that—even though some of the meaning of dreams could not be properly studied till Freud did so—the experience of dreaming and the unconscious mechanisms of dreams should have been very different one thousand years ago, or three thousand. We may think of associative movement of thought and feeling in a poem as modern, but whether it is attributed to the Muse or to sacred powers of an intoxicant, such movement is apparent even in some ancient songs and poems. In Pindar's Olympian 13, the poet suddenly emerges from his ode to say, as himself, not in the voice of the chorus, that he is "a private individual embarked upon a public mission," using a verb that most translators associate with sailing and the sea (maritime metaphors abound in ancient Greek poetry). Then Pindar retreats once more into the substance of the ode and immediately mentions Medea, "who in opposition to her father made her own marriage, / to become the savior of the ship Argo" (13.49 and 13.53–54). That is, the association of the role of the poet, as one who *sets out* to praise, with someone *setting sail* in a ship leads to the next thought, the ship of Jason.

My point is not only that Pindar moves the thinking here by association but also that the movement is interesting and meaningful. There can scarcely have been any poetic era in which some poetic thinking did not move by association, even though in certain periods such movement can be narrowly constrained—such as the English eighteenth century, with its formal and rhetorical poetic conventions. And in contrast, as we see in, for example, twentieth-century French surrealism or some of our own contemporary American poetry, there have been moments when the utmost freedom of movement, without sustaining any single train of thought, is used as a poetic gesture and is prized above a focused meaning. The sheer mobility of a performance of imagining becomes widespread as a poetic mode. Some contemporary American poets have used what we might call the "unconscious" of the Internet to harvest the use of a particular word or phrase, for example, from which they select some "lines" which they present as a poem. Such a piece can seem to move by human free association if the selecting and assembling are done by the poet, because among such assembled fragments of randomly "found" language a human psyche, incapable of functioning in a truly random way, is at work. A second computational device to make that selection would, on the other hand, produce a random sort; yet meaning might be found in it that emerges from a reader's own psyche, if that reader is willing to go to the trouble of slowing down and allowing the random poetic phrases to evoke here and there something meaningful to that particular reader. But no matter how far or far out movement by associative thinking may be taken (even if it's to try to suppress or avoid meaning entirely—which was done in several ways in the twentieth century), we may remain certain that in itself associative thinking is not new.

In fact, by the time of the poets we call the Romantics, associative movement of thought, feeling, narrative, something we often call "dream logic" (Freud's "primary-process" thinking), was becoming one of the core *conventions* of poetic thinking. In his notebooks, Coleridge wrote of what he called "streamy thinking." From 1801, an entry when he was evidently self-drugged, perhaps with laudanum: "Abed— nervous—had noticed the prismatic colours transmitted from the tumbler—Wordsworth came—I talked with him—he left me alone—I shut my eyes—beauteous spectra of two colors, orange and violet— then of green, which immediately changed to Peagreen, & then actually grew to my eye into a beautiful moss, the same as is on the mantle-piece at Grasmere—abstract Ideas—& unconscious Links!"(1957, entry 925). In 1805 he wrote: "Poetry a rationalized Dream"; Wordsworth's "rapid associations of sensuous Images"; "rapid association and combination both of images with images, & of images, & combinations of images, with the moral and intellectual world, and vice versa" (2002, 66, 78, 79).

The poetic justification—or freedom, for this artistic paradox has two poles—of such associative moves can be by many poetic means (paronomasia; structural devices like strophe and antistrophe, refrains, etc.; allusiveness and connotations of names and other words; narrative associations with myth and legend; and other elements of poetic craft). By the twentieth century, the poetic convention that it is appropriate (although not always necessary) for poetry to be fluid in association, dreamlike in movement, finally predominates, even in anti-Freudians.

Charles Baudelaire wrote a short prose poem called "Get Drunk," and a short treatise titled "On Wine and Hashish," in which he praised the Muse (that ancient idea, divinity, or metaphor, invented by the Greeks) who visits the intoxicated or stoned poet. He and Gérard de Nerval were among the poets belonging to a "Club des Hashischins." Baudelaire wrote that hashish "expands a person's individuality beyond all measure ... [and even] people completely unsuited for wordplay will improvise an endless string of puns and wholly improbable idea relationships," and thus he linked himself and everyone else with such experience to Vedic poets and the soma cup (2013, n.p.).

He evoked no supernatural intervention in thought but instead some *other* energy of creation; in our psychoanalytic and neuroscientific era we may think of this other—formerly the Muse—as simply the result of the opening of the mind to its own usually hidden or suppressed intrapsychic resources, which are both individual and also formed by society and culture. (Not all of them of either sort pleasant, of course.) And our accidental spills of thought, feelings, and words, like those of wine onto the floor amid the enthusiastic drinking that Baudelaire urged and ancients also practiced, cannot be regarded by mortals (or still patient immortals waiting for their due honoring) as libations, even though speaking objectively, we would have to say that in seeking altered states of consciousness (even though without divine inspiration), Baudelaire, Nerval, and others before and since were very like their predecessors of twenty and thirty centuries earlier. The modern context negates the great authorization that supported the ancient poet, prophet, oracular priestess or priest, and the high status of such figures. Yet we understand that such movement of thought and feeling from unconscious self-authorizing into the creative process is the nature of our psychic being. Analogously, for the social authorization of ancient poets we substitute this psychic one. We follow some ancient practices even while lacking the powerful, divine, ancient dispensation.

❋

The poetic techniques for making use of altered states of mind, or the skills that those altered states heightened, were all the practices of rhythm and image, sound, trope and tradition that the ancient poet had worked hard to acquire, like many poets since. Oral-culture poets and those who like Pindar lived in eras of transition from oral composition to writing needed a capacious, powerfully retentive memory for story, traditional phrases, formulas, metrical aids (like the epithets "swift-footed Achilles," "ox-eyed Hera" in Greek), knowledge of gods and heroes, and much else. In the language of some modern poetry, and in certain traditional phrases, such as "last but not least" and "oats, peas, beans and barley grow" (Watkins 1995, 29, 47–49), we can recognize ancient techniques that are still in use in English. I'll give a recent example (they are countless) of the poet's organizing of the sounds of words. In the title poem of *Human Chain* (2010), Seamus Heaney describes a "chain" of aid workers slinging "bags of meal passed hand to hand," and remembers the lifting of heavy bags of grain in his youth. He writes: "Nothing surpassed // That quick unburdening, backbreak's truest payback, / A letting go which will not come again. / Or it will, once. And for all" (2010, 17).

This has Heaney's characteristic clarity of description while at the same time it makes much of the words themselves—both their phonemes and their rhythms. Let me point out one phrase in particular: "backbreak's truest payback." We easily hear the reiterated sound of *b*—all three of them. And also the repeated long *ā* in "-break" and "pay-," as well as all the sounds of the word that is repeated whole, "back," and the third *k* in "-break." Note that the pattern of the repetition of the short *a* and the long *ā* is short-long-long-short. This mirror symmetry is ancient; we call it by a word that is in fact (Latinized) ancient Greek, *chiasmus*, which means a "crisscrossing" pattern, *abba* (it's of sounds here, but its four elements could be any element of language, in general, whether in four syllables or many more). Note that in the word "back" the sounds of the two consonants *b-k* begin the phrase and end it; note also that the *b-k* of "back-" and "-back" is reversed into the sound of the intervening *k-b* at the center of Heaney's unhyphenated word "backbreak." And also note that the doubling of the *b* in "backbreak" is echoed in "payback," simply because the *p*, like the *b*, is a "plosive" consonant. But the loveliest of these ear-trained repetitions is the chiasmus-and-a-half (if I may call it that) of the sound of the repeated *st*: "b**a**ckbre**a**k's tru**est** p**ay**back." In this way, even beyond how the sounds in the word "back" frame the phrase, three sounds (four, if we were to count *b-b* and *p-b*) in Heaney's several mirror-symmetry interlocking repetitions, which I label A, B, and C, are paired and nested within each other like verbal Russian dolls:

A [a]	-	B [ā]	-	C [st]	-	C [st]	-	B [ā]	-	A [a]
back-		break's	tru-			est		pay-		back

And at the center, singular and triply nested, is the word "truest." With this gesture, an ancient poet would have been implying "this technique of words is the guarantee of the truth of what I say." It's a sentiment found in Hesiod, in whose era it was a commonplace, a "formula," in much ancient poetry in Indo-European languages: the poet speaks the truth (Watkins 1995, 85–93, 98–101).

Such poetic patterning, Heaney had been prepared to create: he was born into a culture that still uses an ancient language (Irish Gaelic) and that speaks an English that is more musical than the standard English of England itself and of America. Heaney's gift for the word-sounds and rhythms of language allowed him to train his ear and make English-language music at will, especially in ancient ways (hence, I think, his attraction to the project of translating *Beowulf*). His imagination also sought out Irish antiquity — prehistoric corpses discovered in bogs, age-old strife as the precedent for the "troubles" in Northern Ireland, depths of religious practice, and more. For the sake of honoring, or insisting on, a continuity of Irish experience ranging from Iron Age revenge to the present day, he enlisted the continuity of poetic technique itself.

Most contemporary poets, from those of the plain style to those of denser and even disruptive poetic effects, make something of the sound of their lines. It can be artificial to separate the sounds of phonemes from the rhythms of word sequences, so in the following phrases from modern and contemporary English-language poems I boldface *some* of the phonetic figures and underline speech stresses that are especially emphatic because they are adjacent to each other (this is a "spondee" in metrical lines or simply a "rhythmic figure" in free verse): "the bird's fire-fangled feathers dangle down" (Stevens 1990, 141); "my father [...] put his clothes on in the blueblack cold, / then with cracked hands that ached / from labor in the weekday weather made / banked fires blaze" (Hayden 2013, 41); "Fog-thick morning— / I see only / where I now walk. I carry / my clarity / with me" (Niedecker 2004, 181); "I knocked on the door of his fore-head" (Weigl 2012, 27), "muse whose jutting / lips he kissed as he / could ... 'Mouth that / moved my mouth'" (Mackey 2006, 3); "in the high bed her webbed face / her halo of hair past humankind" (Voigt 2013, 18); "the copper pot tipped toward us, the white pitcher / clutched in her hand, the black one edged in red / and upside down" (Tretheway 2012, 7); and so on, almost infinitely. All this is indexical, artistically *intensified deliberateness*. Some poets take for granted the "marking" of language with poetic figures — it is natural to poetry; or in reaction to it, some poets reject the use of it — which also reflects an understanding that it is historically natural to poetry. (Eliminating phonetic figures is not easy to do; nor is it easy to prevent English from falling into an iambic rhythm; conscious deliberateness is required in both cases to not do what English tends to do. As Pope wrote, albeit with more conviction than most modern and contemporary poets might have, "Those rules of old discovered, not devised, / Are Nature still, but Nature methodized" [1988, 38].) That phonetic figures and rhythmic emphasis are an element of poetic practice that originated perhaps five thousand years ago, or five times that long ago, is on scarcely anyone's mind, but, as we see, it's in nearly everyone's practice.

❋

Contemporary poets cite, unselfconsciously and surprisingly often, proper names and other traces of ancient culture, especially from poetry itself. Perhaps they do so in order to authenticate and authorize — sometimes unconsciously, sometimes wittingly — their own right, which in any case poets surely have, to dwell in language as they do, and to make a poem, and the rightness of doing so as a use of language.

The Homeric epics and the earlier traditions from which they emerged (performed first as song, later as recitation [Nagy 2013, 143]) had "divine credentials." Song, in its imagining, its language, its performance, could bring to human "chaos of death and disorder" the consoling idea and presence of "quasi-divine order and beauty" (Greek *kosmos*; Halliwell 2011, 68, 84). Thus Achilles, to calm his own anger at the haughty, disrespectful treatment he has received from Agamemnon, sings in his tent at Troy, and produces for himself a musical and poetic order, accompanying himself on a lyre (*Iliad* 9.185–89). Kirkē and Kalypso, themselves immortals of a dangerous sort, sing at their looms as they weave divinely beautiful, harmoniously ordered fabric. (The ancient poetic portrayal of song itself is not without its ironies, however, and in the *Iliad* and *Odyssey*, these are dazzlingly complex: Achilles' lyre, described as particularly beautiful, is a trophy of his earlier savage depredations. He has taken this prize of victory in war from a king he killed, an ally of the Trojans. This was the same king whose daughter, Andromakhē, is the wife of Achilles' greatest enemy, Hektor. The undying fame, the *kleos*, of all three remains alive today— because the *Iliad* has survived.)

It has been a tremendously long time since poetry, except in some remaining religious contexts, has lost its "divine credentials," even though it has continued to use a "divine" artistic technique, but we can infer from what contemporary poems often do and say that for centuries most poets have felt, and many feel still, a reluctance to give up the idea of a kind of foundational authorization of poetry like what was given by the divine, the immortal. Hence the frequent mention among contemporary poets of the Muse; and they need not be accused of bad faith for invoking as if with real purpose an ancient Greek divinity in whom they do not believe, since for us the Muse is a metaphor that represents access to certain creative intrapsychic resources—"imagination," "inspiration," "flow." Even in the ancient world, although Homer's contemporary, Hesiod, acknowledged and thanked the source of the "poet's truth" as the Muses, that "truth," which derives from the special ability to create song, he also attributed to his own skill as a poet. In Greek he is an *epéōn téktones*, a "craftsman of words." In Sanskrit, the poet's knowledge of how to craft song is "a heavy burden." In Ireland, the poet was one who had the advantage of a father or grandfather who was a bard, plus his own ability and hard study—six years of it in the last known bardic school in a tradition of incalculable age; it was described in the eighteenth century as a "snug low Hut" with windowless cells and daily assignments in oral composition (Watkins 1995, 68–84, 98–101). And in the ancient world, "divine credentials" were the hope of a guarantee of immortal remembrance not only of the subjects of poetry—those figures whom poetry portrayed and honored (or cursed and remembered forever as dishonorable)—but also of poetry itself, and the poet.

Even many poets—including the ones I will shortly quote—who have taken a secular and antitranscendental stance toward language have continued to allude to poetry of the ancient and the Christian past (especially to Dante) that was composed within a culture of belief in the divine. Modern and contemporary poets use such allusions as if implicitly to authorize themselves. Although contemporary mention of Dante in a poem may be ironic, the irony is almost never used to consign Dante to a junk heap of past human religious illusions. (And we recall that standing at Dante's side is Vergil, Dante's own authorizing figure and his guide through hell.)

The prominent symbolic use of the image of a forest or a road (or both) early in a poem seems inescapably Dantesque to me; it authenticates by a consciously or unconsciously deliberate allusion that provides a context for the gravity—whether expressed somberly or flippantly—of a crisis of being. From the 2013 Best American Poetry: "Oh hell, here's that dark wood again" (a first line; and much more in this vein; Kim Addonizio); "groping blindly down a page, like someone lost in a forest" (Billy Collins); "Her first assumption: life's hard, so Mom runs trails / through Amherst's woods" (John Hennessy); "If the road's a frayed ribbon [. . .]" (Adrienne Rich); "I said, 'I'm afraid to go into the woods at night. Please don't make me go into the woods'" (James Tate); "The winter trees offer no shade nor shelter" (Jean Valentine); "What years of weather did to branch and bough" (Richard Wilbur) (Duhamel 2013, 1, 26, 51, 107, 140, 146, 151).

In the same prize anthology from which I take all those lines, many poems advert or allude—beyond Dante specifically—to historically distant, even ancient, worlds (not only Greek): "Dear Thanatos" (Traci Brimhall—but this ancient Greek word may make us think first of Freud); "Before us the Greeks themselves / were not [white] (though the weaker enemy / Persians were)" (Martha Collins); "the builders of the tower of Nimrod wanted / rising up into the heavens [. . .] I built the Tower of Babel" (Timothy Donnelly); "The ancient Indian poets / Had their heads screwed on straight [. . .] And every *gezunte moyd* / In a juvenile honey locust / Will prefer their Hindi distichs / To the Indiana Hoosiers" (Anthony Madrid); "and I swear I see Eden" (Jesse Millner); "Psalm to Be Read with Closed Eyes" (title; D. Nurkse); "Even though I'm an immigrant, / the angel with the flaming sword seems fine with me" (Vijay Seshadri); "The concept of telos in a discussion of / Greek philosophy and the work of Aristotle" (Mitch Sisskind); "Mine has Plato saying man is a featherless biped" (Paul Violi) (Duhamel 2013, 20, 27, 33, 91–92, 101, 103, 116, 123, 147).

❀

Perhaps the reason poetic craft doesn't seem to everyone so difficult to acquire is because so many contemporary poets use a reduced set of devices, compared to earlier poets. Most contemporary poets don't use poetic meter; do keep their rhythms very loose; don't create intricate sound weaving (although it's present in a good many poets' lines); do make use of the ancient poetic addiction to allusion but by going to popular culture rather than to traditions of narratives, heroes, gods, and all their accoutrements, or to canonical poetry in modern languages. And while crafting poetic language in the ancient world required learning a technology of language and protocols of special social and ritual occasions, somber or celebratory, now poetic effects of language can be just for the purpose of making the sale (of the poem itself, and of the poet).

When Karl Shapiro combatively recounted in 1960 his engagement with poetics and literary criticism, he commented in passing, "The real poetry of the modern world is advertising, probably the most debased form of poetry in history but the only authentic poetry we have. [. . .] Advertising is the poetry of the American masses. [. . .] The aim of advertising is not to sell things (nobody believes the claims of the advertisers), but to convince the defenseless victim that he is happy" ([1960] 1989, 109). Poetic technique is the bread (whole grain! fresh!) and butter (organic, no hormones, no RBGH!) — of the *wording* of advertising, one of the most prominent of the human activities that saturate our linguistic environment. But although the cinematic technique of advertising may have influenced film and television, and vice versa, the verbal technique of advertising has often, with its briefest and catchiest phrases, simply drawn on this trick or that from the ancient bard schools. "Juicy Couture" is one example that struck me recently. As if the corporate name were saying languidly, erotically, "ooh, ooh, ooh," this long *ū* vowel is voiced three times. The *j* is a rich consonant, and the last syllable of the three long *ū* sounds in this brand name is sensuously extended; meanwhile "juicy" itself has additional erotic overtones and "couture" suggests expensiveness. And by the way, the rhythm of this brand name, <u>Jui</u>cy Cou<u>ture</u>, happens to be one of the most recognizable of ancient metrical feet, which in Greek was called choriambic. It has the form (in English) of *<u>stressed</u>-unstressed-unstressed-<u>stressed</u>* (*abba* again, like Heaney's phonemes, a mirror symmetry of four elements—so in this instance, a *rhythmic chiasmus*). In "Juicy Couture" I think we hear the added *length* of the first and last syllable, too. (An additional emphasis of the rhythmical chiasmus.) "<u>Glad</u> you've come <u>back</u>!" is an easily found example of how common that rhythm still is, in English. As for Juicy Couture— the words . . . <u>sound</u> like a <u>spell</u> . . . and the . . . <u>spell</u> is so <u>strong</u> . . . <u>Why</u> not go <u>now</u>?

No, let's go back to Baudelaire's intoxication. No, let's go all the way back to wine and to poetic rhythm. Some of the words of prehistoric peoples are still preserved in modern languages almost as they were (like *cow* and others I mentioned earlier) or within modern words. One that whispers of ancient life and of poetry is *spondee*—a metrical term meaning a foot of two syllables both of which are emphasized (by long vowels in Greek, by stress in English). I'll also offer a few more examples of choriambs.

   Our metrical terms were all applied from ancient Greek to English, mostly with awkward and not entirely useful results, since the rhythmical basis of ancient Greek is completely foreign to English because it included the use of pitch as well as a clear differentiation between long and short syllables. Also, Greek poetic language was not a natural language but one that was intensified in one genre or another by the artificiality of its diction, its syntactic compression, its use of even more ancient phrases, epithets, formulas, dialect spellings, and other devices. Greek meter was not, as English meter has been, a regularization of one rhythmic pattern already inherent in the way the language was spoken, but instead a rhythm created for song and for dance. But the Greek terms we still use (iambic, trochaic, and a few more) are useful. Almost everybody who cares about this already knows them, and these terms are not nearly as technical as the terminology of some more recent theories of how to analyze the rhythms of English-language poetry.

In English-language meter, a spondee is two stressed syllables: "first fight," "win war." Scansion is not at all an exact science, but here are a few clear examples of how spondees can show up in lines of iambic pentameter verse. The pentameter line is long enough to allow for much more interesting metrical — that is, rhythmic — variation than is a shorter line, so it has been much used; it also turns out to be roughly the length of ancient and modern poetic lines all across Indo-European languages ancient and modern, so our five-foot line is not arbitrary but must come out of something that we, like ancient poets, intuit about language and bodily rhythms and breath. (Cixous: "poetry is about traveling on foot"[1993a, 64]; and on rhythmic feet, whether to a steady beat or freely.) In the following lines, taken from Gwendolyn Brooks's sequence of five metrical sonnets, "The Children of the Poor," in her larger sequence, "The Woman Hood," I underline all the speech stresses and I put adjacent stresses (here, four spondees and a three-stress sequence) in bold type:

First fight. Then fiddle. [...]
Win war. | **Rise blood**- | y, may- | be **not** | **too late**
When my | **dears die** [...]
$$(1987, 118, 119)$$

And here's the spondee used in free verse as a *rhythmic, not a metrical, device*, and sometimes extended also to three successive stresses, in Brooks's free verse (also from "The Woman Hood"):

He knows his **wish**. **Yes**, but that is not all. [last 4 syllables = choriamb]
Because I **know mine too**. [...]
Or tipping over an **ice box pan** [...] ["over an ice" = choriamb]
$$(120)$$

[...] We are **lost, must**
Wizard a track [...] [another choriamb]
$$(140)$$

Ezra Pound was the first poet, I think, to write *free* verse that contains small *metrical* devices, using them as rhythmic *figures*, separated from any metrical context, and even using them in a musical way as motifs. By motif I mean that the rhythmic figure is part of the meaning of the poem—it enacts something which, in a loose way, can be paraphrased as an expression of an idea. For example, in his 1912 poem "The Return" (2010, 31), which can in fact be "scanned" as entirely metrical although in lines of irregular length, Pound repeatedly used the choriambic rhythm, during this period of finding his way fully toward true free verse, and he also used adjacent stressed syllables (spondees). These emphatic rhythms are the dominant rhythmic motifs, and they enact what the words say about the tentative steps of the pale, perhaps almost translucent, returning gods, who are trying to get back into the real world again. (By the way, *motif* is used not only as a term of craft in music but also in lace making and embroidery—and later I point out some ancient metaphorical links between poetry and the craft of making and ornamenting fabric.)

A few lines taken from Canto XVI, written in 1924/1925, in which Pound's energetic clarity of description is prominent, will show his use of spondees (and multiple adjacent stressed syllables) and choriambs in free verse:

And before **hell mouth**; **dry plain**
and **two moun**tains;
On the **one moun**tain, a running form,
and another
In the turn of the hill; in **hard steel** ["turn of the hill" = choriamb]
The road like a slow **screw's thread** ["road like a slow" = choriamb]
(2010, 155)

Pound would have known the Latin word *spondēus* or the Greek *spondeîo*, so he knew the original meaning of the word, which would have pleased his sense of the value of making the ancient new, just as much as the spondaic rhythmic effect pleased his ear. The original Greek word for our *spondee* meant a metrical "foot consisting of two long syllables used in melodies accompanying *spondai*" (libations). The Greek word comes ultimately, through what stages we don't know, from Proto-Indo-European **spend-*, "to offer a libation," which suggests that at least some of the prehistoric rituals of libation had verbal and dance ("foot") rhythms that included the pattern of two beats. In the earliest surviving book we have on how to write (oratory and poetry), Dionysios of Halikarnassos (modern Bodrum, in Turkey), who lived in the first century BCE, says that this metrical foot has "dignity and solemnity" (1985, 125). Our *spondee* is another example of how "language remembers what we have forgotten," and those words that still remember the forgotten make available to the poet a historical layering of meaning and a historical enactment of poetry.

⊙ 7 ⊙

Simultaneities

THE BOW, THE LYRE, THE LOOM

A quotation is not an excerpt. A quotation is a cicada. It is part of its nature never to quiet down.

OSIP MANDELSHTAM (2004, 108)

Mandelshtam's cicada has in Russian a name that can be used, as here, as a pun on *citation*. In some ancient Greek poems, the cicada, *tettix* (a masculine noun), is a poetic analogue of the nightingale, the greatest singer in nature. John Keats and John Clare, among many other English poets, old and fairly new, assumed or pretended that the singing nightingale was female. (Arabic, Russian, German, and most, I think, Romance languages gender the noun for "nightingale" as masculine; in Romanian it is feminine — *privighetoare*; a Romanian writer told me that the voice of the nightingale is that of a young female singer.) The ancient Greek word for "singer," *aoidós*, is masculine in grammatical gender, but ... this same word as a feminine noun means "nightingale," "songstress," which the Greeks used as a metonym for song or poem. In an elegiac epigram by the Hellenistic poet Kallimakhos, he wrote of the poems of his dead friend Herakleitos, "but your nightingales are still alive." In ancient Greek, "song," or the act of singing, or the theme of the song, or the person of whom the song sings, is a feminine noun, *aoidē* — very like the singing human voice, the word sustains itself almost wholly with vowels. *Aoídimos* means "sung of," or to put it as the Greek does, "songed." There's a Greek word, too, that would serve us as the word for what we think of, in its contemporary version, as a poetry slam, *aoidomákhos*, "fighting with verses."

When the poet—like Herakleitos, above—is male, as most often in ancient Greece, the singing nightingale which was thought to be female, *aoidós*, is a metaphor for him. The word itself seems almost to produce a subtle feminization of poem making. Poetically, ancient Greek culture associated masculine solo singing with the feminine in more than one way. It is not necessarily a contradiction of Greek patriarchy that all the Muses are female.

The triple analogy—used by Pindar and other male poets—of the lyre, with taut strings, the loom, with taut threads of the warp, and the bow, with its one taut string, represented both male and female mastery: the lyre (invented by Apollo, god of poetry) as a metonym for poetry; the loom (of Helen, Andromakhē, and Penelope, of Kirkē and Kalypso, and with Athena as the patroness of the craft) as a metaphor for poetry; and the bow (weapon of Apollo, the "far-shooter," not of Ares, god of war). Pindar's bow (metaphorically song itself) not only launches the fame-giving ode to far audiences but also, after the release, reverberates like a one-string lyre.

Apollo is often invoked by Pindar, who shoots arrows of song (and thus fame) with his bow—sending an athletic victor's renown great distances. Pindar's song arrow transforms the weapon of the archer into a far-reaching word of praise. Sometimes it seems he is shooting *at* the victor—but instead of harming him the arrow of song honors him and glorifies his name. When Pindar wrote, "Weave quickly, sweet lyre, this song" (Nemean 4.44), he combined two of the stringed tropes and by implication evoked the goddess Athena as both battle-strategist and patroness of weavers, and in addition the bivalency of Apollo, too, with his lyre. It's almost as if the deep association that links such apparently disparate elements in the nature of a god is itself the working of a kind of divine poetics of metaphor. In his 1918 piece "Religio" (something between a poem and an essay), Pound defined the Greek divinities by writing that "a god is an eternal state of mind" (1973, 47); within Pindar's odes, warfare is remembered, stories of gods are recounted, athletes are praised, and Apollo and Athena are creative states of mind internalized and also eternalized in part by their survival in this guise in Pindar's odes and elsewhere in ancient Greek poetry.

In metaphors for song and poetic composition (such metaphors being a way of thinking about both) and in discursive thinking about

song and composition (which can include a metaphorizing of it), figures and occupations both masculine and feminine crisscross in the
figures for poetry itself. Pindar presented himself metaphorically as
warrior, athlete, charioteer, singer, and . . . weaver. Not a weaver of
male schemes, stratagems, or plots, but of an artisanal object, a verbal, woman-made, ornamental cloth: a woven or embroidered "varicolored" (Greek adjective *poikílos*) song. Gregory Nagy has pointed
out connections between *poikílos* as applied to cloth and as applied to
song. Hesiod, he has noted, used the adjective *poikilóderos*, related to
poikílos, for the variety of the nightingale's song. Variety of pattern in
cloth and variety of song are both to be prized (1996, 39n1).

Pindar referred to the Homeric rhapsodes this way (note the extended sequence of vowels in the last word in the Greek, which means
"singers" — the sound seems an enacting of what singers *do*, which is to
hold an extended note on a vowel): "Homerídai rhaptōn epéōn [. . .]
aoidoí" (Nemean 2.1–2; Homer's sons, singers of stitched verses). And
among Pindar's own metaphors for poetry, weaving (again, the work
of women, appropriated metaphorically by the mostly male world of
composers of song) is repeated a number of times, as in the lines "for
spear-warriors I weave a multi-colored hymn" (Olympian 2.86–87).

The name *rhapsodes* means that the ancient singers "stitched"
together the lines and episodes of each performance; yet work with
fabric belonged not to the open, public, male world of war, governing,
athletic contests, song festivals, commerce, building and farming and
crossing the sea. By contrast, when Herodotos described the ways in
which Egyptian culture was the opposite of Greek, and therefore bad,
he cited as one of his proofs that in Egypt the weavers were men, not
women. This was because Greek weaving and embroidering of cloth
belonged, especially in Herodotos' time, fifth century BCE Athens, to
the closed, private world of the household, the sphere of women —
from the legally and socially privileged wives of Athenian citizens to
the women captured and enslaved during the centuries of Athenian
war making and brought back to work looms for the warriors' wives
and other wealthy households.

Women who were not wives or daughters of citizens in the heyday
of Athens — women selling in the market and minding small farm-
houses, the servants and slaves, the country girls herding sheep, the
women companions-for-hire in male gatherings (the *symposion*) —
have left no songs or poems, nor were they imagined by poets till the

third century BCE, in poems of Anyte, of Leonidas of Tarentum, and others. The tiniest portion of their work survives. Anyte wrote epigrams, perhaps fictitious, as if for tombs, and the first poems about animals, including an epitaph for a cicada. Leonidas too wrote funerary epigrams, also perhaps fictitious, that memorialized working people. His male subjects included sailors, a gambler, a shepherd, a teacher of rhetoric, a sophist, a composer of comic songs; and his female subjects included a wet-nurse, a seven-year-old girl, and an old and poor woman, Platthis, who spun and wove until her end. For this portion of my explorations, Platthis would be the emblem, alongside the most beautiful, famous, and dangerous woman who ever lived, Helen—the two of them *weavers*, embroiderers. (It's tempting to regard Edwin Arlington Robinson's poems of Tilbury Town and Edgar Lee Master's Spoon River as modern versions of Leonidas.)

❈

In the modern world, weaving as a metaphor for writing is the commonest of clichés. It can be revivified, "made new," as it is implicitly in Ezra Pound's notorious "usura" canto from 1937, in which he weaves his poem with examples that include weaving: "weaver is kept from his loom [. . .] usura / blunteth the needle in the maid's hand / and stoppeth the spinner's cunning [. . .] [Usura] gnaweth the thread in the loom / None learneth to weave gold in her pattern" (Canto XLV in 2010, 184). (Latin *usura*, the word from which our *usury* derives, meant the use of a thing, and then, metonymically, the interest paid on borrowed—that is "used"—money.) This inglorious canto and other such moments of Pound's anti-Semitism, fascist enthusiasms, and crank economics and social policy still undercut his lamentation over the loss of the human touch in the industrialized making of things. Drawing on images from a premodern world, Pound excoriated the modern. (*Excoriate*: to take the skin off; and *skint* means "out of money.") Weaving and spinning Pound rightly used as emblematic crafts related to poetry and belonging to the preindustrial world and to Greek mythology—Arachne, Kirkē, Kalypso.

In Homer, the male poet (or properly, the male singers in the ancient epic traditions) makes an emblem of Helen the female weaver or embroiderer at her loom in Troy, where she in turn is creating scenes of the battles outside the city walls—depicting "many battles of the horse-taming Trojans and the bronze-clad Achaeans" (*Iliad* 3.126–27; Homer 2003, I:139). Helen is Homer's emblem of himself, for with words he is weaving scenes of the war. And in fact using verbal "patterns" to do so. Gregory Nagy has argued that the meaning of the Greek adjective *poikílos*, when applied to cloth, is "pattern-weaving." Helen's patterned weaving is echoed by Andromakhē's, as she weaves a love story which, as Nagy has written, will be tragically truncated, for she is weaving "right before the moment she finds out that her husband, Hektor, has died in the battlefield" (2012, 276). The stitching poet-singer, the woman weaver, and—as I mentioned above—the (supposed) female nightingale, a figure for the poet's song and a singing bird which, with the cicada, is an animal analogue of the poet himself: these feminize the male poet who creates design in epic and ode as he works the cloth of his composition. Such feminization seems to me a profound aspect of the ancient Greek view of the way the poet must harken to the assistance of the Muse, but also an anticipation of modern understanding of the complexity and imaginative capabilities of the creative mind, as well as of the widespread practice of women poets, finally, beginning in the twentieth century.

And Pound, out-Pindaring Pindar's variety of materials, wove his *Cantos* with a Modernist multiplicity, which included the Homeric poems. After the destruction caused by World War I, he achieved a singular and unprecedented patterning of ancient and modern together, as did, in their distinct ways, T. S. Eliot in *The Waste Land*, James Joyce in *Ulysses*, and H.D. in *Helen in Egypt* and other poems. Representing Western civilization as a ruin, Eliot and Pound, especially, brought into their work "fragments" in the form of citations and thematic threads, allusions and implications. To use an American metaphor of cloth, these were like quilting scraps salvaged from beautiful cloth damaged by the destructiveness of warfare. These poets also looked beyond the boundaries of Western culture for more such scraps. Well before publishing the first volume of his *Cantos*, Pound "wove" his (partial) understanding of classical Chinese poetry into the devastated mood of World War I in *Cathay*, and Eliot gathered those famous snippets of Sanskrit to decorate his "varicolored" (Greek *poikílos*) waste land. As a metaphor, weaving (like embroidery, also ancient) serves ancient poetry and song, and these Modernist poems, equally well, because so many different sorts of things are intertwined and stitched. In the ancient works, these are the formal, crafted qualities of the sounds of words and the rhythms in the poetic line; the simultaneous aesthetic, religious, and ceremonial dimensions of poetry; and the threads of the very substance of a poem—characters and catastrophes in tales. Victors, gods, advice, praise, and proverbial wisdom are intertwined in the ancient choral odes of celebration. Athenian tragedies combine several earlier genres into one and make larger-than-life men and women of the epic past step out of the narratives about them and speak for themselves as living presences (actors) as they quarrel with each other, commit decisive crimes, and are punished by the eternal laws of the gods, who themselves may appear (Herington 1985, 103–50). And in the Modernist poems, the achievement is not unprecedented but rather an echo, in a way. But this time the patterns are created by the interweaving of ancient scraps of literary and other works with modern voicings of an impulse to preserve, renew, and reuse. Interweaving or braiding becomes a primary method of achieving not a harmonious work (the ancient Greek goal) but a variegated (*poikílos*) and unresolved asymmetry, internal contention, and improvisational energy, among materials, voices, and ideas. (And, if I may change metaphors: cicadas are buzzing everywhere—just as they were already in Homer, in the form of even more ancient narratives, formulas, epithets, and so on; in Pindar, as incorporated quotations from earlier oral traditions, as well as more lore of gods and heroes, and other materials; and in Sophokles and his fellow tragic poets, as a braiding of different earlier genres of song, epic lore, and ceremonial purposes.)

Among the several layers of allusion (for which poetry has and has always had an appetite) that Pound weaves or stitches into Canto XXXIX (published in 1934) is an evocation of the keenly engaging moment in the *Odyssey* (in book 10) when the hero and his men land their ship unwittingly on the island of the enchantress Kirkē:

> In hill path: "thkk, thgk"
>   of the loom
> "Thgh, thkk" and the sharp sound of a song
>   Under olives

(1986, 193)

Pound is alluding to the supernatural weaver of Odysseus' first island of dangerous enchantment by the feminine. The sound of the shuttle in the loom and the accompanying beautiful singing by a goddess, Kirkē, draw Odysseus' men into a trap from which Odysseus, with the aid of the god Hermes, will then free them, when he finally has had enough of Kirkē's beauty and attention. Greek mythical women — whether mortal or deathless — always sing as they weave. (Perhaps they sing *so that* they can weave? — an idea to which I will return.)

Although the story of Kirkē and her island is recounted in Book 10, yet in the sequence of events in Odysseus' return to Ithaca it takes place *before* the tale of Kalypso that is narrated earlier, in Book 5. This crisscrossing of narrative chronology is another of the techniques that anticipate modern narrative. The story of Kirkē also layers almost vertiginously the *levels of narration* in the *Odyssey*, again anticipating modern narrative technique. Odysseus himself tells this story later — or rather *recites* it, in Homer's lines, of course; thus the warrior Odysseus, the man of many skills, himself *becomes* a bard for a while. He tells it to the Phaiakians, a people blessed in all ways who — like Kirkē and Kalypso — live on an island, but in their case it is a remote, even undiscoverable place of safety and self-sufficiency, so the poem *thinks* with its settings, as poets and novelists still do. And the narrative sophistication of this episode would be called metafictional today, when such devices flourish at three millennia's remove from their source.

Kirkē's story is two levels deep in the structure of the narrative: Homer's level is the narration of Odysseus with the Phaiakians; there, Odysseus must listen to the court bard, Demodokos, sing of Troy. This performance, because of the episodes of the suffering and death of companions, deeply disturbs Odysseus, himself one of the heroes who already enjoys a fame that is achieved and sustained by epic song like that of Demodokos. As the *subject* of epic narration, Odysseus must hide his face as he weeps. As a *performer* of epic narration, Odysseus himself later relates his story of Kirkē (masterfully, of course, since he is chanting or reciting in Homer's poetic lines, as *we* know, but as the Phaiakians do not hear). The Phaiakians already know what followed, for Odysseus has arrived on their island naked and alone, having lost every one of his men.

Some of Odysseus' men fearfully explore the unknown island on which they have landed, and they discover a household from which tame wolves and lions come out to them, and they hear Kirkē singing as she weaves. That the site of divine weaving can be hazardous to men is a kind of under-trope in this scene, linking the female agency of weaving itself with the sorceress' power over animals and men.

> They stood there in the forecourt of the goddess with the glorious
> hair, and heard Circe inside singing in a sweet voice
> as she went up and down a great design on a loom, immortal
> such as goddesses have, delicate and lovely and glorious
> their work. Now Polites, leader of men, who was
> the best and dearest to me of my friends, began the discussion:
> "Friends, someone inside going up and down a great piece
> of weaving is singing sweetly, and the whole place murmurs to the
>   echo
> of it, whether she is woman or goddess. Come, let us call her."

The *subsequent* island where Odysseus will remain a while, as recounted *earlier* (Book 5), is Ōgygía, where the goddess Kalypso lives. (Because the *Odyssey* begins by narrating the journey of Telemakhos in search of his father Odysseus, it does not embark on its tales of Odysseus until Book 5, where it starts with the next-to-last leg of the hero's journey—from Kalypso to the Phaiakians.) The name of Kalypso's island is an ominous play with sound and iconic effects: its auditory and visual shape implies or sensuously embodies ideas. The name Ōgygía begins with the last letter of the Greek alphabet, Ω, *omega*, and ends with the first, α, *alpha*, suggesting a backward or upside-down reality. (And perhaps very subtly hints at the *Odyssey*'s own delightfully upside-down narrating of Odysseus' journey.)

Hermes is sent by Zeus to Kalypso, "loveliest among goddesses" (as Odysseus says in Book 9), to instruct her to release Odysseus so that he may continue his journey home. Hermes finds her at home in her great cave (all these lines from Richmond Lattimore's translation):

> [. . .] She was singing inside the cave with a sweet voice
> as she went up and down the loom and wove with a golden shuttle.

Kalypso accedes to the will of Zeus. The next morning when she takes Odysseus to the island shore, her divine aura is figured in the cloth she has woven:

[. . .] the nymph mantled herself in a gleaming white robe
fine-woven and delightful, and around her waist she fastened
a handsome belt of gold, and on her head was a wimple.

She shows him how to build the raft on which he will leave her. She
brings him woven sailcloth, which he himself crafts into the sail, and
she puts "fragrant clothing upon him" and provisions him before he
sails away (*Odyssey* 10.220–28, 5.61–62, 5.230–32, 5.264; Homer 1967,
158, 89, 94, 95). Like Kirkē's female identity, dangerous power, and
creativity, the loving Kalypso's magical powers are figured in cloth.
Kalypso produces many kinds of cloth, from the most delicate veil to
the sturdy heavy sailcloth.

Anthony Tuck has pointed out that in the narrative about Kirkē
in Book 10, the description "indicates that Polites is outside Kirkē's
house when he speaks, yet he knows that she is weaving. In fact, he
seems to recognize that she is weaving not from what he sees but
rather from what he hears—her singing" (2006, 541). That is, women's
song of some unique quality is so associated with weaving that when
Polites recognizes the sort of song he hears, he knows that a woman
is weaving. Because of the antiquity of archeological, textual (Homer,
the *Rig-Veda*, and more), and even etymological and philological
evidence, and the documented use even in modern times of weaving songs among preliterate populations, and other ancient narratives
that speak of storytelling cloth, woven and embroidered, Tuck wonders whether the origin of metrical poetry itself, in the mother language from which all the Indo-European daughter languages developed over millennia, may have been in the songs that accompanied
weaving. Why metrical poetry? Because the complex metrical patterns
of the singing and chanting of women at the loom may encode some
aspects of the complex fabric that the women are weaving. The preliterate weaving song might be a mnemonic enactment of, a memo-
rized set of instructions for, the pattern or part of the pattern of the
weaving itself. Such song and its lyric wording would be a confluence
of rhythmic language, meaning, and bodily movement—a dance of
hard-working hands at the loom. Also, Elizabeth Barber has written
that in ancient warp-weighted looms, the shifting of the warp threads
would have moved the many weights slightly and produced a musical
clinking (1991, 102). Weaving is a site of rhythm and melody.

Tuck mentions some of the qualities of the weaving songs he has heard (in India, where he had an interpreter): such songs can change rhythms and tones, can communicate a verbal coding of arithmetical sequences that specify which strings of the warp the shuttle must go over or under when it pulls the weft after it through the growing fabric, and can also narrate stories related to what is portrayed on the rug (if the pattern of a rug includes figural representations).

If we imagine for a moment that what Tuck has hypothesized about the possible origins of poetic meter in weaving songs is true, then the analogy of poem and cloth (both of these implying the muses of memory and of music), works in two directions. The complexity of woven patterns, and of the manifold images, from geometric or abstract to figurative, to say nothing of borders, colors, and so on, is like the complexity of the poet's verbal and narrative weaving (his "stitching together" or "piecing"), and the complexity of the verbal texture is like that of the fabric.

Having brought together some of the connections between weaving and writing, and between weaving as a feminized metaphor for writing, I want to suggest that in the several passages of Homer that I have quoted, and in innumerable others, what we see is a *simultaneity of multiple thought processes*. This characteristic of poetry begins at the beginning, it seems, and characterizes poetry still. This is the very nature of the poetic use of language.

As an art, poetry exploits the multiple meaning-making produced by its *technē*, its devices, structures, and strategies. Poetry thinks in simultaneities—semantic, phonetic, rhythmic, temporal, allusive, narrative, psychical, historical. When a figure of repetition, for instance, is completed—a sound chiming with an earlier sound, a word or a visual image with its earlier iteration—the effect may be not only the marking of the language but also a sudden concurrence of two ideas, two associated feelings. Rhyme, citation, and allusion in poems create a second thought, and in a more self-contained way, so do metaphor and metonym.

Some of the simultaneities may be allusive only. In several of Sappho's poems, the materials of epic are reshaped in such a way that her song revalues them; in fragment 16 she reverses the epic view of Helen and seems to praise her for her world-shattering abandonment of Agamemnon, and she asserts that the absent Anaktoria is more beautiful to her than what would presumably be, for a man, the thrilling sight of troops, horsemen, and ships massed for battle. And in Book 23 of the *Iliad*, the chariot race during the funeral games for Patroklos has a complex subtext that implies many aspects of hero cult in Homer's time, not in the time of that legendary war (Nagy 2013, 169–234).

Sometimes the movement of thought and feeling in poetry has a reasoned completeness—developing, filling in, describing closely, with linguistic textures ranging from the very visual to the sonically rich to the abstract and discursive. But if there are simultaneous movements forward in time as words, phrases, clauses, sentences come into the reader, and backward in the poem as words, images, feelings, ideas already present resonate again, then such complex movement is not likely to be of a sort that one can describe as if it were only a step-by-step argument, or consisted of only one train of thought, or one stage of feeling at a time.

The well-worn phrase "poetic logic," in which "logic" only means "a way of thinking," tends to signify anything that moves a poem forward other than by rational argument. Connotation and association are supremely important in producing a second and third thought and conjuring an elided intermediate thought. Eliot's definition of the "music of poetry" as the "music of the secondary meanings of words" suggests both the sonic and the ideational at once (as does Pound's "logopoeia"). Apophatic poetics and Mandelshtam's image-metaphor airplanes and Tsvetaeva's "word-root dialectics" also create simultaneities of thought. Secondary, subliminal, unconscious thought and feeling may not all come to the conscious awareness of the reader (as they did not to the conscious awareness of the poet), especially since the reader has an idiosyncratic individual history as a reader and as a person. But many such under-ideas and under-feelings are in the poem itself and so can become apparent, can "dawn" on us, in a closer reading, a focused rereading, even a recollection. Our thinking simultaneously follows different paths—William James and Sigmund Freud came at this from different positions to articulate the significance of such under-thinking. For poetry to have enacted a similar, but of course differently furnished, complexity thousands of years ago, is one of my points. (No poets or readers had any conceptual frame for this, or analytical vocabulary for it, until James and Freud, yet it has been present in us and in poetry all along.) Repeating the sound of a part of one word in a second word that begins a new idea; bringing in a word with the same root as an earlier word but a different meaning; alluding to and citing a variety of texts, ideas, historical events, places, and so on, outside the poem; suggesting visual similarities ("rhymes," but of image, not of sound), conceptual ones, poetry approximates simultaneities of our inner life, which is not itself "poetic." And not only lyric, first-person poetry perhaps of all eras, but in subtler ways even third-person poetry like the Homeric epics, and "impersonal" and "abstract" poems of the twentieth century.

Simultaneity of thought processes is one of the notable characteristics of the surviving poems of Pindar. Calvert Watkins has noted of Pindar that "in some of his formulas and themes, some of his genres and subgenres, some of his training and his role in society, he was still part of a cultural tradition, verbally expressed, which reached back thousands of years" from *his* era (1995, 11). This might be one reason he is notably metapoetical—he composed while looking back, or rather listening back, at a long history of poetry that had been preserved orally, so inevitably he was led to think about poetry itself, simply because its characteristics and function in his society were changing. Considering how extensive the now lost ancient traditions of poetry must have been, I think Pindar received a greater historical legacy of poetry than we have now of English poetry. In his odes are many lines about poetry itself, too—his own and the poetry of others—and about the question of what poetry is for and how it should comport itself.

We cannot reconstruct more than a tiny fraction of his knowledge of gods and heroes (in all the variety of narrative that is typical of ancient Greece), Greek religious practice, and the activity of poet and chorus in Greek life. Nor can we be certain of his distinguishing qualities as an individual poet, because we have almost nothing to which his work can be compared. His odes give us only glimpses of his world, and only by the inferences of scholars who have read very deeply. His poetic language is allusive and artificial, but in the midst of it he may shift suddenly to what seems the impulse of a personal statement (yet of course such a line or two is in fact his metapoetic composition of the performative simulation of such an impulse). He will suddenly shift the register of his diction. He breaks into a train of thought to announce his intentions and boast of his poetic prowess. He swerves from topic to topic—sometimes no less abruptly than do many poets of our day—although he moves within a loose but somewhat consistent range of impulses that can be seen in almost all the odes (each includes celebration of the victor, his family, and his town; episodes of gods and heroes; often a genealogy that links the celebrated athletic victor with heroes and gods; appeals to gods and the Muse; proverbial statements). His rushing and the motion this way and that was later likened by the Roman poet Horace to a loud mountain river with such cascading momentum that it was bursting over its banks (Ode 4.2).

Pindar's first-person statements in the odes can't be assumed to be more than partly autobiographical. But precisely this seems one of his modern characteristics. (Ancient commentators debated such issues, too.) He wrote with an air of personal presence, and yet his subjectivity as a human being is not the substance of what he wrote. The complex interrelationship in poetry of simultaneous trains of thought, which the modern era has brought us to appreciate with our conscious attention, had already become in Pindar not only part of his practice but also one of the subjects of the ode. I think that in a way, only the twentieth century could come to read Pindar well, because earlier readers—even though English poets wrote loose "Pindaric" odes (like Wordsworth's "Tintern Abbey") and more carefully controlled odes, too (Keats)—could not think about the complexity of inner life with the tools that we have for it (from James and Freud and their descendants).

I'll offer a comparison of old and new. Here are the first twelve lines—six lines plus six lines—of Pindar's Olympian ode number 7, written to celebrate Diagoras of Rhodes, who was said to be the most famous boxer in antiquity after he won the contest at Olympia in 464 BCE. Pindar's commission was to spread the fame of Diagoras by praising it in a memorable song, a song so beautiful that it would be remembered longer than bronze and stone might endure. (Which again happens to be the case, in fact.) In the Greek choral ode, the first stanza (the *strophe*) is matched symmetrically in rhythm by the second (the *antistrophe*), as with exactness the antistrophe must repeat the strophe foot by foot and line by line for the sake of the repetition of the sung melody and the performance of the dance (music and choreography also having been provided by the poet). This metrical precision is part of the poet's *sophía*, his artistic knowledge, while the complex metaphorical profusion (a verbal cornucopia which Pindar clearly delights in providing) is part of poetry's own *kharis*—the charm, beauty, grace, generousness of its meaning-making effect on us, the delight it provides us.

These two stanzas are filled with radiant charm. Pindar's antistrophe provides symmetry in substance, too: the wine in the strophe and the nectar in the antistrophe. The wine is imagined as real, but it is always, in such a setting, sacred as well. The nectar is a metaphor for the song. The harmony of the marriage in line 6 is matched by the harmony of the music in line 12. The joy of the imagined symposium of line 5 is matched by the good fortune of good repute in line 10 and the favor of the goddess Kharis in line 11. All is *woven* with symmetry and bright verbal colors.

And note that the extended simile with which Pindar opens the song is about how a powerful man's *hand*, rather than striking a blow (in a poem which, in its recounting of gods and men, includes temporary insanity that produces murder; flight and exile; and the birth of Athena, who immediately gives a battle cry that horrifies Heaven and Earth), is making a generous and peaceful gesture of hospitality and a pledge of affiliation, and doing so with a wine bowl which, as it is pure gold, is an emblem of purity as well as wealth. My translation:

> The way a man from his
>   own wealthy hand presents
> his crowning possession, a drinking bowl—
>   made wholly of gold,
> poured full of the frothing dew of
> vineyards—to his new son-in-law,
>   with a toast from the one

to the other, house unto house, honoring
this concord and the good happy grace
of the men's feast, putting the groom amidst all
the friends' envy of the marrying bed:

So I too, sending poured
nectar, the Muses' gift,
sweet fruit of my mind, to champions of the
games — I ingratiate
Olympian and Pythian victors.
That man is blessed of whom what's said
keeps him in high regard.
For Grace, who with goodness lifts life into bloom,
over one man watches now, but then
over another — often with all the sweet-
voiced tones of the lyre, notes of the *aulos*.

A poem "unfolds" in time. "Poetry is the essential word in the dimension of time," wrote Antonio Machado, with a poetic consciousness keenly attuned to both the ear and the page ([1964] 1989, 164).
In Greek, Pindar's syntax seems to unfold in space, too — like a beautiful cloth. This itself is one of the main pleasures of the opening
strophe and antistrophe, turn and counterturn. The Greek original
shows us poetic resources familiar to us: Pindar repeats and *shifts* the
meaning of the Greek word *kharis*, which in line 5 is used to mean a
joyous quality of experience, while in line 11 it becomes the proper
name Kharis, the minor divinity who joins her two sisters as the Three
Graces. As I noted earlier, there is no end-rhyme in ancient Greek
poetry, but Pindar creates a texture of repeated phonemes that gives
the lines of the song the musical authority, the poetic justification,
that conveys great deliberateness of composition. (He uses an ono-
matopoeic word, *kakhládzoisan*, the sound of which might suggest the
pouring, like English "glugging," of the wine into the cup. However,
because the wine is already in the cup, I have translated it as "frothing," simply because I have learned that English — unlike Greek or, for
that matter, Russian — likes best an articulation in which everything
really does make material and temporal sense. I may be mistaken in
this decision. Maybe Pindar wanted to violate a temporal expectation
that he was well aware of, to create a simultaneity of the pouring of
the wine and the handing of the cup to another.)

Pindar's metrical intricacy can't be achieved in English or, I would think, any modern European language; we don't have the resources for it because in modern languages meter is so much simpler than it is in ancient Greek. It's rare for any of us to dance to a poem; and poets don't write poems for that purpose or any corresponding social occasion.

We have no trouble with Pindar's metaphors (the "dew" of the grapevine; the bowl that is a "crown" of the father-in-law's wealth) and metonyms (the "hand" that is wealthy, rather than the man — or this is hypallage, in that "wealthy" would normally modify "man"; the "marrying bed" for "marriage" and for the financial alliance of the two "houses," which stand for the families), or with his symbolic object (the bowl made entirely of gold). In the antistrophe, Pindar's lines leap into an implicit metacommentary on song itself, *even as the chorus is singing the song*: they sing in the voice of the poet that his song itself is (metaphorically) a "poured nectar," that is, a natural liquid with the sweetness of flowers, not a text composed and thus artificial (which of course it is); the song is raw not fermented (even though it has been painstakingly "cooked," we might say); and it is a gift from the Muses, even though Pindar, quietly, makes sure that everyone will acknowledge his having composed it, for the very next words mean the "sweet *fruit*" (here a metaphor, something between the natural and the cultivated) of his *mind* (here a metonym for his practice, his expertise, his talent as a composer of song).

After sweetened wine, sweet dew and nectar, sweet fruit, then of course the lyre's sound is sweet, and that of the *aulos* (a reed instrument). The poem is ancient and other in its occasion, its purpose (I mean the transaction that it represents between him who commissioned it and him who created it, and its place as a gesture in the relationship between the human and the divine), and its social use in performance; but its devices or modes of poetic thinking are immediately recognizable to any modern reader of poetry and are used by modern poets.

We can regard Pindar's extended but cohesive syntax as one of the remotest precursors of the extended and supple clauses of the three books that achieved C. K. Williams' originality and poetic power: *With Ignorance, Tar*, and *Flesh and Blood*. In these he explores the subtle simultaneous development of associations and counterfeeling that characterize our movement of mind as we try to experience them.

They can only be represented or articulated with simultaneous sinuosities on different levels—personal, social, ethical, and historical, as in "Combat," or intimate, as in the opening of this poem:

> Until I asked her to please stop doing it and was astonished to find
>   that she not only could
>
> but from the moment I asked her in fact would stop doing it, my
>   mother, all through my childhood,
>
> when I was saying something to her, something important,
>   would move her lips as I was speaking
>
> so that she seemed to be saying under her breath the very words I
>   was saying as I was saying them.
>
> Or, even more disconcertingly—wildly so now that my puberty had
>   erupted—*before* I said them.
>
> (1983, 6)

This is the sinuously constructed opening of "My Mother's Lips," which, like Pindar's opening, so deftly creates more of a floating of simultaneities than does any usual speech or everyday writing. In an intimate tone, with simple diction, Williams extends a sentence that is very satisfyingly complex in what it gets hold of. No one could represent in coherent language the thinking that comes to our consciousness so suddenly, unexpectedly, and fleetingly that we usually miss, because we can't listen to it all, what we ourselves had evidently been saying to ourselves. And much of what we do hear, we forget almost at once. But Williams found a way to sequence thinking in an energetically comprehensible and discursive, not imagistic, way, while preserving somehow the elusiveness of thinking it all at once. The recollection of an apparent simultaneity of thought between mother and boy is infused with the oedipal erotic element implied by the words— if we take them all together—"please," "astonished," "stop," "lips," "breath," "wildly," and "puberty." The syntactic deferral of the topic— the mother's lip-synching of her son in lines 3–4—enacts a movement of thought ("as I was saying them . . . before I said them") catching up to itself with a leaning, balancing dance of syntax that provides the reader with the pleasure of comprehending this complex, uncanny experience that is painful to this poetic self.

Pindar extends his first sentence for the sake of bringing along several simultaneous ideas in order to seem to unite them at the end of the strophe—as groom and bride unite—on that marriage bed (which is the last word of the strophe in Greek); then the sentence continues in the antistrophe and finds its completion as the second half of a very extended simile. The strophe ends with the bride and groom of the united households, and the sentence ends with a readiness to praise the leaf-wreathed boxer, Diagoras, whom the ode as a whole honors.

What Pindar does with a braiding of marriage, charm, Grace, wine, and nectar, Williams does with the verbs "speak" and "say" intertwined around the contest of personal autonomy between the mother and the teenage boy. The boy feels a disturbed but only half-conscious awareness of the erotic, while the adult poetic self who narrates is aware of everything.

All the punctuation in ancient Greek poetry has been put there not by the poets but by later editors who began working on textual matters during antiquity and have continued to our day, so my analysis of Pindar's sentences, although not of his syntax, is dependent on decisions others have made as recently as the edition of the Greek text that I am using. However, like the syntactic sequencing of Pindar's first strophe and then the conclusion of that long first sentence, followed by short second and third sentences, the sequencing of Williams' syntax, the long sentence and then the short one, is an ancient poetic device of the rhythm of thought.

Dionysios of Halikarnassos was the contemporary of the ancient Roman poets Horace and Ovid, and the ancient Roman orator, politician, and philosopher Cicero. By that time, the craft of poetry was discussed in prose by poets themselves, sometimes even in poems. "[I]t seems that the choral poets, Pindar and Bakkhylides, were the first in Greece to use the metaphor of weaving to designate poetic activity. They are thereby clearly distinguished from Homer, who," according to John Scheid and Jasper Svenbro, "never explicitly defined song as fabric, although he was familiar with the metaphor of language weaving" (1996, 119). Gregory Nagy, however, proposes that there can be a link between song and weaving even as early as Homer, for in the

Homeric phrase *aoidēs humnon*, "'humnos [hymn] of song' at *Odyssey* viii 429 [...] the noun *humnos* can be explained as a derivative of the verb-root that we see in *huphainō* 'weave,' in the metaphorical sense of 'web' or 'fabric' of song [...]. The point is, metaphors referring to the craft of fabric-workers pervade the usage of *humnos* in archaic Greek poetics" (2002, 70–71). Hundreds of years later, Dionysios, writing in Greek, and although no poet himself, proposed in his essay "On Literary Composition" some rules for literary writing—especially oratory and poetry—that draw on this traditional metaphor, advising (among many other things):

> The writer who is intending to leave a pleasant impression upon the ear should, I think, see that he observes the following rules in his composition. Either he should *link* to one another words which are melodious, rhythmical and euphonious, by which our sense of hearing is affected with a feeling of sweetness and utter softness, and is completely won over; or he should *intertwine* and *interweave* those which have no such natural effect with those which can so bewitch the ear that the unattractiveness of the one is overshadowed by the charm of the other. [...] [B]eauty in literary arrangement must be pursued by the aid of all those elements that constitute attractiveness. Here, as before, the cause resides in the nature of the letters and in the *phonetic* effect of the syllables, which are the raw material from which the *fabric* of the words is *woven*. [...] The most elegant writers of poetry or prose have understood these facts well, and both *arrange their words by weaving them together* with deliberate care, and with elaborate artistic skill adapt the syllables and the letters [phonemes] to the emotions which they wish to portray. [...] [After citing Homeric lines of special phonetic skill:] Countless such lines are to be found in Homer, representing length of time, bodily size, extremity of emotion, immobility of position, or some similar effect, by nothing more than the artistic arrangement of the syllables; while other lines are wrought in the opposite way to portray brevity, speed, urgency, and the like. [...] [On a song by Sappho, frag. 1:] The eloquence and charm of these verses arises from the continuity and the smoothness of the connections: the words lie close to one another and *are woven together* according to certain natural affinities and combinations of letters [i.e., phonemes]. (1985, 87–88, 91, 109, 111, 199; my italics and brackets)

This emphasis on sound is entirely apart from end-rhyme; Dionysios listened for a sonic texture within poetic lines and in the whole weave of a poem.

While the rules or at least advice of Dionysios cannot anticipate all that poets have added to poetic technique over two subsequent millennia, many of his observations could be made as justly of later poetry as of ancient. He went on to mention the effectiveness of words that sound like what they mean, the importance of etymology (which of course we understand better, with the advantage of philology), and the relation of sound to sense. Some of Dionysios' ideas about nature and art lead us directly to the "neoclassical" (in given name as well as in practice) Alexander Pope. In "An Essay on Criticism" (1711) Pope articulated his principles of the general nature of poetry, and gave his own illustrations of the use of sound and rhythm, in effect implying rules of poetic craft in his lines, as Dionysios had done with lengthy analysis and citation in his essay. (Not long afterward, Pope would begin translating Homer.) Among the best-known lines are bravura demonstrations for all the less skilled, less brilliant poets whom Pope satirized (lines 337–83). Dionysios cited lines in Homer to show how certain sounds create certain effects; Pope composed his own lines. Regarding poetic mistakes, he briefly mocked predictable rhymes, clumsy meter, and a lack of ideas; then he illustrated his ideals of excellent poetic craft, to show that "The sound must seem an echo to the sense":

> And ten low words oft creep in one dull line [...]
> A needless Alexandrine ends the song,
> That like a wounded snake, drags its slow length along. [...]
> Soft is the strain when Zephyr gently blows,
> And the smooth stream in smoother numbers flows;
> But when loud surges lash the sounding shore,
> The hoarse, rough verse should like the torrent roar.
> When Ajax strives, some rock's vast weight to throw,
> The line too labors, and the words move slow;
> Not so, when swift Camilla scours the plain,
> Flies o'er th'unbending corn, and skims along the main.
> (Pope 1961, 278, 280, 282–83)

Pope's lines about slowness and swiftness enact the same qualities of verbal rhythm that Dionysios remarked in the Homeric passage about Sisyphus (*Odyssey* 11.593–96). Dionysios analyzed the slow rhythm created by shorter words, the fast rhythm created by polysyllabic words, and anticipated, or rather provided, Pope's conclusions (Dionysius 1985, 158–65). Enlightening me, Lawrence Lipking wrote to me that it was in the second edition of Pope's "Essay" (1713) that he added this couplet: "See Dionysius Homer's Thoughts refine, / And call new Beauties forth from ev'ry Line!" (Pope 1961, 314); and that Pope's "Preface" to his translation of the *Iliad* "specifically credits Dionysios for pointing out beauties of the agreement of sound and sense." The continuity of ancient poetics has reached into the modern world through the study and learning of later poets such as Pope, but much of what I am displaying in my cabinet of more recent curiosities cannot be accounted for in that way.

While Dionysios argued for beauty, elegance, and proportion — and perhaps helped the English eighteenth-century poets formulate their own poetics — what he most emphasized is the effect on poetic composition of a careful listening to language, and the "weaving" of elements of composition into the poem, which are technical virtues found in English in all places and literary periods. Especially in Homer, garments and other material objects produced by literal weaving are described with luxurious pleasure, although as Scheid and Svenbro noted, Homer did not explicitly use weaving as a metaphor for the composition of song, even though he did use it for speech — meaning for instance to tell a tale, argue, or scheme against someone. One instance: in the *Iliad*, when Helen is pointing out the principal Greek warriors from the vantage of the high walls of Troy, one of the Trojan elders, Antenor, recalls that when Menelaos and Odysseus came to request that the Trojans give Helen up, these two ambassadors from the Greek forces "wove" or "spun" their speech, their arguments (3.212).

I believe there is no surviving work earlier than Dionysios' essay that sets out to *teach* the craft of writing. The Stoic philosopher Epictetus, an ex-slave who perhaps had direct knowledge of weaving, may have written of the weaving of syllogisms; and men and women, gods and goddesses, have woven with guile and persuasiveness their designs on others in Homer and later in tragedies; and Pindar and Bakkhylides wove song; but the later Dionysios of Halikarnassos wrote of weaving *words* and the *sounds* of words, and different *sorts* of words, together.

❈

For a notable modern instance of poetic weaving, I'll begin by quoting
a little more fully the opening of Pound's Canto xxxix:

> Desolate is the roof where the cat sat,
> Desolate is the iron rail that he walked
> And the corner posts whence he greeted the sunrise.
> In hill path: "thkk, thgk"
>   of the loom
> "Thgk, thkk" and the sharp sound of a song
>   under olives.

(1986, 193)

("The cat: Conflation of many memories including the sound of the
looms on the hill path leading up from Rapallo [where Pound lived
during his last years], E.P.'s many years of feeding hungry cats, and,
most important, the sound of Circe's loom overheard by Odysseus'
men as they approached her house of 'polished stone'" [from a discussion of the *Odyssey*, Book 10, in Terrell 1993, 160; my brackets].)

Robert Duncan later weaves these two little threads—cat and
loom—from Pound into his own poem about poetic composition, "At
the Loom." Duncan evokes the whole fabric of remembrance of heroic
exploits and suffering—Odyssean looms, Iliadic battles, Achilles and
Hektor—and he layers his own present moment of composing this
poem over his reading of Pound's poem and over Homer's telling of
ancient warfare, moving by "increment[s] of associations" and explicitly incorporating etymologies and foreign words to do so: "word-
ness" itself. Such poetic weavings are, like material weaving, both thematic and sensuous—they unfold in time as we read or listen; as we
apprehend the sounds, rhythms, word-forms, structures of language,
and threads of thought and story in language; and as we imagine the
sensuous "imagery" of sight, sound, touch and taste.

Duncan's poem "At the Loom—*Passages* 2" includes (perhaps
"presents" would be a more accurate term) the Old Norse word for
the shuttle, "*skutill* 'harpoon'—a dart, an arrow / or a little ship," and
the Latin word for it, *navicula*, which means "small boat," and the German word *weberschiff*, which means "weaver-ship/vessel." The shuttle
is "crossing and recrossing from shore to shore" of a poem and of

the Aegean Sea. Duncan writes of the "cords that bind / meaning in the word-flow / the *rivering* web" (my italics). The poem is substantial, and I will quote it in full to show the breadth of the web Duncan creates:

A cat's purr
in the hwirr thkk   *"thgk, thkk"*
of Kirke's loom on Pound's Cantos
"I heard a song of that kind . . ."

my mind a shuttle among
set strings of the music
lets a weft of dream grow in the day time,
an increment of associations,
luminous soft threads,
the thrown glamour, crossing and recrossing,
the twisted sinews underlying the work.

Back of the images, the few cords that bind
meaning in the word-flow,
the rivering web
rises among wits and senses
gathering the wool into its full cloth.

The secret!   the secret!   It's hid
in its showing forth.
The white cat kneads his paws
and sheathes his eyes in ecstasy against the light,
the light bounding from his fur as from a shield
held high in the midst of a battle.

What does the Worm work in His cocoon?

There was such a want in the old ways
when craft came into our elements,
the art shall never be free of that forge,
that loom, that lyre —

the fire, the images, the voice.

Why, even in the room where we are,
reading to ourselves, or I am reading aloud,

sounding the music,
                    the stuff
        vanishes upon the air,
                line after line thrown.

Let there be the clack of the shuttle flying
        forward and back,   forward and
                    back,

warp, *wearp, varp:*   *"cast of a net, a laying of eggs"*
        from **warp-*   *"to throw"*

            the threads twisted for strength
                    that can be a warp of the will.

        "O weaver, weaver, work no more,"
            Gascoyne is quoted:
        "thy warp hath done me wrong."

And the shuttle carrying the woof I find
        was *skutill*   *"harpoon"*   —a dart, an arrow,
                or a little ship,

            navicula   *weberschiff*

crossing and recrossing from shore to shore—

        prehistoric **skutil   **skut-*
            "a bolt, a bar, as of a door"
            "a flood-gate"   ·

                        but the battle I saw
was on a wide plain,   for the
        sake of valor,
the hand traind to the bow,
        the man's frame
withstanding,   each side

facing its foe for the sake of
        the alliance,
allegiance, the legion, that the
        vow that makes a nation
one body not be broken.

> Yet it is all, we know, a mêlée,
> a medley of mistaken themes
> grown dreadful and surmounting dread,
>
> so that Achilles may have his wrath
> and throw down
> the heroic Hektor who raised
> that reflection of the heroic
>
> in his shield . . .
>
> Feb 4–11   1964
>
> (1968, 11–13)

Duncan was writing this poem as the as yet limited American involvement in war in Vietnam was becoming more known outside the armed forces and the CIA, and in it he undercuts the honor even of ancient heroic warriors with an awareness of how "it is all, we know, a mêlée, / a medley of mistaken themes / grown dreadful and surmounting dread." The loom—ancient medium of feminine creativity—is the metaphor of the poet's work, which celebrated the warrior in the ancient world but had no role in combat. Duncan's poem makes a figure for itself in the realm of women: the household in which the performance of the poem "stitches" episodes together and "weaves" with sensuous qualities of language. The poem trails away at the end, unable to redeem suffering, although at crucial moments in both the *Iliad* and the *Odyssey*, and in much of all subsequent poetry, song charms mourning and pain to the surface, entertaining—in the fullest human way, inviting each listener's inner life to follow the shuttling movement of the tale or poem.

Poetry that remembers and praises the fame of heroes and athletic victors *is* that fame, in the ancient Greek view; the poetry *is* the glory that it sustains. So the *kleos* of Achilles and Hektor is at the heart of the Greek epic and victory poems, and is not absent from Robert Duncan's poem, either. It is still "crossing and recrossing from shore to shore," and in it a fundamental kind of human accomplishment, remembrance, still flows from the past to the present. Duncan's poem preserves the figures of Kirkē, Pound, Gascoigne, Achilles, Hektor (and a cat); especially in what it says and implies about poetic composition itself, "At the Loom" also presents an implicit image of the poet to the reader. For a few moments, the reader's inner life (and sub-vocalizing of the words) is evoked by Duncan's sequencing of image, sensuous qualities of language, idea, and remembrance; the poem renews that remembrance in the reader, who in the moments of reading it is thinking and feeling by the woven pattern of the poem.

⊙ 8 ⊙

Onyx-Eyed Odalisques

Onyx-eyed Odalisques
and ornithologists
observe
the flight
of Eros obsolete

From "Lunar Baedeker,"
by MINA LOY (1997, 82)

It might be that the first line in this quotation plays against the frequent Homeric epithet for the goddess Hera, "ox-eyed" (for example, at *Iliad* 1.551), which suggests human eyes open wide. (With feminine mock innocence? With erotic excitement?) The English *ox-eyed* reproduces the compound Greek word *bo-ōpis*. There might be an iconic *auditory* aspect to the Greek word, in the way the first *o* sound, Greek letter omicron (literally "little *o*"), in the first syllable, from *bous*, "cow" or "ox," opens wider to the second *o* sound, the Greek letter omega (literally "great *o*") in the second syllable, for *ops*, "eye." When the word *boōpis* is said aloud, Hera's left eye opens wider. (Our English *eye* is *visually* iconic, with its two half-lidded eyes separated by some kind of nose.) In Loy's "onyx-eyed," we see a poetic move like those so often made by Marina Tsvetaeva in Russian, bringing one word out of another—and the "ox" is still there, inside "onyx." In Loy's poem, amid drugs, death, obliviousness, doomsdays, hallucinations, and sex, what is the *o* that these four lines reiterate nine times after the first one? A blank state of mind? An orifice? Earlier I mentioned the name of Kirkē's island, Ōgygía (Greek *Ōgŭgía*, with a hard *g*); its breadth, from omega to alpha, suggests an infinite realm, even though its narrative meaning is that it is small and dangerous. The gagging sound of the word, and the gagging sensation of saying it, seem just right if we think of the astonishment and dread in the disgruntled men who, approaching her house, were greeted uncannily by those desperately friendly lions and wolves.

Most poetry has used language so as to make it as fully present as possible — its clarities, obscurities, ambiguities, and ambivalences; its surprising way of evoking what it does not explicitly state; and the sensuous aspects of words. For millennia, iconic and etymological effects have been part of the pleasure of the simultaneity of poetic thinking. In poetry, language can even try to save a word for the sake of a meaning that has so weakened that the word should already be in a linguistic ambulance to an emergency room of sense and nonsense. Poetry can momentarily revive it, for a late fullness of meaning, before it's lying in a word-hearse to continue on its way to the cemeteries of words either dead or so wronged by new usage — as the word might feel in its etymological bones — that it cannot survive as it was. (But younger poets take it as it is, and make more of it in its new sense.) Williams Carlos Williams solicits a double meaning in his poem "Pink Confused with White," in which the sense of *fused* is added to the everyday meaning of *confused*. In Robert Duncan's "At the Loom" (which I quoted earlier in full), after mentioning the loom and the lyre (i.e., the "woven" song and the musical accompaniment), the poem refers to the "stuff" of the voice that "vanishes upon the air"; *stuff* is from Middle English and its cognate words in Romance languages mean "cloth" or "a piece of rich textile fabric." In C. K. Williams' poem "My Mother's Lips" (quoted earlier in part), the word for how disturbing the mother's verbal behavior is to her son is "disconcertingly"; the verb *disconcert* is ironic here, or at least the English language itself is ironic in providing it, since to do things in *concert* means to do them *together* — hence the English noun *concert*, meaning a collaborative musical performance.

A poem can express (articulate and deliver) new words, too, and find a meaning in a fusing or confusing of one word with another. Words have life narratives; poetry likes such narratives. Or, to put it as Pindar might, "such narratives love poetry." (He sometimes inverted the expected agency of subject and verb: "victory in the games loves song most of all" [Nemean 3.7; Pindar 1997, 2:23].)

As I mentioned in chapter 1, *etymon* means "the primary word which gives rise to a derivative." Already in Greek antiquity, conjecture about etymologies informed both poetry and philosophy. The etymology of the word *etymology* is that it derives from *etymon*, which in turn is simply an anglicization of ancient Greek *etumos*. But the Greeks were limited to conjecture, often fanciful; only the modern understanding of the life history of words and their family relations in constantly evolving languages makes of etymology a truer search for accuracy.

In the Athenian tragic drama *Bakkhai* ("women followers of Dionysos, in a trance of worship"), Euripides gave a brief etymological discourse to the character, Teiresias, the seer, who lectures the young king Pentheus on the folly of his angry zeal to reject the god Dionysos (2009, 255; Greek lines 286–97). An engagement with a word's etymology is a gesture often repeated in English poetry, and sometimes a way of thinking, as in the work of Gerard Manley Hopkins, who was born in 1844 and flourished just when philology itself began to flourish in England and Germany, as new evidence and theories were bringing to light the common ancestors of apparently different words and the development of modern languages from prehistoric ones. Hopkins could weigh slight differences in words with perhaps a common root, as he thought, for example, as in this 1863 notebook entry:

> *Flick, fillip, flip, fleck, flake.*
> *Flick* means to touch or strike lightly as with the end of a whip, a finger, etc. To *fleck* is the next tone above flick, still meaning to touch or strike lightly (and leave a mark of the touch or stroke) but in a broader less slight manner. Hence substantively a *fleck* is a piece of light, colour, substance, etc. looking as though shaped or produced by such touches. *Flake* is a broad and decided *fleck*, a thin plate of something, the tone above it. (1959, 11)

In his poem "Inversnaid" (1881), he seems to have coined the compound word "beadbonny," and while Norman MacKenzie suggests that it means "the mountain ash (rowan) gay with scarlet berries in autumn" (Hopkins 1992, 426), the earlier sense of *bead* can also remind us that the word is religious in origin and meant a prayer.

(Prayers themselves, counted out by the use of a rosary, became the "beads"—a metonym, in other words, for the prayer with which each "bead" was associated). The beauty of the "beadbonny ash" tree in Hopkins' poem also has to do with its posture—in a stance as if of praying. (Nothing could be more in keeping with Hopkins' devotional mentality.) By the late nineteenth century the age of a word could seem to throw a light onto the ruins of the cultures from which the word had survived. Hopkins was a precursor of the Modernists who made more use of the very age of a word as an expressive resource.

❋

The palpable reality of things loves English. The way we make language itself seem palpable, or at least make that which it describes seem palpable *through* the words, is to favor words with Old English roots. Basil Bunting's "Ode 17" (dedicated to Mina Loy) contrasts the Germanic roots of English in Anglo-Saxon and Norse, on the one hand, and the origins of other words in Latin, on the other. These two groups of words mark the history of English; after the invasion in 1066 by the French and their occupation afterward, Latinate words came to be woven into the English fabric. Here are some of the lines of the poem:

> Now that sea's over that island
> so that barely on a calm day sun sleeks
> a patchwork hatching of combed weed
> over stubble and fallow alike
> I resent drowned blackthorn hedge, choked ditch,
> gates breaking from rusty hinges,
> the submerged copse,
> *Trespassers will be prosecuted.*
>
> Sea's over that island,
> weed over furrow and dungheap [...]
>
> Over face, thin eyebrows wide of the eyes,
> a premonition in the gait
> of this subaqueous persistence
> of a particular year—

for you had prepared it for preservation
not vindictively, urged
by an economy of passions. [...]

Weed over meadowgrass, sea over weed,
no step on the gravel.
Very likely I shall never meet her again
or if I do, fear the latch as before.

(1994, 95)

The first stanza is almost completely made of words deriving from Old English, until the last line, in which the voice of law stops it short with its two threatening Latinate words. The last stanza is again mostly Old English. And in between, the linguistic tone of the interior lines is very Latin, so that the poem enacts an etymological contrast as it sketches, only very implicitly, Bunting's feeling by representing it as landscape, within which there is "a woman walking alone in her garden." Among the words with Old English roots are "now" (*nu*), "sea" (*saē*), "day" (*daeg*), "sun" (*sunne*), "sleeks" (from *slick*, probably from an earlier Old English word), "patchwork" (the origin of "patch" is uncertain), "work" (*weorc*), "combed" (*camb*), "weed" (*wéod*), "fallow" (of uncertain, perhaps Old English, origin), "alike" (*anlic*), "drowned" (of obscure origin, perhaps from an Old English word that has not survived), "blackthorn" ("black" of uncertain original form, although similar words are found in other early Germanic languages, first attested in Old English as *blac*; and "thorn," *þorn*), "hedge" (*hecg*), "choked" (probably Old English), "ditch" (*díc*), "gates" (*geat* or *get*), "breaking" (*brecan*), "rusty" (a very ancient word, going back far beyond Old English, but in the latter, already *rust*), "hinges" (probably an Old English word *hencg* not found), and more words, too. Even words like "calm" (from French, thus ultimately from Latin), and "hatch" (from French, in the sense Bunting uses), and "stubble" (from Old French) have been anglicized in *sound*: one or two syllables, richly consonantal.

The Latin etymological tone — discursive, abstract, polysyllabic — crescendos suddenly from "submerged" to "*Trespassers* will be *prosecuted*" (Latinate words are, after all, the heart of legalistic and bureaucratic language in English). Later, this tone intensifies: "a *premonition* in the gait / of this *subaqueous persistence* / of a *particular* year— / for you had *prepared* it for *preservation* / not *vindictively, urged* / by an *economy* of *passions.*" ("Economy," though, comes into English *through* Latin from Greek.)

Thus can the ancient lingo (and more) *show itself* as ancient in a modern English poem, and *function* as an echo of ancientness, almost of timelessness, yet create a fresh effect. Some of the Modernists interwove such materials so as to create effects of rapidity, depth of thought, and linguistic energy. Bunting did not have to be consciously deliberative to create the etymological effects of "Ode 17," for in all his work his famously fine-tuned ear is evident as one of his gifts, sharpened no doubt by the qualities and tune of the Northumbrian English in which his ear was trained.

Bunting's weaving conveys meaning: it's less like the montage of Eliot's barren culture-scape and Pound's *Cantos* and more like a meditative exercising of the English language itself. When Bunting's Latinate language, after overtaking the Germanic with which the poem begins, is then displaced in turn by the Germanic again, ideas and abstractions are overcome by something more earthy, more palpable, just as lowly weeds and the sheer thinginess of the world as it changes physically may overcome the generalities into which we so often put everything. The use of the Latinate words in English is mostly abstract, hence Latin's large-scale use in law, philosophy, and structures of thought, as, for example, medical terminology and animal and plant taxonomy. But English seems to have used its Old English words almost like things themselves; they have given a vernacular naming to the physical realm of preindustrial technologies of metallurgy and woodcraft (the sword, the shield, the bow, the arrow, the spear,), agriculture and villages (the barn, cow, barley, rope, the farm, the house, the path, the ditch), ships and sailing, and to the natural world. (The *technē* of poetic language, too, is preindustrial, of course.) English names much of what is small scale in social and institutional structures. In these words there's thinginess in their very sound, hence the pleasant linguistic sensation of "palpability" English style (not the same as the Russian palpability created by metaphor, discussed earlier). Curiously, Latin did produce a philosophical word for the *idea* that things and persons have inherent, essential qualities, *quidditas*, which in English is *quiddity*, even though Latin—whose daughter Romance languages today act similarly—did not generate the richly discriminating taxonomic vocabulary of an earthier language like ancient Greek or, well after the Romans had abandoned Britain, early English.

One might call Bunting's poem an interweaving of two different-colored threads—Germanic words and Latinate words—of the weft (OE *wefta*) or woof (OE *owef*), together woven (from *weave*, OE *wefan*) on the warp (OE *wearp*) of the poem's structure, its shape, its "unfolding" over the duration of one's hearing or reading it. Old English and Latin—that's the varied pattern of the words as words.

Such choice of words, which, in echoing their origins, also echo metaphors, attitudes, and ideas from an earlier time, is not at all a new device. Pindar himself fashioned (in both senses of the word) his commissioned narratives of gods and a heroic ancestry for the athletic victor, while listening in his memory to the longstanding poetic traditions he knew, and using them in several ways. He sustained certain values and ideals, and certain words, remembering the work of other poets—predecessors and contemporaries—and the already long life of poetry itself.

Elizabeth Arnold's book *Effacement*, a poem sequence, overlays illness, surgery, and the loss of identity in the poet's present onto several scenes, including an English World War I hospital for the reconstruction of terrible facial injuries. A brief quotation cannot show the rich effect of the complexity of these overlays, which are how the sequence thinks. One poem describes a present-day hospital ward, perhaps organized by the armed forces, in which an "Iraqi Boy" has a facial injury and is also in a wheelchair. Among its terrible resonances in American life, Iraq is a metonym of the most ancient human world. There have been countless wounded Iraqi boys over the many millennia. The poem begins:

> What appear to be
> peach-white, overwashed pajamas
>
> in a washed-out newspaper photo
>
> on one side droop
> like a monk's hood,

the upper half of that leg

raised with the other whole one
and the hands

they're there!

(2010, 38)

The boy's hands are not damaged; in a later line, the poem hints that his face is very damaged. One of Arnold's metaphors for both literal and metaphorical "effacement" is in these opening lines: "overwashed," "washed-out," "less washed-out."

Let me start a second train of thought here by going back to ancient experience again — ideas, practices, mentalities. Even though we cannot naturalize these in our own minds and experience, they remain, as I have been describing, as remnants in poetry — more, I believe, than in any other art. The Homeric formula *kleos aphthiton*, "unwilting" (that is, "undying," "imperishable," "unfailing") fame, has a cognate in Sanskrit, *áksita-*. In the *Rig-Veda*, this idea produced such elevated poetic metaphors as "rain from the celestial 'fountainhead' of thunderclouds [being] compared with the urine of prize-winning stallions," as Gregory Nagy has shown (1974, 233). He also says that from "all the Greek nouns (except *kleos*) which are described by *aphthito-*, we may posit a least common denominator in context: an unfailing stream of water, fire, semen, vegetal extract (wine)," as well as milk, soma sap, and even light. (244, 231–36). In Greek, that everflowingness becomes associated with the glory that is disseminated — note the apt (Latin) root of that English word, *semen*, "seed" — by the poem, and at the same time *it is a characteristic of "the powers that are inherent in the Singer's craft,"* too (233, 229; my italics). Thus song and *kleos* (and libation, too) are interlinked, as pouring, running, liquid. In this context, Pindar's song-nectar is not far-fetched, even though we fetch it from afar. And even in antiquity, this phrase need not be stated explicitly for the underlying metaphor to be active; Pindar uses the metaphor of liquid for his songs, writing "I too am glad to pelt Alkman" — a Greek mythical hero — "with wreaths and sprinkle him with song" (Pythian 8.56–57; Pindar 1997, 1:333).

Proceeding from the metaphor of the "washed" in Arnold's poem, I think I can now point out this metaphorical juxtaposition of *liquid* and *remembrance* as one of the most curious survivals of all, even though we can have no sense of the experience and ideas of the realms in which it was created and sustained for a very long time. After reading Nagy, I began noticing the mention of water in contemporary poems, and from time to time I saw something uncanny: the flowing of water was sometimes associated — by sheer proximity or by phonetic figure or some other device with which poems think — with remembrance. We tend to think that in the literary survival version of the game of paper/scissors/rock, what has most endured has been memory, and after memory, paper. As for "Not marble nor the gilded monuments / Of princes, shall outlive this powerful rhyme" (sonnet 55), might a new Shakespeare brag, "Not scissors nor the lanes of governors' / new toll roads shall outlive this powerful . . . tweet"? We produce an extreme contrast between writing for a great dissemination through time and for a broad dissemination for a day. In Greece, poetry was for all time, and human beings were "creatures of a day"; now perhaps poems have migrated toward being creations of a day, while human beings remain as fragile and mortal as ever. But I do mean that a poetic utterance may possibly outlive steel and cement. Although unknown poems must lie sedimented in thick geo-literary deposits on the ocean floor of oblivion, Shakespeare's boast is also proven by such survivals as the poems of Osip Mandelshtam in the memory of his widow Nadezhda and a few friends. And although Keats asked that his gravestone say only "Here lies One / Whose Name was writ in Water," it is curious, nonetheless, that the most ancient poetry to which we have access, even indirectly, associated remembrance — "undying fame" — with liquid. This metaphorical moving water flows with equal ease over paper, metal, and stone.

The last five poems in Arnold's book mention "the sea Odysseus was whirled around in / by the gods" and the poet's father "on the heaving deck of [a] submarine chaser, / a Coast Guard cutter"; a burial vault like a swimming pool; "a barnacle's feathery body reaching / from its shell / into the river water"; a "salmon run, / the stream out of hearing [. . . where the salmon] struggled in loud water"; and Thor Heyerdahl on his raft in the Pacific (2010, 68, 70, 71, 72, 73, 74). Her book is a remembrance of many: the poet's father, the "defaced" or "effaced" soldiers of World War I and later, and her own former self.

Elizabeth Bishop's "At the Fishhouses," in which the "cold dark deep and absolutely clear" water of the sea with gentle waves is "swinging indifferently above the stones," ends with a deservedly well-known passage about our ability to know and about knowledge itself. The poem's tone is attentive and elegiac; where there was liveliness in coastal Nova Scotia there is now decline. There are "small old buildings," "an ancient wooden capstan," rusted ironwork, and "the decline in the population / and of codfish and herring." Her focus is on an old man "down by one of the fishhouses" beside the ocean, a friend of her grandfather (in ancient Greek, he would be regarded as someone linked to her as *philos*: friend, ally, "kith and kin" — an Old English poetic figure). About the cold water of the ocean, Bishop writes:

> It is like what we imagine knowledge to be:
> dark, salt, clear, moving, utterly free,
> drawn from the cold hard mouth
> of the world, derived from the rocky breasts
> forever, flowing and drawn, and since
> our knowledge is historical, flowing, and flown.
>
> (1983, 66)

Ancient Greek *aphthitos* and Vedic *áksita-* become an apt "flowing" that is remembered by and through poetry, simultaneously with Bishop's remembrance of the fisherman. The poem — and poetry itself — remember a diminished *good*, even if it is not *glory*, of a faraway place imagined briefly but with persuasive fullness. In the plain but musical style of Bishop, the last four lines are of equal length (four speech stresses hovering in a loose iambic rhythm) like a slow drumbeat, and marked also by choriambic rhythmic figures (utterly <u>free</u>; <u>drawn</u> from the <u>cold</u>; <u>flow</u>ing and <u>drawn</u>; <u>flow</u>ing, and <u>flown</u>) and phonetic figures (**d**ark, **d**rawn, **d**erived, **d**rawn; be, **f**ree; forever, **flow**-ing, **flow**ing, **flown**). Bishop's elegiac remembrance of a man and a place, and the elegiac tone of the way she characterizes her own presence there, are clearly *associated* with water. To the *mind of poetry* the association of undying remembrance with the flowing of water or another meaning-laden liquid is familiar over millennia and is present here, while to the mind of the poet and the reader, it is unfamiliar, even alien.

Are such collocations of liquid and remembrance an engrained but unconscious association in all of us, by virtue of how language works, how we are formed by language, and how we experience remembrance? Is it an archetype? A kind of improbable species memory in us, like the fearsomeness of snakes (those little dragons)? Song itself is a flowing *sound*. Might the ancient song that accomplished the dissemination of the remembrance of a glorious accomplishment (the *Iliad*, Pindar's victory odes, and the old traditions within which such poems were composed) be an enactment of a metaphorical association inherent in our human experience of song and rivers, rainstorms . . . ? I once heard a recording of an indigenous woman in the Amazon forest singing what was described as a duet with a burbling stream.

A startlingly clear linking of water and remembrance infuses Robinson Jeffers' early poem "Juan Higera Creek": "Neither your face, Higera, nor your deeds / Are known to me; and death these many years / Retains you, under grass or forest-mould. / Only a rivulet bears your name." Jeffers alludes to Shakespeare's sonnet 55 in order to praise the anonymous, shapeless durability of water over even Shakespeare's proof of poetry's power to outlast what seems the durable remembrance of monuments: "Not bronze, Higera, nor yet marble cool the thirst; / Let bronze and marble of the rich and proud / Secure the names; your monument will last / Longer, of living water forest-pure" (2000, 61). This poet may have wished to reject Shakespeare (and behind him, Horace) and the urbanity of bronze, marble, *and* poetry, for Jeffers chose wild water as the ultimate preserver—although not of a name but of an identity (Higuera is identified with the presumed purity of forest living, of wild places).

Alert now for something I had never thought to look for, I take from my shelves some books of poems. I am repeatedly surprised. Muriel Rukeyser opens her great documentary/lyric elegy, "The Book of the Dead," with an Adamic description of arriving in the valley of the disaster in West Virginia, where a long tunnel had been drilled "[t]o divert water (from New River) / to a hydroelectric plant" (1992, 12), and two thousand men had been required to labor in silica dust and many of them sickened and died for the sake of the project to use the energy of "the hard and stone-green river / cutting fast and direct into the town" (11). The poem preserves a memory of named, individual, historical men and women.

Linda McCarriston's *Little River* is uncannily named as if, echoing something ancient, it intended to float its many remembrances (of people and animals) on water. Bringing together, in a gesture of remembrance of the dead, the two meanings available in *gravely* (the *grave* that derives from an Old English word, meaning a burial place, and the *grave* that derives ultimately from Latin, meaning "weighty, serious"), she writes:

> The waters though
> find their own way deep
> in the runnels that their toil
> has made going about going
> elsewhere gravely
> though their music is gay.
>
> (2002, 11)

In Joshua Weiner's recent "Rock Creek (II)," the six hundred or so short lines river down the page, except where they run underneath some obstructing passages in prose. Rock Creek, in the meandering park named for it in Washington, DC, flows to different sorts of contemporary and historical events and persons. The beginning:

> Cutting a way through stone
> to see what's there, not
> how things appear, earth-blood,
> without style, never
> at rest, what settles in it [...]
>
> (2013, 3)

And after 17 lines of description of the moving water a first name appears: Leonardo (da Vinci), apropos of how the latter saw running water itself ("a motion resembling hair," Weiner writes); at line 43 the streaming poem reaches a second name: the narrowing gorge in which Rock Creek flows "driving that motion / like Coltrane stretching / tight vibrato / phrases [...] cascades / of smaller scales [...]." At line 59, "prisoners of / Guantánamo / flooding cells in protest / each drinking / eighteen bottles of water / in an hour." And then a brief quote from Genesis, "the breath moved / upon the face of the waters." And a few lines further on, George Washington is named. The poem finds its way to many names. It does not seem fanciful to me to regard as unexpectedly just right this echo of the watery sense of Greek *aphthitos* (undying, unwilting) and its cognate Vedic *ákṣita-*. Weiner's whole poem threads (this word associates itself with both weaving and with water) history like beads on Rock Creek. Walt Whitman, jazz and blues musicians, prehistoric flora and fauna, political Washingtonians, Civil War hospitals, Teddy Roosevelt, John Quincy Adams, a young woman murdered near Rock Creek in 2001, the Duke Ellington Bridge, and so on: recent events, scandals, outrages, everyday life, and long-ago settlement, history. It is all remembrance, and it is all along and near the little river.

Even though few of the ancient poetic purposes survive in the modern world, the residue of such purposes in poetic technique is everywhere underfoot; along with the *technē* that has survived, this is the ground, the body, the Gaia of poetry. In "From Dragon to Worm," Calvert Watkins turns from his analysis of the ancient formula "man kills dragon (or serpent)"—which seems to take every possible form, including inversions and negatives, in a wide variety of ancient poems in various Indo-European languages—to the tiniest form of a dragon or serpent: the worm. "As a symbol of disease," however miniature, it was nevertheless a monster (1995, 519–24). Dwelling within us, however, it must be defeated within us, even though it cannot even be seen nor can it be slain by courage and brute heroic force. Poetry was a weapon against an inner monster—as it still is today, although not so literally. A charm for healing can be tried, and sometimes it must have seemed to suffice.

The poet Heidy Steidlmayer wrote to me in 2010 about Watkins' chapter on the worm, drawing out a parallel with the modern and making a balletic leap from the worm to words themselves:

> Here, the epic struggle of man vs. dragon takes its most interior (and perhaps darkest) turn—how to kill the dragon within us—the wyrm, the worm, the disease and ultimately, the death. And language itself is the *bana* or "slayer" of old, in a battle where words must incant a cure (to kill the dragon within us, but not by killing) and extract from language its promise to bring that which is invidious to the surface so that the worms "will out" as it were (ascending layer by layer—as if by their own accord). (And the worms rise to the surface, I imagine,

as if the words were a long rain.) It is almost as if the implicit reasoning of these worm charms is that the slaying of such an adversary (death, disease) were impossible without language's uncanny ability to join "bone to bone, blood to blood, joint to joint" as evinced in another spell to heal serious wounds.

"[W]ords must [. . .] extract from language its promise to bring that which is invidious to the surface": if we expand the category of "invidious" to everything that is hidden, could one find a better definition of one of poetry's special powers of articulation, from ancient to modern? Each age has its own understanding of what is hidden inside us and how it got there.

In English the senses of *charm* are still the ancient Greek ones, as in the passage I quoted earlier from Pindar's ode: grace, warmth, kindness, and perhaps even Grace, Kharis, the minor goddess. But in English a "charm" is also human will that is magically effective over something or someone. It would be impossible to list all the poems of our moment which in effect are new versions of a charm against illness. The very charm (meaning the appeal to one's inner life) of poetry is created, is effected, by reading or hearing such a poem. The poem may not charm illness away, and of course cannot. Yet the charm (the grace and emotional intensity, or warmth) of the poem can itself accomplish a momentary enactment of resistance or respite. And with its inherent power of multiplying the implications of words singly and in combination, of sustaining simultaneous trains of thought, a poem enacts a plenitude of meaning that is a kind of assuaging metonym for the plenitude of health itself—even if what the poem narrates or conveys is not health but the presence of illness. Of the worm.

As one of his examples, Watkins offers an Old Saxon charm against the worm (preserved in a tenth-century manuscript) that I will arrange in lines so we can see (and almost hear) the rhythmic integrity of each line of this chant or song:

> gang ût, nesso, mit nigon nessiklînon,
> ut fana thema marge an that bên,
> fan theme bêne an that flêsg,
> ût fan themo flêsgke an thia hûd,
> ût fan thera hûd an thesa strâla.

(Go out, worm, with nine little worms, / from the marrow to the bone, / from the bone to the flesh, / from the flesh to the skin, / from the skin to this arrow. [Watkins 1995, 522–23])

If the language of the charm could draw the illness out, then a metaphorical *arrow* would slay that worm, or a physical (and metonymical) arrow, a talismanic arrow as from shamanic practice in Tibet. In the arrow, is there a faint trace of a far-traveling Apollo?—not only because charm is a chant or song, and Apollo is the Greek god of poetry and song, but also because, as we see in the *Iliad*, he can send sickness to the Greeks with his arrows and yet is also a divine healer.

The worm and the dragon, ancient poetic figures, are very much alive still, remembered from their use in our inherited Judeo-Christian religious culture, certainly—the redoubtable serpent with legs, mind and language, who is neither killed by the first man nor kills him. The genealogy of the dragon-snake runs for millennia, through ancient mythic systems to *Beowulf* and the English St. George and countless other myths and poems to the various immense, fire-breathing, winged creatures in the films of imaginary worlds that fill movie theaters with lovers of mayhem. I would not be surprised if a census of American poems of, say, 1950 to 2000 turned up many unrepentant, repellant, reptilian monsters.

⊙ 9 ⊙

"Had I a Hundred Mouths,
a Hundred Tongues"

One sonata by Franz Schubert thinks in its own way and another in another way—and in both, the same Schubert is thinking. I remember hearing Hélène Cixous remark that she liked Beethoven's "sentences." What might we say about Shostakovich's symphonic play of one mood against another or Webern's spiky and disconcerting aphorisms, or Duke Ellington's instrumental narratives, or Thelonius Monk's satires? How does Charlie Parker use quotation? What such thinking is like can be analyzed in comment on musical scores, and its moods can be approximately characterized in language; the thinking itself can be transferred to another medium, such as dance; but it cannot be translated. But what *is* the thinking except the performed notes? It can be somewhat described but is not expressible in language. Poetry's medium is the very substance of most thinking—words—so if it pursues that which cannot quite be thought, its pursuit must be strenuous and will use ways of "turning" language to suggest more than words say; if it pursues a not-thinking, it might be either laconic (a word derived from the reserved habits of speech of ancient Spartans) or garrulous (a word derived directly from Latin). Words may be a performance of word-ness and also of wordlessness (nonsense sounds), rather than of meaning. (This was one of the paths of avant-garde poetry in the early twentieth century, and is still followed by some poets.)

I see a continuity between what Curtius called an "inexpressibility topos" in classical and medieval literature (1963, 159) and the attempts of nineteenth- and twentieth-century poets to approach saying something that remains inexpressible or that can be expressed only in ways not subject to paraphrase, not reformulable as discourse. This became one of the characteristic gestures of the poetry of the last 150 or even 200 years. The "topos" is the confession that what the poet wants to say can't be articulated; later poets often acknowledge that they create only an approximation of full expression (with more recently devised kinds of movement of thought and feeling). The inexpressible is not something prohibited but rather an idea or feeling or reality (especially the latter, in ancient and medieval literature, but also, albeit very differently, in Russian Metarealism) that is situated beyond the powers of language.

An illuminating stage of this poetic progress occurred in France in the shared attention to this impulse that we see in the individually distinct work of Baudelaire, Arthur Rimbaud, Gerard de Nerval, Stéphane Mallarmé, and Jules Laforgue. The communicative function of poetry was shifted away from representing lived experience, reason, and the world and toward creating an imaginative experience unique to the poem, by means of evocation, ellipsis, allusion, mood, impressionistically presented feeling, and so on. Later, this poetic mode was pursued by some poets and not by others — developed, pushed further toward vitiating the communication to the reader of anything but a mood, and perhaps a mood not to be found outside the poem. By now, perhaps mood too has been discarded in favor of a kind of unmistakable poem-ness, we might call it, that has no referent or purpose beyond providing the reader with an experience of a particular way of suggesting a meaning that cannot be thought, or of not being meaningful at all in any expected way. Decades ago, Jonathan Culler argued that a (well-chosen) sentence taken literally from a newspaper and arrayed like the lines typical of William Carlos Williams could be found to behave like a poem. A step further would be to argue that any exercise of the poetic function even in its most random-seeming progress from line to line may be found to behave as if it were meaningful, even if the meaning cannot be determined except vaguely. The inexpressible began as a poetic encounter with what language was not adequate to express; the poems of the French poets I mentioned above beat a path to the exploration of that stage, and to what poetic language could propose as almost uninterpretable. Perhaps in recent decades the inexpressible, which has proliferated, has become a way of devising a response to the stimulus of reality without any desire to represent that stimulus; perhaps it has become the devising of what has no connection to any reality outside language. It's not silence; it's related to the endpoint of the work of Beckett and other writers who shared his fascination with the way language can deliquesce or evaporate away from itself, and away from something in us, in our response to the world. For Paul Celan, the articulation of what was inexpressible, of a wrestling with and against inexpressibility, was not an effort to express inaccessible feeling and thought (although he did so), nor was it about attending to another kind of reality that cannot be directly perceived and thus must be approached apophatically; the lived reality to which Celan responded had been overwhelmingly present but had no precedent. As is well known, Celan's experience of his languages, and of what was said and done in those languages, led him to choose to write in that language which had been used as an instrument in the murder of his own parents and millions of others, through edicts, decrees, orders, rules, memoranda, building plans, extensive documentation, "sentences" that produced the physical murderousness. The regulatory function of language having been given a demonic thoroughness and intent, it produced the specifications for construction of machines for manufacturing into nothingness what had been human life, for manufacturing death; it had recorded the success of that manufacturing. Celan recovered his portion of that language from its horrific use, but used it differently. Of his choice of German, he wrote:

> Reachable, near and not lost, there remained in the midst of the losses this one thing: language.
>
> It, the language, remained, not lost, yes in spite of everything. But it had to pass through its own answerlessness, pass through frightful muting, pass through the thousand darknesses of deathbringing speech. It passed through and gave back no words for that which happened; yet it passed through this happening. Passed through and could come to light again, "enriched" by all this. (2001, 395)

Here is a small poem by Yannis Ritsos, "Remolding" (translated by Edmund Keeley). We might entertain a reading of it in which the "you" is Celan, and another in which it is the German language:

> What you call peacefulness or discipline, kindness or apathy,
> what you call a shut mouth with teeth clenched,

indicating the mouth's sweet silence, hiding the clenched teeth,
is only the patient endurance of metal under the useful hammer,
under the terrible hammer—is your knowledge
that you're moving from formlessness to form.

(1979, 17)

The starting point of all this was already present in the most ancient poetry. One version of the topos of the idea of expressing indirectly the inexpressible, or withdrawing from the task entirely, is among the oldest of recoverable ideas about poetry, but it belonged to almost entirely irrecoverable cultures—well before the Greeks—and to very ancient ideas about poetry and gods. As Gregory Nagy has written, the earliest poetry was:

> an art-form grounded in religion. The ostensible audience is divine, not human, so that even human comprehension is not a prime consideration. Words in a prayer might no longer be understood by us mortals, but the prayer remains efficacious and so the words must be right. Granted, [ancient] secular poets also use incomprehensible traditional elements, but they cannot keep their audience if they go beyond mere flavoring of their diction with arcane language. There is not such compunction [however] in Vedic ritual, where arcane language is a precious heirloom that keeps on inspiring language that is even more arcane. (1974, 16–17; my brackets)

Also ancient is the idea of something inexpressible simply because it exceeds human powers to convey it. In the *Iliad*, the epic poet wished to honor the glory of heroes and also remember the due fame of the multitude of Greeks who had come in their black ships to the shore of Troy, but there were so many of them that he said: "Tell me now, you Muses [. . .] who were the leaders and lords of the Danaans. But the multitude I could not tell or name, not even if ten tongues were mine and ten mouths, and a voice unwearying, and the heart within me were of bronze, unless the Muses of Olympus, daughters of Zeus who bears the aegis, call to my mind all those who came beneath Ilios" (*Iliad* 2.484–92; Homer 2003, I:97). Pindar made a similar gesture when he wrote, for the purpose of a metaphorical comparison, that he "would not know how to state a clear number for the pebbles of the sea" (Olympian 13.46; Pindar 1997, 1:30;).

In his *Aeneid*, Vergil upped Homer's numbers when he commented, in the midst of narrating Aeneas' journey to the underworld, that the multitude there of the dead who are punished cannot be counted. As John Dryden translated this passage (his *Aeneid* 6.851–54; Vergil's 6.625–27): "Had I a hundred Mouths, a hundred Tongues, / And Throats of Brass, inspir'd with Iron Lungs, / I could not half those horrid Crimes repeat: / Nor half the Punishments those Crimes have met" (Vergil 1997, 170).

I don't think we should too quickly rule that the category of Homeric and Vergilian inexpressibility because of sheer quantity is so different from the inexpressibility of what is less definably "beyond words," syntax, or even fragmentary utterances. After all, it's not the factual number of the Greeks at Troy that is inexpressible but rather the sense of awe in the poet, and perhaps in the men too, at the magnitude of the war and of the suffering and death, and also of courage and especially *kleos* of the great warriors, which, if it finds its poet, will be undying. And it did find its poet, and it has been undying. (This scene of a massive Greek gathering at Troy of ships, men, arms, chariots, and horses is the one that Sappho played against in her fragment 16, rejecting any of those as the emblem of the most glorious thing in the world, and preferring instead the remembrance of the step and face of one young woman, who is absent. Sappho conceded to Homer only a challenging deference, I think, when she evoked not the famed Greeks at Troy but "the host of cavalry [...] infantry [...] the Lydians' chariots and armed infantry" — the army of the Persians, the worst of Greek enemies. By substituting an otherwise unknown or even fictional young woman for the expected image of male Greek military power and glory, she veered away from the expected idea of what her word, Greek *kallistos* ["most beautiful, most excellent, finest, best, noblest"], meant and replaced it with ideals of feminine beauty and desire.)

Modern poetic obliquity, "displacement" (as in Freud's theory of dreams), metaphor, metonymy, and so on, are devices of thought which, from the individual and social complexity of our unconscious, allow what cannot or is not to be said directly, what cannot be thought or even felt directly, to be brought into articulation. A poetic trope "turns" articulation to indirectness. "Slant," Emily Dickinson called it. In Catullus' Latin translation (his poem 51) of part of Sappho's fragment 31, he either did not know or he subtracted the last lines of her poem and added a stanza that swerves sharply away from his subject. The poem does not say why. The force that pushes the poem off its path is what is inexpressible.

I track the words for their meaning in my English, and I cannot represent the subtleties—typical of poetry composed in highly inflected languages like Latin or Greek or Russian—of how the sequencing of the words creates tensions of meaning and additional meaning because it differs from the order of the overall sense of a phrase or sentence:

> I see him as the equal of a god,
> That man—if it's permitted to surpass the gods, he does—
> Who sitting across from you looks at you over
>   And over and listens to you
>
> Laughing sweetly . . . which rips out of me
> Every sense I have, for from the instant
> I looked at you, Lesbia, nothing is enough for me
>   [missing line]
>
> But tongue thickens, thin flame ripples
> Along the limbs, the ears din
> With their own noise, [my] twin eye-lights
>   are cloaked by the night.
>
> Doing nothing, Catullus, is what gets to you.
> You enjoy it, you love it, too much.
> Long before now, idleness has destroyed kings
>   And fortunate cities!

The first-person pronoun drops out of the poem after the first two stanzas. The bodily sensations of intense desire are articulated without their belonging to anyone; then in the last stanza the poet addresses himself, or, in a way, the poem addresses Catullus, as "you." A complete reversal of perspective has been achieved by the way the pronoun transforms the voice of the poem into the voice of someone else addressing Catullus.

❋

Nagy's distinction between ordinary language and an arcane language of the gods that men cannot understand is perhaps still echoed in Russian to the extent that "[t]he language of the Russian Orthodox Church is Church Slavonic, a liturgical language with its own alphabet, developed originally in the ninth century from Slavic dialects spoken in Thessaly and Bulgaria, which is only partly comprehensible for Russians" (Tolstoy 2008, 1238n25). This is not the problem of poetic obscurity (which, however, is related) but rather a suggesting with words used in particular ways of what simply cannot be said in ordinary discourse, by a priestly caste that has maintained a language marked as special and thus appropriate for ritual. (We might say that religion began with poetry, and required poetry for millennia, and uses it still in hymns and prayers, but that later poetry has required religion only here and there in modern times.) The modern problem of poetic obscurity has nothing to do with the sacred versus the everyday, but such a polarity is re-created somewhat by our trying to represent the movement of thought and feeling—belonging to us, and yet not, in that so much of it is inaccessible to us in the unconscious, where creativity begins, that it cannot be articulated in everyday discourse. It requires poetic devices and simultaneities.

Confronted by the poetry of Charles Baudelaire, Gérard de Nerval, and others, the nineteenth-century French critic Charles Augustin Sainte-Beuve became aware that poetic thinking had perceptibly changed. I don't assume that this change in poetic thinking represents a change in all human thinking, but rather that it demonstrates that poetry can express, indirectly, that which previously had not been conceived, or had been considered inexpressible, because of earlier understandings of what thought is, and because of poetic convention, too. (Surely English poets of the eighteenth century had nightmares as irrational and awful as the ones Fulke Greville described much earlier, but they could not regard them as suitable subjects of poetry.) Change in poetic thinking must almost always be a combination of a genuinely new exploration and at the same time an echoing of aspects of past poetic thinking, for each change immediately produces its newly visible precursors, whose work is clarified or intensified in some aspect that earlier was probably seen—if seen at all—as minor or eccentric. Each turn in the many distinct histories of poetry in many languages has added some resources, purposes, and modes to the composing of poems, and has subtracted others. Precursors are valued because of the artistic practices of their successors. (I'm only rephrasing something that Eliot [1960] said in his 1919 essay "Tradition and the Individual Talent," and that Jorge Luis Borges [2010] put somewhat differently in "Kafka and His Precursors," first published in 1951). But necessarily, only giants can create or unveil their precursors; in part, they become giants by doing so. All other writers are cicadas.

In the nineteenth century, by exploration, invention, and changes in poetic conventions, English and French poetry, along with poetry in some other places, was transformed from a discourse that had most often (but not always) moved more or less logically or by narrative from one moment to the next. Yet with the advantage of our methods of reading and our understanding of the mind, we can see simultaneities and movement by association in poems by poets who themselves did not see them with conscious awareness, because even before there was any artistic awareness of the full powers of a mind concentrated both consciously and unconsciously on its task, artists, like other makers and builders, must have worked this way. The eighteenth-century emotional and intuitive intensities in Rousseau's *Confessions* seem surprisingly modern; but then so do those in the confessions of Augustine. Pindar too had moved portions of his odes by association, but out of a different mentality of such movement. He did it not so much psychologically (and yet there are subtle markers of this, too, in my view) but by repeatedly swerving in the sequence of his topics, registers of diction, points of view, and more, which must have created in the performance of the ode a sense of improvisation and immediacy, of a song that was somehow spontaneous. In poetry of almost any era, one can find movement by association underneath the first-level linking of one thought to the next by logic, narrative, or sequence of thought or feeling.

The development of associative poetic thinking happened earlier in France than in England or America. Later, the Modernist poets working in English — drawing on some of that earlier French poetry and unearthing precursor poetics from the work of all the past — shifted poetic composition toward montage with longer leaps of association, toward fragment, linguistic excess, the etymological or morphological use of words, and other techniques, along with what came to be called by some critics "pseudo-reference" and "pseudo-statement."

And in avant-garde movements in several European languages, poets explored the possibilities of not making discursive sense at all.

The epicentric poem of new effects and new movement of thought in poetry might have been the sonnet titled "El Desdichado" (c. 1853) — this Spanish word means "the unfortunate one" or "miserable one" — by Gérard de Nerval.

Je suis le ténébreux, — le veuf, — l'inconsolé,
Le prince d'Aquitaine à la tour abolie:
Ma seule *étoile* est morte, — et mon luth constellé
Porte le *Soleil noir* de la *Mélancolie.*

Dans la nuit du tombeau, toi que m'as consolé,
Rends-moi la Pausilippe et la mer d'Italie,
La *fleur* qui plaisait tant à mon coeur désolé,
Et la treille où la pampre à la rose s'allie.

Suis-je Amour ou Phébus? . . . Lusignan ou Biron?
Mon front est rouge encor du baiser de la Reine;
J'ai rêvé dans la grotte où nage la syrène. . . .

Et j'ai deux fois vainqueur traversé l'Acheron:
Modulant tour à tour sur la lyre d'Orphée
Les soupirs de la sainte et les cris de la fée.

(Nerval 1993, 645)

A first-level decoding into English would read something like this:

I am the dark one, the widowed one, the inconsolable one,
The prince of Aquitaine at the ruined tower,
My only *star* is dead, and my constellate [covered with stars] lute
Bears the *Black sun* of *Melancholy* [we might say depression].

In the night of the tomb, you, who consoled me,
Give me back Posillipo and the Italian Sea,
The *flower* that so used to please my grieving heart,
And the arbor where the vine and the rose intertwine.

Am I Eros or Phoebus? . . . Lusignan or Biron?
My forehead is still red from the Queen's kiss;
I dreamed in the cave where the siren [or mermaid] swims . . .

> And twice I have crossed the Acheron, victorious:
> Modulating by turns on the lyre of Orpheus
> The saint's sighing and the fairy's cries.

In Nerval's poem, allusion and pseudo-allusion become the dominant poetic device. They are constellated so that their combined effect
is more important than their meanings taken individually. (It's a similar effect of simultaneities, in part, that Denise Levertov is echoing
when she mentions a *"constellation* of perceptions" [see chap. 4].) The
dense allusiveness and rapid swerving of this poem, simply as a pace
and manner of thought, may first differ more in degree than in kind
from Pindar's allusiveness and instant shifts of direction and tone of
voice. But something else is happening here, too—an attending to,
or a performance of, or a creating of, a movement of thought with no
single direction or goal set or achieved. By contrast, Pindar had his object (or objectives) clearly in sight—praise for, reverence of, and good
stories about gods and heroes, the offering of flattering genealogies of
the victor and traditional apothegms and ideas, and establishing his
own status as a preeminent maker of song.

A stark contrast, even an internal dissonance, is created by the way
the strict sonnet structure, metrical consistency, and rhymes of the
poem remain traditional and predictable, while inside that structure
the conceptual and emotional movement from image to image, allusion to allusion, is unpredictable and perhaps without poetic precedent. The poem mostly alludes to what it does not identify. It seems
private, associative by links that it does not intend us to know.

The poem itself is the "constellated lute"—the lute a metonym for
the poem itself, so this poem is melody, the "song," that the lute accompanies. The proper names and capitalized nouns form the "constellation." Perhaps (in a somewhat Russian way?) the allusions are
not alternatives between which we cannot decide but are all to be
held in mind together for the shape they make—like a constellation
of stars in the night sky. They may be intended to form an unthinkable
idea that is inexpressible directly. The poem cannot say what it wants
to say. (Baudelaire was clearer about wanting what cannot be made
clear when he wrote in his 1861 sonnet "Obsession": "O night!—how
you would please me if you had no stars / Speaking with light a language already known! / What I seek is the void, pure darkness, de-
nuded nothingness!" [Baudelaire 1975, 75–76; my translation].)

Nerval's poetic thinking moves very fast from one image or allusion to the next, from rhyme to rhyme, even from word to word, in what may seem non sequiturs rather than a "logic" of syntax, line, narrative, setting, or argument. Is there meaning in the movement from formal structural element to formal structural element (from octet to sestet or stanza to stanza)? If so, it's at a very deep associative level. As an old professor of mine once said, "The specifically modern element of this poem *is* its obscurity." No wonder T. S. Eliot must nod to Nerval by quoting the second line of this sonnet at the end of *The Waste Land*, almost like a credit at the end of a movie, since *The Waste Land*—all the more so after Ezra Pound edited it by making many cuts—was the first great montage poem. It may well be that many aspects of modern and even postmodern poetry descend and develop from the effects produced in this one poem by Nerval. By later poetry Nerval's poem was made even more visible as a precursor.

An early and acute response to the shift in consciousness from the classical to the romantic and beyond to the characteristically modern, which in effect developed out of a European and English preoccupation with the fragment, with consciousness itself, with intense states of feeling, with indirect, even inexplicable movement of thought and feeling, can be found in the article by Sainte-Beuve, originally published in April 1866, at which I hinted earlier. For Sainte-Beuve, the greatest French writing had come from such neoclassicists as the seventeenth-century poetic dramatist Jean Racine, who was among Sainte-Beuve's paragons of literary ideals and achievement, and to whom he dedicated one of his widely read newspaper essays, "The Last Five Months of the Life of Racine." At the end of this homage, Sainte-Beuve turned surprisingly to poetry in general:

Our ideas of poetry have in effect changed almost entirely in the last few years. It is no longer a question of classic or romantic, if you wish; one is dealing with something quite different from an ornamental cockade, from the parts and the whole, from forms and colors: one is dealing with the very basis and substance of judgment, of the dispositions and customary principles in virtue of which one feels and one is affected. Might I succeed in describing this new state, this direction now shared by so many intelligent persons? In earlier times, during that correct literary period called classic, one esteemed the best poet as him who had composed the most perfect work, the poem that was most beautiful, clearest, most pleasant to read, most fully realized in every way—the *Aeneid, Jerusalem*, a beautiful tragedy. Today one sees something else. For us, the greatest poet is he who, in his works, has given the most to his reader to imagine and to dream, who has most excited the reader himself to participate in making the poem [*poétiser*]. The greatest poet is not he who has done the best: it is he who suggests the most, he of whom at first sight one does not really know what he wanted to say and express, and who leaves one a great much to desire, to explicate, to study, a great much to complete in one's own turn. There is nothing that excites and feeds our admiration more than these poets of the incomplete and the inexhaustible, because henceforth, one wishes poetry to be almost as much in the reader as in the author. (1880, 390–91; my translation)

By 1866, then, at least to Sainte-Beuve, it was clear that some poems would be valued for qualities of *incompleteness*, for what they did not or could not say; such poetry invites and even requires the reader to (try to) complete the poet's articulation. Later in Sainte-Beuve's essay he implied that criticism itself was being led by such poetry to go back to "Faust, Beatrice, Mignon, Don Juan, Hamlet, these figures of double or triple meaning, subjects for discussion, mysterious in some way, indefinite, indeterminate, extensible in some manner, perpetually changing and mutable" (391–92). What Sainte-Beuve suggested about the new "greatest poet" is that he floats undecided simultaneities toward the reader. The French critic, he believed, would also have to reexamine such literary characters as Faust, Hamlet, and others by looking at what had seemed obscure in their fictional nature, exceeding as it does what can be analyzed or understood as clearly revealed. That is, the critic could return to earlier poetry with an eye toward reading the qualities of the indefinite or indeterminate. (Again we see how precursors or precursor qualities of poetry come into view for later readers.)

Signing only with the initial F., and writing of himself in the third person, Freud published in 1920 a brief essay on the "prehistory of the technique of analysis," in which he included a quotation from another book:

In 1857, Dr. J. J. Garth Wilkinson, more noted as a Swedenborgian mystic and poet than as a physician, published a volume of mystic doggerel verse written by what he considered "a new method," the method of "Impression." "A theme is chosen or written down," he stated; "as soon as this is done the first impression upon the mind which succeeds the act of writing the title is the beginning of the evolution of that theme, no matter how strange or alien the word or phrase may seem." "The first mental movement, the first word that comes" is "the response to the mind's desire for the unfolding of the subject."

Freud added: "Those who are familiar with psycho-analytic literature will recall at this point the interesting passage in Schiller's correspondence with Körner in which (1788) the great poet and thinker recommends anyone who desires to be productive to adopt the method of free association." And he told of another very early instance of free association in writing from 1823, quoting the German writer Ludwig Börne: " 'Take a few sheets of paper and for three days on end write down, without fabrication ["deliberation"?] or hypocrisy, everything that comes into your head' " (Freud 1959, 101–3; my brackets).

If an external context is lost, as with Pindar, obscurity is a result of allusiveness and elision regarding now unfamiliar or ambiguous referents, and of lost poetic purposes and social practices. When poetic thinking moves through allusions, images, sounds, and verbal gestures rather than language that is more discursive or narrative, obscurity is the upshot of that poetic technique of floating simultaneities and indeterminate choices toward the reader and thinking by "free" association. (While free association is less constrained by self-censoring, it cannot be entirely free, simply because it emerges from a psyche that always is constrained by prohibitions; hence its interest to the psychoanalyst and its richness for the reader.)

If we think about incompleteness, obscurity, and ellipsis (in this case, the absence of connectives between stages of feeling or thought in a poem), the gaps between words and their unfamiliar or unknowable referents, the poet's attempt to say what is not quite sayable, to discover allusions and images which as a *constellation* achieve a feeling or idea that the poet can't otherwise articulate but that the reader can't quite bring together into a single train of thought, to offer the poem to the reader as a gesture rather than as a fully communicative utterance, then we're still partly within the frame of remote antiquity's poetics of a language that the poet finds *necessary* even though it cannot be understood on the reader's plane of thought and feeling.

For us that different plane of thought is not constituted by the minds of gods. At times and in some poets and readers the different plane of thought may be that of what can be called the secular sacred—a thinking without articulation, an intuiting in braids or knots or webs of feeling that we experience in the presence of "that which *compels* the poet's, the writer's, attention," and the reader's. Those words are from W. H. Auden's essay "Making, Knowing and Judging," about the sacred imagination. He surveys the imagination's response to a range of psychologically, not doctrinally, sacred objects, events, and ideas. "Some sacred beings seem to be sacred to all imaginations at all times. The Moon, for example, Fire, Snakes and those four important beings which can only be defined in terms of non-being: Darkness, Silence, Nothing, Death." At the other end of the scale, he notes that a "sitting room is not merely a place to sit in; it is also a shrine for father's chair" (1968, 55–56, 59). Linda McCarriston's portrait-poem "My Mother's Chair: 1956" sacralizes the merely secular household chair of the woman who sat in it to recover herself from the traps of exhaustion and suffering both physical and emotional: "As a child beats a stick / on the cage of an animal, so a certain / world was playing on her soul" (2002, 18–19).

The sacred (religious or secular) might be thought of as residing in the human unconscious, or in the mind of language itself, as a whole—all its possibilities not of form and relation but of expressive meaning and of stance toward external reality and inner life. Some believe that the sacred can be named (cataphatically), but even such naming may be thinkable only in clusters of those knots or braids or webs of feeling and thought that straightforward language cannot represent. If they could be disentangled they would not mean what they mean *as tangles.*

But inexpressibility does not always present itself as failure of expression. An apparently simple original poem, in simple language, may create an effect of the inexpressible because of how the simplicity and even the grace (*kharis*) are at the edge of an inexpressibility. Perhaps I am trying to gather too much in my net, but I will offer for consideration Goethe's most famous poem, his little 1780 "Über allen Gipfeln" (from "Wandrers Nachtlied II"; "Over all the peaks," from "Wanderer's Nightsong"), which evokes an overflowing of feeling that remains, or that is expressed so as to seem, serene:

> Über allen Gipfeln
> Ist Ruh,
> In allen Wipfeln
> Spürest du
> Kaum einen Hauch;
> Die Vögelein schweigen im Walde.
> Warte nur, balde
> Ruhest du auch.
>
> (Goethe 2012, 37)

An inescapably linear decoding without achieving any simultaneity of braided overtones, ambiguities—or amphibologies—and more: "Over all the peaks [heights, hills] / there is rest [stillness, peace, quiet, sleep, calm.] / In all the treetops / you follow [discover, feel, experience] / scarcely a breath [breeze]. / The little birds are silent in the forest. / Only [but] wait, soon / you too will rest [sleep]."

The simplicity of expression that the poem seems to create is simultaneously both a calm effect and a dark thought sweetened by that simplicity. A graceful translation might be possible, but is it possible to make it say in English or another language what it says to the German reader or listener? Translation—as is often the case—seems to hold the poem back from its approach toward the inexpressible; translation often only substitutes banal expressibility. In this light, the German poem seems inexplicably potent as poetic thinking. And in closing with this poem, perhaps I have come to the near side of the shifting border on the side of which poetry pursues what it cannot say.

The idea that when the poet is writing, composition is happily beyond any complete supervision of the poet's conscious mind comes fully into play in the Romantic movement. But consider the opening of this victory ode by Pindar (Olympian 10.1–3), written sometime not so long after the year 476 BCE. Pindar calls to the Muse—sort of:

> The victor at Olympus: read it to me —
> it's the son of Archestratos — from where, in my mind,
> it's written, for I owe him sweet song
> and had forgotten.

Pindar's first strophe apologizes for having taken too long to compose this very song. It had been commissioned to celebrate Hagesidamos, who had won the boy's boxing competition and whose family and town were very far from Pindar, in the southern tip of Italy.

The complexity and variety of Pindar's odes suggest that the invention of writing, which before his time had already preserved the Homeric epics as compilations of episodes, had also begun, by the time Pindar was composing his odes, to inflect the process of composition itself. Poets could write and revise on a wax tablet and "publish" by means of inked texts on papyrus. The process of composition must have remained both mental, by memory, and written, in stages. Writing made it possible for Pindar to send a commissioned victory ode to be learned, choreographed, and sung elsewhere; and in fact, he mentions this in an ode, and among his metaphors for poetry itself, he uses the ship: "This song is being sent like Phoenician / merchandise over the gray sea" (Pythian 2.67–68; Pindar 1997, 1:239); "My heart, to what alien / headland are you turning aside my ship's course?" (Nemean 3.26–27; Pindar 1997, 2:25).

Commenting on Olympian 10, William Race says that "the opening strophe and antistrophe use the language of business (record-keeping, debts, interest, repayment) to discuss the lateness of this ode" (Pindar 1997, 1:163). But the idea of what's written in the mind is not limited to Pindar's playful use of the mundane metaphor of a debt owed.

Elsewhere Pindar calls himself "a private individual embarked upon a public mission" (Olympian 13.49; Pindar 1997, 1:195) — that is, a poet whose work, however much it makes use of traditional materials and however much it conforms to the expectations created by its genre, is uniquely his own yet is created for the sake of public occasions. Glenn Patten has argued that from our perspective this passage about a name written already in Pindar's mind is about subjectivity: "Pindar undertakes here the first attempt in European literature to understand the relationship between writing and subjectivity, and he does so by linking writing with memory in a metaphor that occurs in this poem for the first time. The text connects it with two requests, to read out a name (*anágnōté moi* ['read to me'], 1) and to find a place (*póthi* ['where'], 2). The question of the whereabouts of writing foregrounds its spatiality; the request for reading out loud implies that mere writing alone does not suffice to create living remembrance" (2009, 219).

Gregory Nagy has analyzed the metaphorical meaning of Pindar's verb *anagignōskō* by its component parts (the prefix *ana-* plus the main verb) as to

> know again, recognize. [. . .] To "read" is to "know again" by reperforming to oneself and potentially to others the last in a series of preexisting performances—this last one having been written down rather than spoken, whereas the previous ones had been spoken. The act of *reading* here is a metaphor for the activation, through public performance, of the composition. To *know again* the composition, that is, to *recognize* it, is to be performing it. Such a *recognition* takes place in the mind of both performer and audience as one hears the words being read out loud. In Pindar's *Olympian* 10, the song starts with the command to "read out loud" (verb *ana-gignōskō: anágnōte* 10.1) the Olympic winner, who is "written down" inside the *phrēn* "mind." Thus the image of reading out loud can even serve as the metaphor for the public performance of a composition, and the image of writing, as the metaphor for the composition itself. (1990, 171)

If performance can be a metaphor (it could also be a metonym) for composition, and the mind is a space within which knowledge, memory, and technique are directly accessible only in part, and accessible otherwise only indirectly, then the model of poetic composition implied by Pindar is as complex as anything we might imagine in present-day terms. Pindar asks the Muse to read the name to him, as if he himself cannot do so. Yet he is only pretending that he is unable to do so, in order to give his ode more of the illusion of spontaneity when later it is performed. It's the spatial metaphor that is so interesting: the name is "written" in his mind where he cannot get access to it. He has imagined a place in the mind where some part of his own knowledge is inaccessible to him.

So I will surprise no one if I say that Pindar's implicit concept of subjectivity seems to me already to include the idea—even though no one would be able to *analyze* it for many centuries—of the unconscious. It certainly seems to include the idea of what has been called the preconscious—information that we can remember if we try, or if reminded, even though we can't bring it to mind before that effort. In the midst of the somewhat disconcerting advent of writing, this poet, drawing so much from earlier poetry and traditions that had been preserved and transmitted orally, registers a sense of a concerted working of different kinds of thinking in the creation of poetry.

In his world, poetry's very purpose is to guarantee remembrance!—of the victor's *name*, first of all, which Pindar pretends to have forgotten, as if illustrating that even for the poet, it is not memory alone but rather poetry, the ode, that preserves the name through time. The process of composing that ode enables the mind to articulate remembrance as it would not otherwise do, in the fame-sustaining way. Pindar creates an ode which in choreographed performance also choreographs knowledge and feeling for his listeners. He does not give them the victor's name—which everyone who is listening to the performance of course knows—right away. (Nor does he give it to us—the readers who validate his purpose and his promise, these many centuries later, that he has successfully preserved the fame of the victor.) In other odes, too, Pindar holds off naming the victor, but in this one his chorus, voicing the poem on his behalf and on their own, first explicitly say that the name has eluded memory. There follows a delicious delay not of information but of feeling. In line 2 Pindar names the victor's father, and then, in line 13, the town, and then finally, in line 17, the victorious youth. One imagines that moment of sociable pride in the audience. The song's unfolding in the dimension of time requires the listeners, who have gathered at a ceremony in Western Lokria to hear their own chorus perform it, to wait for the moment when the boy—he is standing there before them—is named.

Homer was blind: in the mythology of poetry the absence of physical vision is often twinned with heightened awareness of the sounds and rhythms of language. Everyday thinking and feeling belong to the upright head, so let's imagine that Pindar when composing this ode closed his eyes and inclined his head, forward or back. And he asked the Muse (elusive, both singular and multiple) to *read* to him a name which at some earlier moment he had evidently *written* in his mind. Then he can begin—as if he were performing the ode himself, spontaneously, rather than composing it beforehand. These first lines of the ode are a choral performance of a crafted simulation of a mnemonic performance — and then, *in* performance by others, the lines become a crafted simulation of the presence of the poet.

❋

Even among ancient Greek scholars — the authors of the often isolated comments on poems and poets that have come down to us as marginalia ("scholia") — there was debate about whether the first-person poem was to be understood as being voiced by the poet or not. There were other — impersonal — voices in a song or poem, too. There were traditions that spoke *through* poets: "Hesiod," "Homer." A poet also could inhabit the tradition of an earlier, known poet's work, as in the case of the many poems written imitatively and attributed to Anakreon, centuries after his death. We are uncertain about Theognis, one of the earliest poets, almost 1,440 lines of whose work survives, but much of it written by other poets who were collapsed by later readers into one putative author. Some of Sappho's poems (fragments) seem very modern, individual, and psychological, like the famous fragment 31 that Catullus translated, "He appears to me the equal of a god, that man . . . ," but this seemingly subjective poem about the bodily sensations of desire and jealousy in the speaker, "Sappho," is also deeply embedded in traditional ideas about an epiphany of a god (echoed by the Greek verb for "appear") and about mythological bridegrooms and brides; the description by "Sappho" of how she feels physically, as if she were dying, echoes myths of erotic initiation (Nagy 2013, 109–39). Arkhilokhos (whose work survives in a few fragments), the earliest lyric poet, presents a very interesting case of uncertainty, from our perspective, about who is speaking in the poem. He lived from around 680 BCE to around 650 BCE; he may have died in battle. We have a fair amount of information about him, and we know that "much of the language of [his] poetry belongs to the epic tradition" (Campbell 2003, 136–39). His poems are intimate and first person, sometimes surprisingly modern sounding. The unique virulence of his satire made Pindar call him "Arkhilokhos the blamer" (Pythian 2.55). Yet it seems that the individuality implied by what Pindar knew about him cannot be regarded as certain. His well-known poem (frag. 6) on throwing his shield away (which implies that he ran from battle) was sufficiently compelling to three later poets, Alkaios (also in fragments), Anakreon, and Horace, for them to copy it, claiming to have thrown their shields aside, too; or alternatively, they used a psychological rhetorical figure—we might call it—that was older than Arkhilokhos: the cowardice that proves the prudence of the good warrior. And yet, on the other hand, the individuality of the poetic self (real or fictional) in the four lines by Arkhilokhos, their mood still fresh today, suggests that whatever individuality is, it did not have to wait until the Renaissance, looking backward at antiquity, rediscovered it, or until Early Modern English writers, anticipating it, looked forward to modernity. And the resolve of Yeats, Eliot, Pound, and others to write from outside the expectation of Romantic self-presentation reminded us again, not for the first time in the history of poetry, to consider the difference between the person who writes the poem and the implicit "image" of that person that the poem presents.

David Campbell has noted that D. L. Page, one of the great editors of ancient lyric poetry, "suggests that those iambic and trochaic poems [by Arkhilokhos] in which there is little or no traditional element were composed with the help of writing, whereas the elegiac pieces and others in which traditional language is predominant were oral compositions. This may be true, and it seems certain that Archilochus' poems, especially those which were appropriate to only a single occasion, survived simply because they were written down by Archilochus or a friend" (2003, 139). It might be that the use of writing in poetic composition must imply in itself a greater individuality of the poet than could ever be possible in oral traditions. (Even the ghazal, with its poetic "signature" in the form of the poet's unique name in the last line, has been subject to further variation by anyone who sings it.) And through the centuries of poetry and commentary both in antiquity and in the modern world, poetic individuality, as it is caught in the poem itself, cannot have been exactly the same as the psychological individuality of the person who wrote the poem. There is that self-alienation of which I wrote in chapter 2, which was explicitly formulated by Rimbaud in the nineteenth century, and yet I think it has been enacted by poets, however subtly, for millennia.

Only particular portions of the poet are present in a victory ode—that seems obvious, because the genre requires other elements to be present too that are impersonal. And yet it would seem very unlikely that the configuration of the impersonal material in Pindar's odes and even certain aspects of the language of the ode were exactly like that in the odes of the other choral poets whose work has disappeared. Bakkhylides, the one remaining substantial comparison, does not seem to be Pindar. So maybe I'll be permitted to suggest now that, as it seems to me, what happened after poetry had emerged from collaborative traditions (Hesiod and Homer), and even alongside later collaborative traditions like the poems written in imitation of Anakreon, is that individuality of poetic composition was secured by at least some poets. I don't know if or how they particularly prized this, or were aware of it—they might not have been, as a modern poet would be. Of all the continuities of poetry, this one seems right for the conclusion of this exhibition of some varieties of poetic thinking. The details of individuality in ancient poems and in modern ones may have not the relationship of fact or of fiction to the historical person of the poet, but instead a relationship of analogy and of a psychic investment, rather than a representation, of experience, emotional repertoire, and impulse.

Even in the ancient world, an aspect of the poet, an identity, a mask, is what the poet's poems inescapably create, just as most of the modern world's novels—of Dickens or Faulkner or Morrison, or Maxwell or Goyen or Cixous—suggest in the aggregate of each writer's work an idea of the identity or of an "authorial mind" that can be somewhat distinct from the mind of the person. In contemporary American poetry and fiction, we may have gotten as close to a full overlap as is humanly possible, because of some qualities of the way we are formed as subjects of American media and history and behavior, drawing us toward making nearly every individual action an audition for status, an offering for public *consumption*.

Also, the nature of the psyche rather than the rules of art require that poet and poetic self be somewhat or very different. The achievement of the concerted, complex simultaneities of meaning in a literary work simply exceeds what conscious deliberateness can do. Not only an intuitive synthesis of elements of practiced craft but also aspects of identity pour from the unconscious into the composing of poems. A poet could be psychoanalyzed with poems as additional evidence, and a body of poetry could be psychoanalyzed (after a fashion) with the poet as additional evidence, but there is no reason to suppose that the resulting profiles would be exactly the same. It was appropriate and wise for us as readers to have separated ourselves from interpreting poems as factually autobiographical documents, even though so many poets invite us to do so. The person and the poetic self are not likely to be drastically different from each other, but even that is possible. It is a dance of three: the poet's linguistic energy, craft absorbed into the intuition, and feeling and thought; the poem itself, its nature as genre, gesture, and form, as a formal "other"; and as they move, finding their images and their articulation together while holding hands with the third dancer: language itself.

Afterword

A DEMONSTRATION

How would I, with ancientness on my mind, as well as aspects of poetic thinking from earlier in this book, read a poem by a modern poet? Let me illustrate with what might seem an improbable example, a simple, modest poem by William Carlos Williams.

This untitled poem is a section of Williams' sequence *Spring and All* (1923), his vigorous poetically revolutionary rejoinder to Eliot's poetically revolutionary *The Waste Land* (1922). In *Spring and All*, Williams set out to refute, to supplant, Eliot's poem, to correct its lack of American materials and language and its superfluity of European ones. Two different ideas of starting over: one using diverse cultural materials from the past and extraordinarily allusive language (pseudo-allusive, sometimes), the other using everyday stuff, almost the roadside trash of America, and a simple vocabulary inflected from time to time by the absurd. Eliot went against the grain of America, and Williams, acting on behalf of the American language and American realities, went against the grain of Eliot. Both poems presented a wealth of poetic possibilities that have proven to be endlessly fruitful for later poets. And this contest, if we are to judge by the poetry published today, was won by Williams, for better and worse.

Eliot looked back at antiquity several times in *The Waste Land*. Yet Williams did so too, albeit in a way that is not nearly as noticeable, and cannot be accounted for by what we might suppose could have been his conscious intention, for this poem runs a little against Williams' belief that he was coining new poetic usage. Here's the poem:

Pink confused with white
flowers and flowers reversed
take and spill the shaded flame
darting it back
into the lamp's horn

petals aslant darkened with mauve

red where in whorls
petal lays its glow upon petal
round flamegreen throats

petals radiant with transpiercing light
contending
> above

the leaves
reaching up their modest green
from the pot's rim

and there, wholly dark, the pot
gay with rough moss
> (Williams 2011, 13)

The reader follows a panning view from top blossoms down to flower-pot. (Williams' "Young Sycamore" describes from bottom to top a hardy, weedy, even insolently energetic sort of tree that out of urban pavement has risen as a growth of green. The lines of that poem go down the page, of course, while the poem raises its imaginative gaze from the foot of the tree to its top. The contrary motions contradict and complement each other. Paradox loves poetry, as Pindar might say.) In this poem of the flowerpot, feeling modulates from a real, not mental, con-fusing of pink and white — vibrant but not transcendent, only "transpierced" by an apparently antique lamplight — to the gaiety of humble, lowly moss. As the mind's eye moves down, colors (pink, white, mauve, red, "flamegreen") dim to "modest green."

This poem says that modesty has its grace. By the deftness and im-plications of its language, in a subtle way Williams' poem still brings to us that modest divinity, the ancient Greek *kharis*, the grace of an "unsolicited kindness." A little celebration, the poem figures *itself* as the modest pot and leaves and flowers, owning up to its own modesty.

In addition to the pink and white there are other pairs: the color of the petals and the green light from the oil lamp (with a chimney of green glass?); the living flower and the manufactured lamp (the chimney's color might resemble that of horn, or I suppose might even be made of it); flowers and flowers reversed; and so on, including the gay insouciance of the humble plant and even that of the dark pot and the rough moss. Imagistic contrast loves poetry, too.

Words have double meanings: "confused" and "con-fused," "reversed" and "re-versed." And what could be older than the poetic theme of flowers? (Our word *anthology* still preserves within it the Greek word *ánthos*, "flower"; "the delighting flower of my hymn," Pindar wrote [Olympian 6.105].) Repeated phonemes give the language a richer sound than it may seem to have on first reading or hearing, and they vouch for the deliberateness (conscious and unconscious) of the poet's choices. (Much of this, in the poet whose mind and ear are trained to hear the *sounds* of the words we say every day while the rest of us hear only their *meaning*, requires of that poet no conscious working out.) Thus "flowers and flowers reversed" repeats a whole word with all its phonemes, and then repeats yet again the *-ers* in "reversed." "Take and spill the shaded flame" repeats the long *ā*, the *s*, the *l*, and the *d*, and picks up from the previous line the consonant cluster *fl* and repeats that, too. And so on through the poem — vowels and consonants sounded twice or more, chiming like faint, very small, bells.

The repetition of phonemes can also produce rhythms, but those of speech stress are much more emphatic. To my ear, the most noticeable repeated rhythmic pattern — in this "free verse" poem which might have been thought not to produce any patterns at all, but does — is a sequence of four syllables in the pattern *stressed*-unstressed-unstressed-*stressed* that I have pointed out several times as a choriamb, the ancient metrical figure in Greek that surprisingly shows up in English too as a pattern easy to recognize (without needing any metrical terminology to justify its existence): "Juicy Couture."

In ancient Greek, the pattern was based on vowel length, which we English speakers can't hear, and which, several centuries after Pindar and Sophokles, even the Greeks couldn't. So: flowers and flow(-ers), flowers reversed, darting it back, petals aslant and darkened with mauve (two in a row), red where in whorls, gay with rough moss (and a few more, subtler). In English *meter*, this is the pattern of trochaic foot (or trochee) followed by iambic foot (or iamb), often found at the beginning of a line of pentameter, as in Shakespeare's sonnets, or after a pause (caesura) somewhere in the middle of the line. Shakespeare: "When in disgrace with fortune and men's eyes" (sonnet 29), "Like as the waves make toward the pebbled shore" (sonnet 60), "They that have pow'r to hurt and will do none" (sonnet 94).

To go all the way back: the first four syllables of the first line of Sophokles' famous "ode to man" (lines 332–75 in *Antigone*) instance this pattern: "polla ta deina kouden [. . .]." And it's still with us, and not at all absent from free verse, for Ezra Pound took it from metrical verse and used it as a rhythmic figure in free verse, and it seems to be a rhythmic figure inherent in English. And perhaps it needed no one poet or another to preserve its later use outside the context of meter. I would think that it is older than Greek, and persists because of something in the persistent rhythms of (some?) languages in the Indo-European family. It is part of how English works, anyway, even if it is not present in modern languages with rhythms not based on speech stress (like French). So we can easily hear the choriamb in contemporary poems, too, although its use is undoubtedly a result not of the poet's study but of careful listening, of tuning the poetic craft to our language. Some recent first lines: "Sheldon decided" (Sherman Alexie); "First your dog dies" (Kwame Dawes); "Cartloads of corn" (Campbell McGrath) (Duhamel 2013, 3, 29, 96). The rhythmic figure is present in English and simply awaits use (for instance, as a way of marking a strong beginning of a line).

There is some iambic rhythm in Williams' language (lines 1, 3, 14), for English itself is generally iambic, which is why iambic penta- | meter | has been | the met- | er dom- | inat- | ing po- | etry | in Eng- | lish. We | might say | it is | a rhy- | thm nat- | ural | to English. But in metrical poetry the iambic line is used as an abstract pattern with and against which the natural rhythms of English are organized in such a way as not to violate the abstract pattern too much while, at the same time, at least after the early poems of William Wordsworth and S. T. Coleridge, keeping the spoken language lively and natural. It's another version of the aural poetic dance, this time with speech and meter as partners, each gently pulling and pushing the other a bit to create a rhythm that is pleasurable rather than monotonous.

And in fact, Williams used another pattern that converts a metrical figure into a rhythmic one in his free verse, and, like the first, this one allows him to keep the iambic within hearing distance while not seeming to use it at all. I think this variation on the iambic foot was introduced into free verse as a discernable rhythmic figure by Ezra Pound ("and the slow feet," "on that swart ship" (Pound 2010, 31, 127). It's two unstressed syllables followed by two stressed ones. In meter, it sounds like this: in Shakespeare's sonnet 73, line 11, "As the death-bed whereon it must expire"; in John Keats's "Ode to Melancholy," line 13 (I italicize the figure, to make it more visible), "That fost*ers the droop-head*ed flowers all"; in William Butler Yeats's "Leda and the Swan," line 3, "By the dark webs, her nape *caught in his bill*" (I have italicized the choriamb of the last four words), and line 7, "And how can body, laid in that white rush" (and in that sonnet there's at least one more, and one that sounds like it is but isn't; this is a kind of syncopation by a master drummer) (Keats 1995, 197; Yeats 1997, 214). In Williams' poem, this rhythmic figure sounds like this: "into the lamp's horn" and "from the pot's rim."

And I should mention that the word "white" in line 1 and the words "wholly dark" in the next-to-last line subtly exemplify a frequently encountered ancient device of poetic structure called "ring composition," in which a phoneme (or several), a word, an image, or something else placed at the beginning is repeated at the end—or it is changed in a way that still makes the pairing perceptible; here it's an opposition of light with dark. And since the poem associates gaiety with the dark, it's also a reversal of a conventional idea that light is best and darkness worst. (This was the received idea at the heart of Greville's sonnet "In night when colors all to black are cast" and also the idea that Lord Edward Herbert subverted thoroughly in his "Sonnet of Black Beauty," both of which I quoted in chapter 4.)

Williams' stance toward writing poems was to use everyday life where other poets privileged high subjects, elevated language, classically or traditionally poetic proportions or shapes or forms, and European materials from the whole history of poetry and art. Williams wanted to redeem from neglect or lack of notice or conventional deprecation many objects and aspects of everyday life, to celebrate that which is modest, ordinary, even ugly, if it was alive to him and if it seemed *American* in some way. Hence his powerful, well-known poem, "By the road to the contagious hospital," also from *Spring and*

All. But is there something more than a touch of craft, a reader might ask, to link this poem with ancient ideas and practices of poetry? And I ask in return, is it too farfetched to attribute to the image of the living plant flush with bloom and green of leaf a faint trace of that which is "unwilting"? No persevering "fame" adheres to any human figure in this poem, and yet the green itself suggests something more than the leaf. The "crowns" of the victors in the four holy Greek athletic games were braided or woven of green leaves of the wild olive (Olympian victors), laurel (Pythian, at Delphi), green parsley (Nemean), and pine or dry parsley (Isthmian) (Race 1986, 19). These were signs of their having been favored by the gods, and, as the color green suggests, by life itself. In another imaginative quarter, Andrew Marvell imagined an eternal realm in which one can find that "green thought in a green shade" (see chap. 4). With the words "Verde que te quiero verde" (Green I so love you green), Lorca's famous gypsy horseman begins his life-sustaining monologue—we can think of him murmuring the poem's lines to himself or shouting them into the wind as he rides as fast as he can on horseback, after having been stabbed in a fight, and wanting to reach the young woman he loves, who is waiting for him. Green life is the object of desire, green life is what he loves in the woman, green is the color even of the wind as he is losing consciousness. The sheer force of Lorca's opening line has been alive in nearly everyone who has ever heard or read the poem in Spanish, even once (Diego 1962, 413).

Finally, I'll cite a few memorable words of Pindar again, from what's left of a song for a chorus of girls on some occasion when gods were honored. From Pindar's Partheneion 1, lines 14–15, here is another cicada (in Mandelshtam's sense): "Immortal for human beings, / some days, but the body is mortal." (In Greek, *athánatai dè brotois / hamérai, sōma d'estì **thnatón**.*) I have translated this into English in such a way as to preserve the most important aspect of the word order, so that it's clear in English too that the deeply felt human opposites "immortal" and "mortal" are at opposite ends of the sentence. "Human beings" (Greek *brotois*) falls at the end of the first of these two lines and then "days" (Greek *hamérai*) at the beginning of the second, just as in Greek, where this simultaneous *juxtaposition* in the sequence of words and *division* by the line break gives more poignance to the idea of the transience of "human days." What this tiny passage says is that "we do have our immortal days, but the human body is mortal."

In his poem, Williams is giving the mere transience of the light from a lamp on a short-lived flowering potted plant its immortal *moment*, and its (in a way, even in our world) immortal (even though known by only a few) *articulation* in a poem. This is what the poem implies without saying. Williams mythologizes the flowers, we might say. Words like "flame," "darkened," "glow," "flamegreen," "throats," "radiant," "transpiercing" can all be associated with the fragility of life and ideas of transcendence of mortality, whether by association with light, the source of which was once the god Helios and, in some more potent sense, Zeus himself, or by association with darkness, the Greek realm of death ruled by Hades. Mere moss is merely mortal, and in the pot, it too is short-lived. In Williams' poem, the mortal plants are given the very close attention which, in another era, would have been given to something self-evidently sacred (whether in a religious sense or a looser anthropological one). For Williams, the flowers and moss, and even the pot, are in fact to be treated as a sacred object; here the imagination, as Auden would say, is compelled to acknowledge them. And in rescuing the humble potted plant from oblivion, Williams performs an ancient poetic role, rescuing for a moment those of us who look at the potted plant with him. A moment (now immortalizing, in memory) for the plant, a moment for the reader or listener. *Athánatai dè brotois / hamérai, sōma d'estì thnatón.*

Acknowledgments

Earlier versions of chapters 1 through 5 were published in *American Poetry Review*; a small portion of my comment on Hélène Cixous is drawn from an essay published in *New Literary History*; the translation of Ilya Kutik's poem "Hunchback" and an earlier and much shorter version of my commentary on it were published in *Poetry* magazine. I am grateful to the editors of these journals for their interest in my work, especially to the late Stephen Berg, of *American Poetry Review*. I am grateful also to Provost Daniel Linzer and former dean Sarah Mangelsdorf at Northwestern University for research support. I thank Gail Browne and Frances Sjoberg for having invited me to give two lectures at the Poetry Center at the University of Arizona, some points of which eventually found their way into this book. With great affection, I send thanks to Ellen Bryant Voigt, Peter Turchi, and Debra Allbery of the MFA Program for Writers at Warren Wilson College, and to many fellow faculty and students there; with them I was able to try out some of these ideas and analyses in lectures before an audience that was always alert, exacting, and generous. I am grateful to Jay Barksdale of the New York Public Library for providing me with access to working space and borrowing privileges in the library's Wertheim Study, during several stays in that city, and to Matthew Santirocco for the same privileges at New York University's Institute for the Study of the Ancient World. I especially thank Gregory Nagy, the director of the Center for Hellenic Studies in Washington, DC, and the amiable and thoughtful CHS staff for a tremendously fruitful atmosphere and setting for research, thinking, and writing when I was at work there on the chapters that discuss ancient poetry. My thanks to Cornelia Spelman are without end.

To my colleague and fellow poet Ilya Kutik, who has helped me absorb some understanding of Russian poetic thinking into my English-language head, I owe tremendous thanks, which I gladly pay; it is obvious that chapter 3 owes a key illumination to him, and that chapters 4 and 5 began in my conversations with him about our translating Russian poems together; our collaboration led me to reread English and American poetry for instances of the apophatic. When Ilya and I eventually publish our joint project of translations of Russian poems, with accompanying essays, we hope we'll be able to help all English-language readers who have no Russian to see more of what's going on in the fascinating and dazzling poems of those Russian poets whose poetic thinking is so different from ours that rarely has it survived translation into English.

Poems that I quote in full are: Sappho's "Fragment 16" from *The Poetry of Sappho*, translated by Jim Powell (New York: Oxford University Press, 2007), © Jim Powell; "A Wreath" and "Remolding" by Yannis Ritsos, from *Ritsos in Parentheses*, translated by Edmund Keeley, © 1979 by Edmund Keeley, reprinted by permission of Princeton University Press; Arun Kolatkar's "The Priest's Son" published by *New York Review of Books*, © 1974 by Arun Kolatkar, all rights reserved; "At the Loom, *Passages 2*" by Robert Duncan, from *Bending the Bow*, © 1968 by Robert Duncan, reprinted by permission of New Directions Publishing Corp.; "Pink Confused with White" from "Spring and All" (Section 2) by William Carlos Williams, from *The Collected Poems, Volume I, 1909–1939*, © 1938 by New Directions Publishing Corp., reprinted by permission of New Directions Publishing Corp. and Carcanet Press Limited.

References

Adonis. 1990. *An Introduction to Arab Poetics*. Translated by Catherine
   Cobham. Austin: University of Texas Press.
———. 1994. *The Pages of Day and Night*. Translated by Samuel Hazo.
   Marlboro, VT: Marlboro Press.
———. 2010. *Selected Poems*. Translated by Khaled Mattawa. New Haven, CT:
   Yale University Press.
Agamben, Giorgio. 1999. *The End of the Poem: Studies in Poetics*. Translated by
   Daniel Heller-Roazen. Stanford, CA: Stanford University Press.
American Heritage Dictionary of Indo-European Roots. 2011. 3rd ed. Edited by
   Calvert Watkins. New York: Houghton Mifflin Harcourt.
Arnold, Elizabeth. 2010. *Effacement*. Chicago: Flood Editions.
Auden, W. H. 1968. *The Dyer's Hand*. New York: Vintage Books.
Barber, E. J. W. 1991. *Prehistoric Textiles: The Development of Cloth in the
   Neolithic and Bronze Ages*. Princeton, NJ: Princeton University Press.
Baudelaire, Charles. 1975. *Oeuvres Complètes*. Edited by Y.-G. Le Dantec and
   Claude Pichois. Paris: Gallimard.
———. 2013. *Writings on Hashish and Alcohol*. Elektron Books. E-book.
Bishop, Elizabeth. 1983. *The Complete Poems, 1927–1979*. New York: Farrar,
   Straus and Giroux.
Bollas, Christopher. 2002. *Cracking Up*. New York: Hill and Wang.
———. 2011. *The Christopher Bollas Reader*. New York: Routledge.
———. 2013. *Being a Character: Psychoanalysis and Self Experience*. New York:
   Routledge.
Bonnefoy, Yves. 2004. *Shakespeare and the French Poet*. Edited by John
   Naughton. Chicago: University of Chicago Press.
Borges, Jorge Luis. 2010. "Kafka and His Precursors." In *On Writing*, edited by
   Suzanne Jill Levine, 85–87. New York: Penguin Books.
Brewer, E. Cobham. 1898. *Dictionary of Phrase and Fable*. Accessed July 6, 2014.
   http://www.bartleby.com/81/.

Brodsky, Joseph. 1986. *Less Than One: Selected Essays.* New York: Farrar, Straus and Giroux. See esp. "The Child of Civilization" (on Mandelshtam), "A Poet and Prose" (on Tsvetaeva), and "Footnote to a Poem" (also on Tsvetaeva).

———. 1995. *On Grief and Reason.* New York: Farrar, Straus and Giroux. See esp. "An Immodest Proposal" and "Wooing the Inanimate."

———. 2000. *Collected Poems in English.* New York: Farrar, Straus and Giroux.

Brooks, Gwendolyn. 1987. *Blacks.* Chicago: The David Company.

Brown, Clarence. 1978. *Mandelstam.* Cambridge: Cambridge University Press.

Bunting, Basil. 1994. *The Complete Poems.* Edited by Richard Caddel. Oxford: Oxford University Press.

Campbell, David A. 1988. *Greek Lyric II: Anacreon, Anacreonta, Choral Lyric from Olympus to Alcman.* Loeb Classical Library. Cambridge, MA: Harvard University Press.

———. 1992. *Greek Lyric IV: Bacchylides, Corinna, and Others.* Loeb Classical Library. Cambridge, MA: Harvard University Press.

———. 2003. *Greek Lyric Poetry.* London: Bristol Classical Press. Originally published 1982.

Celan, Paul. 1975. *Gedichte.* Vol. 2. Frankfurt, Ger.: Suhrkamp Verlag.

———. 2001. *Selected Poems and Prose of Paul Celan.* Translated by John Felstiner. New York: W. W. Norton.

Cixous, Hélène. 1991. "The Author in Truth." In *"Coming to Writing" and Other Essays,* edited by Deborah Jenson, translated by Sarah Cornell, Ann Liddle, Susan Sellers, and Susan Rubin Suleiman, 1–58. Cambridge, MA: Harvard University Press.

———. 1993a. *Three Steps on the Ladder of Writing.* Translated by Sarah Cornell and Susan Sellers. New York: Columbia University Press.

———. 1993b. "We Who Are Free, Are We Free?" (excerpted). *Critical Inquiry* 19 (2): 201–19.

———. 1998. "Writing Blind." In *Stigmata: Escaping Texts,* 139–52. New York: Routledge.

Cixous, Hélène, and Mireille Calle-Gruber. 1997. *Rootprints.* Translated by Eric Prenowitz. New York: Routledge.

Coleridge, Samuel Taylor. 1957. *The Notebooks of Samuel Taylor Coleridge.* Vol. 1, *1794–1804.* Edited by Kathleen Coburn. Princeton, NJ: Princeton University Press.

———. 2002. *Coleridge's Notebooks: A Selection.* Edited by Seamus Perry. Oxford: Oxford University Press.

Cruz, Víctor Hernández. 2001. *Maraca: New and Selected Poems, 1965–2000.* Minneapolis, MN: Coffee House Press.

Curtius, Ernst Robert. 1963. *European Literature and the Latin Middle Ages.* New York: Harper and Row.

Darwish, Mahmoud. 2003. *Unfortunately, It Was Paradise.* Translated by Munir Akash and Carolyn Forché. Berkeley: University of California Press.

————. 2009. *If I Were Another*. Translated by Fady Joudah. New York: Farrar, Straus and Giroux.

David, A. P. 2006. *The Dance of the Muses: Choral Theory and Ancient Greek Poetics*. Oxford: Oxford University Press.

Davie, Donald. 1972. *Collected Poems, 1950–1970*. New York: Oxford University Press.

————. 1982. *Ezra Pound*. Chicago: University of Chicago Press. Originally published 1975.

————. 1977. *The Poet in the Imaginary Museum: Essays of Two Decades*. Edited by Barry Alpert. Manchester, UK: Carnanet.

————. 1979. *Trying to Explain*. Ann Arbor: University of Michigan Press.

————. 1982. *These the Companions: Recollections*. Cambridge: Cambridge University Press.

————. 1990. *Collected Poems*. Chicago: University of Chicago Press.

————. 2004. *Modernist Essays: Yeats, Pound, Eliot*. Edited by Clive Wilmer. Manchester, UK: Carnanet.

Davis, Dick. 2002. "All My Soul Is There: Verse Translation and the Rhetoric of English Poetry." *Yale Review* 90 (1): 66–83.

Dickinson, Emily. 1999. *The Poems of Emily Dickinson*. Edited by R. W. Franklin. Cambridge, MA: Harvard University Press.

Diego, Gerardo, ed. 1962. *Poesía española contemporáea (1901–1934)*. Madrid: Taurus.

Dionysius of Halicarnassus. 1985. "On Literary Composition." In *Dionysius of Halicarnassus: Critical Essays*, vol. 2, *On Literary Composition. Dinarchus. Letters to Ammaeus and Pompeius*, translated by Stephen Usher, 3–243. Loeb Classical Library. Cambridge, MA: Harvard University Press.

Donne, John. 2000. *Major Works*. Edited by John Carey. Oxford: Oxford University Press.

Douglass, Frederick. 1982. *Narrative of the Life of Frederick Douglass, An American Slave*. New York: Penguin.

Duhamel, Denise, ed. 2013. *The Best American Poetry, 2013*. New York: Scribner Poetry.

Duncan, Robert. 1968. *Bending the Bow*. New York: New Directions.

————. (1969) 1989. "Notes on Poetic Form." In *The Poet's Work: 29 Poets on the Origins and Practice of Their Art*, edited by Reginald Gibbons, 260–62. Chicago: University of Chicago Press.

Eliot, T. S. 1960. "Tradition and the Individual Talent." In *The Sacred Wood*, 47–59. London: Methuen.

Elytis, Odysseus. 2004. *The Collected Poems of Odysseus Elytis*. Translated by Jeffrey Carson and Nikos Sarris. Baltimore: Johns Hopkins University Press.

Euripides. 2009. *Bacchae [Bakkhai]*. Translated by Reginald Gibbons and Charles Segal. In *The Complete Euripides*, vol. 4, *Bacchae and Other Plays*, edited by Peter Burian and Alan Shapiro, 197–346. New York: Oxford University Press.

Florensky, Pavel. 1996. *Iconostasis*. Translated by Donald Sheehan and Olga Andrejev. Crestwood, NY: St. Vladimir's Seminary Press.

Fowler, Alastair, ed. 1992. *The New Oxford Book of Seventeenth-Century Verse*. Oxford: Oxford University Press.

Freud, Sigmund. 1955. *Beyond the Pleasure Principle*. In *The Standard Edition of the Complete Psychological Works of Sigmund Freud*, vol. 18, 1920–1922, edited by J. Strachey, 7–64. New York: Vintage.

———. 1959. *Collected Papers*. Vol. 5, *Miscellaneous Papers, 1888–1938*. Edited by James Strachey. New York: Basic Books.

Gardner, Helen, ed. 1967. *The Metaphysical Poets*. New York: Penguin.

Gerber, Douglas E. 2002. *A Commentary on Pindar Olympian Nine*. Stuttgart, Ger.: Steiner.

Gibbons, Reginald, ed. 1989. *The Poet's Work: 29 Poets on the Origins and Practice of Their Art*. Chicago: University of Chicago Press.

Gibbons, Reginald, and Terrence Des Pres, eds. 1992. *Thomas McGrath: Life and the Poem*. Champaign: University of Illinois Press.

Ginsberg, Allen. 1986. *Howl*. Edited by Barry Miles. New York: Harper and Row.

Goethe, Johann Wolfgang von. 2012. *Poems of Goethe*. Edited by Ronald Gray. Cambridge: Cambridge University Press.

Goyen, William. 1975. *The Collected Stories of William Goyen*. New York: Doubleday.

———. 2000. *The House of Breath*. Evanston, IL: Northwestern University Press. Restored original 1950 edition.

———. 2007. *Goyen: Autobiographical Essays, Notebooks, Evocations, Interviews*. Edited by Reginald Gibbons. Austin: University of Texas Press.

Greville, Fulke. 2009. *The Selected Poems of Fulke Greville*. Edited by Thom Gunn. Chicago: University of Chicago Press. Originally published 1968.

Hadas, Pamela White. 1998. *Self-Evidence: A Selection of Verse, 1977–1997*. Evanston, IL: TriQuarterly Books/Northwestern University Press.

Halliwell, Stephen. 2011. *Between Ecstasy and Truth: Interpretations of Greek Poetics from Homer to Longinus*. Oxford: Oxford University Press.

Hayden, Robert. 2013. *Collected Poems*. Edited by Frederick Glaysher. New York: Liveright.

Heaney, Seamus. (1979) 1989. "Feelings into Words." In *The Poet's Work: 29 Poets on the Origins and Practice of Their Art*, edited by Reginald Gibbons, 263–82. Chicago: University of Chicago Press.

———. 2010. *Human Chain*. New York: Farrar, Straus and Giroux.

Herbert, George. 2004. *The Complete English Poems*. Edited by John Tobin. New York: Penguin.

Herbert, Zbigniew. 2007. *The Collected Poems*. Translated and edited by Alissa Valles. New York: Ecco/HarperCollins.

Herington, John. 1985. *Poetry into Drama: Early Tragedy and the Greek Poetic Tradition*. Berkeley: University of California Press.

Homer. 1967. *The Odyssey of Homer.* Translated by Richmond Lattimore. New York: Harper and Row.

———. 2003. *Iliad.* 2 vols. Translated by A. T. Murray. Revised by William F. Wyatt. Loeb Classical Library. Cambridge, MA: Harvard University Press.

Hopkins, Gerard Manley. 1959. *The Journals and Papers of Gerard Manley Hopkins.* Edited by Humphrey House. Completed by Graham Storey. London: Oxford University Press.

———. 1992. *The Poetical Works of Gerard Manley Hopkins.* Edited by Norman MacKenzie. Oxford: Clarendon Press.

Hutchinson, G. O. 2001. *Greek Lyric Poetry: A Commentary on Selected Larger Pieces.* Oxford: Oxford University Press.

Jackson, Angela. 1998. *And All These Roads Be Luminous: Poems Selected and New.* Evanston, IL: TriQuarterly Books/Northwestern University Press.

Jakobson, Roman. 1981. "Linguistics and Poetics." In *Selected Writings,* vol. 3, *Poetry of Grammar and Grammar of Poetry,* edited by Stephen Rudy, 18–51. The Hague, Neth.: Mouton Publishers.

Jarrell, Randall. 1969. *The Complete Poems.* New York: Farrar, Straus and Giroux.

Jeffers, Robinson. 2000. *The Collected Poetry of Robinson Jeffers.* Vol. 4, *Poetry 1903–1920, Prose, and Unpublished Writings.* Edited by Tim Hunt. Stanford, CA: Stanford University Press.

Juan de la Cruz. 1991. *Obra Completa.* 2 vol. Edited by Luce López-Baralt and Eulogio Pacho. Madrid: Alianza Editorial.

Keats, John. 1995. *Selected Poems and Letters.* Selection by Robert Gittings. Oxford: Heinemann.

Kharms, Daniil, and Alexander Vvedensky. 1987. *The Man with the Black Coat: Russia's Literature of the Absurd.* Edited and translated by George Gibian. Evanston, IL: Northwestern University Press. (For more Kharms, also see Eugene Ostashevsky, ed., *Oberiu: An Anthology of Russian Absurdism* [Evanston, IL: Northwestern University Press, 2006].)

Kirk, G. S., and J. E. Raven. 1957. *The Presocratic Philosophers.* Cambridge: Cambridge University Press.

Klinkenborg, Verlyn. 2007. "The City Life: Remembered Spaces." *New York Times,* July 17.

Kolatkar, Arun. 2005. *Jejuri.* New York: New York Review Books.

Kutik, Ilya. 2006. "Hunchback." Translated by Reginald Gibbons and the author. *Poetry,* April.

———. 2007. "The Age and Courage of Evgeny Baratynsky" and commentaries on poems by Baratynsky. Translated by Peter France. *Fulcrum,* no. 7, 503–14, 535–69. Issue dated 2007 but published 2011.

Levertov, Denise. (1965) 1989. "Some Notes on Organic Form." In *The Poet's Work: 29 Poets on the Origins and Practice of Their Art,* edited by Reginald Gibbons, 254–59. Chicago: University of Chicago Press.

Liddell, H. G., and R. Scott. 1996. *A Greek-English Lexicon*. Revised by H. S. Jones. Oxford: Oxford University Press.

Livingstone, Angela. 2014. "Donald Davie and Boris Pasternak: Essex and Russia." *Memory Maps* (Victoria and Albert Museum web series). Accessed June 17. http://www.vam.ac.uk/content/articles/m/memory-maps -donald-davie-and-boris-pasternak-essex-and-russia/.

Lossky, Vladimir. 1957. *The Mystical Theology of the Eastern Church*. London: James Clark.

Loy, Mina. 1997. *The Lost Lunar Baedeker*. Edited by Roger L. Conover. New York: Farrar, Straus and Giroux.

Machado, Antonio. (1964) 1989. "From 'Notes on Poetry.'" In *The Poet's Work: 29 Poets on the Origins and Practice of Their Art*, edited by Reginald Gibbons, 161–69. Chicago: University of Chicago Press. Text first published in 1964 but composed approximately 40 years earlier.

Mackey, Nathaniel. 2006. *Splay Anthem*. New York: New Directions.

Mallarmé, Stéphane. 1959. *Selected Poems*. Translated by C. F. MacIntyre. Berkeley: University of California Press.

Mandelstam, Osip. 1977. *Osip Mandelstam: Selected Essays*. Translated by Sidney Monas. Austin: University of Texas Press.

———. 1979. *The Complete Critical Prose and Letters*. Edited by Jane Gary Harris. Ann Arbor, MI: Ardis.

———. 1996. *The Voronezh Notebooks: Poems, 1935–1937*. Translated by Richard and Elizabeth McKane. Newcastle-Upon-Tyne, UK: Bloodaxe Books.

———. 2004. *Selected Poems of Osip Mandelstam*. Translated by Clarence Brown and W. S. Merwin. New York: NYR Books Classics. Reprint of 1974 edition.

Maxwell, William. 1996. *So Long, See You Tomorrow*. New York: Vintage.

McCarriston, Linda. 2002. *Little River: New and Selected Poems*. Evanston, IL: Northwestern University Press.

McGrath, Thomas. 1997. *Letter to an Imaginary Friend*. Port Townsend, WA: Copper Canyon Press.

Mehrota, Arvind Krishna. 2007. "Death of a Poet." *Fulcrum*, no. 7, 49–79. Issue dated 2007 but published 2011.

Nagy, Gregory. 1974. *Comparative Studies in Greek and Indic Meter*. Cambridge, MA: Harvard University Press.

———. 1990. *Pindar's Homer: The Lyric Possession of an Epic Past*. Baltimore: Johns Hopkins University Press.

———. 1996. *Poetry as Performance: Homer and Beyond*. Cambridge: Cambridge University Press.

———. 1999. *The Best of the Achaeans*. Baltimore: Johns Hopkins University Press. Reprint of 1979 edition.

———. 2002. *Plato's Rhapsody and Homer's Music: The Poetics of the Panathenaic Festival in Classical Athens*. Washington, DC: Center for Hellenic Studies.

————. 2012. *Homer the Preclassic*. Berkeley: University of California.

————. 2013. *The Ancient Greek Hero in 24 Hours*. Cambridge, MA: Harvard University Press.

Nerval, Gerard de. 1993. *Oeuvres Complètes*. Vol. 3. Edited by Jean Guillaume and Claude Pichois, with the collaboration of Jacques Bony, Michel Brix, Antonia Fonyi, Lieven d' Hulst, Vincenette Pichois, Jean-Luc Steinmetz et Jean Ziegler. Paris: Gallimard.

Niedecker, Lorine. 2004. *Collected Works*. Edited by Jenny Penberthy. Berkeley: University of California Press.

Notley, Alice. 2013. "At the Mercy of My Poetic Voice: An Interview with Alice Notley." By Lindsay Turner. *Boston Review*. Accessed January 13, 2014. http://www.bostonreview.net/poetry/lindsay-turner-alice-notley -interview-feminism-mojave-collage.

Patten, Glenn. 2009. *Pindar's Metaphors: A Study in Rhetoric and Meaning*. Heidelberg, Ger.: Universitätsverlag Winter.

Pausanias. 1979. *Guide to Greece*. 2 vols. Translated by Peter Levi. New York: Penguin.

Pindar. 1997. *Pindar*. 2 vols. Edited and translated by William H. Race. Loeb Classical Library. Cambridge, MA: Harvard University Press.

Plutarch, 1960. *The Rise and Fall of Athens: Nine Greek Lives*. Translated by Ian Scott-Kilvert. London: Penguin.

Pokorny. 2014. "Indo-European Lexicon: Pokorny Master PIE Etyma." Accessed October 5. http://www.utexas.edu/cola/centers/lrc/ielex/.

Pope, Alexander. 1961. *The Twickenham Edition of the Poems of Alexander Pope*. Vol. 1. *Pastoral Poetry and an Essay on Criticism*. Edited by E. Audra and Aubrey Williams. New Haven, CT: Yale University Press.

————. 1988. *Selected Poetry and Prose*. Edited by Robin Sowerby. New York: Routledge.

Pound, Ezra. 1963. *Translations*. New York: New Directions.

————. 1973. *Selected Prose, 1909–1965*. Edited by William Cookson. New York: New Directions.

————. 1986. *The Cantos of Ezra Pound*. New York: New Directions.

————. 2010. *New Selected Poems and Translations*. Edited by Richard Sieburth. New York: New Directions.

Princeton Encyclopedia of Poetry & Poetics. 2012. Edited by Roland Greene, Stephen Cushman, Clare Cavanagh, Jahan Ramazani, and Paul Rouzer, with Harris Feinsod, David Marno, and Alexandra Slessarev. 4th ed. Princeton, NJ: Princeton University Press.

Proffer, Carl R., ed. 1976. *Modern Russian Poets on Poetry*. Selected and introduced by Joseph Brodsky. Ann Arbor, MI: Ardis.

Pseudo-Dionysius the Areopagite. 1920. "The Mystical Theology." In *Dionysius the Areopagite On the Divine Names and the Mystical Theology*, translated by C. E. Rolt, 200–201. London: Society for Promoting Christian Knowledge;

New York: Macmillan. Accessed July 1, 2014. https://archive.org/stream /dionysiusareopag00pseu#page/200/mode/2up.

Race, William H. 1990. *Style and Rhetoric in Pindar's Odes*. Atlanta, GA: Scholars Press.

———. 1986. *Pindar*. Boston: Twayne.

Ritsos, Yannis. 1979. *Ritsos in Parentheses*. Translated by Edmund Keeley. Princeton, NJ: Princeton University Press.

Rukeyser, Muriel. 1992. *Out of Silence: Selected Poems*. Edited by Kate Daniels. Evanston, IL: TriQuarterly Books.

Sainte-Beuve, Charles-Augustin. 1880. "Les cinq derniers mois de la vie de Racine." In *Nouveux Lundis*, 10:356–92. Paris. Accessed July 20, 2014. http://gallica.bnf.fr/ark:/12148/bpt6k2014120.r=sainte-beuve+%22les +cinq+derniers+mois+de+la+vie+de+racine%22.langEN.swf.

Sappho. 2007. *The Poetry of Sappho*. Translated by Jim Powell. New York: Oxford University Press.

Scheid, John, and Jesper Svenbro. 1996. *The Craft of Zeus: Myths of Weaving and Fabric*. Translated by Carol Volk. Cambridge, MA: Harvard University Press.

Scherr, Barry. 1986. *Russian Poetry: Meter, Rhythm and Rhyme*. Berkeley: University of California Press.

Shakespeare, William. 2005. *Shakespeare's Sonnets*. Edited by Katherine Duncan-Jones. London: Arden Shakespeare.

Shapiro, Karl. (1960) 1989. "What Is Not Poetry?" In *The Poet's Work: 29 Poets on the Origins and Practice of Their Art*, edited by Reginald Gibbons, 92–109. Chicago: University of Chicago Press.

Snyder, Gary. 1965. *Six Sections from Mountains and Rivers without End*. San Francisco, CA: Four Seasons Foundation.

———. 1996. *Mountains and Rivers without End*. Washington, DC: Counterpoint.

Sophocles. 1998. *Antigone*. Edited and translated by Hugh Lloyd-Jones. Loeb Classical Library. Cambridge, MA: Harvard University Press.

———. 2008. *Selected Poems: Odes and Fragments*. Translated by Reginald Gibbons. Princeton, NJ: Princeton University Press.

———. 2011. *Antigone*. Translated by Reginald Gibbons and Charles Segal. In *The Complete Sophocles*, vol. 1, *The Theban Plays*, edited by Peter Burian and Alan Shapiro, 1–190. New York: Oxford University Press.

Stevens, Wallace. 1974. *The Collected Poems of Wallace Stevens*. New York: Alfred A. Knopf.

———. 1990. *Opus Posthumous*. Edited by Milton J. Bates. New York: Vintage Books.

Terrell, Carroll F. 1993. *A Companion to the Cantos of Ezra Pound*. Berkeley: University of California Press.

Tolstoy, Leo. 2008. *War and Peace*. Translated by Richard Pevear and Larissa Volokhonsky. New York: Vintage.

Tretheway, Natasha. 2012. *Thrall*. New York: Houghton Mifflin Harcourt.

Tuck, Anthony. 2006. "Singing the Rug: Patterned Textiles and the Origins of Indo-European Metrical Poetry." *American Journal of Archeology* 110 (4): 539–50.

Vallejo, César. 1988. *Obra Poética*. Edited by Américo Ferrari. Madrid: Colección Archivos.

Virgil. 1997. *Virgil's Aeneid*. Translated by John Dryden. New York: Penguin.

Voigt, Ellen Bryant. 2013. *Headwaters*. New York: Norton.

Wachtel, Michael. 2004. *Cambridge Introduction to Russian Poetry*. Cambridge: Cambridge University Press.

Watkins, Calvert. 1994. "Language of Gods and Language of Men: Remarks on Some Indo-European Metalinguistic Traditions." In *Selected Writings*, vol. 2, *Culture and Poetics*, edited by Lisi Oliver, 456–72. Innsbruck, Austria: Innsbrucker Beiträge zur Sprachwissenschaft.

———. 1995. *How to Kill a Dragon: Aspects of Indo-European Poetics*. New York: Oxford University Press. See esp. "The Field of Comparative Poetics: Introduction and Background," 3–96.

Weigl, Bruce. 2012. *The Abundance of Nothing*. Evanston, IL: Northwestern University Press.

Weiner, Joshua. 2013. *The Figure of a Man Being Swallowed by a Fish*. Chicago: University of Chicago Press.

White, Patrick. 1994. *Voss*. New York: Knopf Doubleday. Originally published in 1957.

Whitman, Walt. 1982. *Complete Poetry and Collected Prose*. Edited by Justin Kaplan. New York: Library of America.

Williams, C. K. 1983. *Tar*. New York: Random House.

Williams, William Carlos. 2011. *Spring and All*. New York: New Directions.

Wordsworth, William. 1979. *The Prelude: 1799, 1805, 1850*. Edited by Jonathan Wordsworth, M. H. Abrams, and Stephen Gill. New York: W. W. Norton.

———. 1994. "'Preface' from *Lyrical Ballads* (2 vols., 1802)." In *Romanticism: An Anthology*. Edited by Duncan Wu, 250–69. Oxford: Blackwell.

Yeats, William Butler. 1997. *The Collected Works of W. B. Yeats*. Vol. 1, *The Poems*. 2nd ed. Edited by Richard J. Finneran. New York: Simon and Schuster.

Index

Except for a very few of the most familiar ancient Greek names (e.g., Helen, Homer, Hesiod), Greek names are indexed by the English transliteration followed by the Latinized version in parentheses—for example, "Sophokles (Sophocles)." Since quotations in the text may use the Latinized version, any such name may appear in the text in either spelling.

kharis/Kharis (Grace), 163, 164, 167, 189, 204, 214
Kharms, Daniil, 116
Kinnell, Galway, 24
Kirkē (Circe), 14, 143, 151, 153, 155–58, 171, 172, 174, 176
kleos (heroic fame; poem of fame), 133, 143, 151, 156, 162, 174, 183, 184, 194, 195, 208, 218
Klinkenborg, Verlyn, 87
Kolatkar, Arun, 103–4, 117
Kunene, Mazisi, 72
Kutik, Ilya, 3, 6, 7, 10, 13, 67–72, 73, 74–78, 80, 81–86, 97, 105, 107–9, 112, 115, 121, 221, 222

Laforgue, Jules, 29, 192
Larkin, Philip, 24
Latin, 2, 12, 14, 19, 20, 26, 31, 39, 59, 95, 96, 132, 140, 148, 153, 171, 179, 180–82, 183, 187, 191, 195, 196
Leonardo da Vinci, 187
Leonidas of Tarentum, 153
Levertov, Denise, 16, 97–98, 200
libation, 136, 139, 148, 183
Lincoln, Abraham, 93
Lipking, Lawrence, 170
Lispector, Clarice, 36
Livingstone, Angela, 8
Lomonosov, Mikhail, 68
Longinus, 16
loom. *See* weaving
Lorca. *See* García Lorca, Federico
Lossky, Vladimir, 113, 114, 115, 121
Lowell, Robert, 15, 107–9, 118–21
Loy, Mina, 30, 176, 179
Loyola, Saint Ignatius of, 93

MacDiarmid, Hugh, 24–25
Machado, Antonio, 15, 81, 164
MacKenzie, Norman, 178
Mackey, Nathaniel, 142
Madrid, Anthony, 145
Mallarmé, Stéphane, 7, 15, 30, 34, 81, 192
Malraux, André, 3

Mandelshtam, Nadezhda, 2, 184
Mandelshtam, Osip, 2, 3, 6–7, 8, 10, 14, 34, 58, 63–64, 64–65, 67, 69, 72–74, 76, 78, 82, 85, 96, 113, 120–21, 125–26, 131, 150, 160, 184, 218
Mann, Thomas, 25
Marcuse, Herbert, 23
Marvell, Andrew, 90, 96, 98, 218
Masters, Edgar Lee, 153
Maxwell, William, 44–46, 211
Mayakovsky, Vladimir, 85
McCarriston, Linda, 95, 186–87, 204
McGrath, Campbell, 216
McGrath, Thomas, 64
memory, 3, 6, 15, 21, 28, 33–34, 38, 42, 45, 46, 59, 79, 89, 101, 102, 108, 109, 116, 121, 130, 131, 132, 133, 134, 136, 140, 144, 149, 151, 158, 159, 160, 163, 166, 171, 174–75, 182, 183–88, 190, 191, 194, 195, 206, 207, 208, 209, 219
Merwin, W. S., 16
metaphor, 3, 5, 6, 7, 12, 17, 26, 34, 38, 40, 49, 60, 61, 68, 71–75, 76, 81–83, 90, 92, 98, 105, 108, 109, 112, 113, 116, 117, 118, 119, 125, 126, 130, 136, 137, 139, 143, 148, 151–55, 159–60, 163, 165, 167–68, 170, 174, 181, 182, 183–84, 186, 190, 194, 195, 206, 207
Metarealism/metarealists, 71–72, 74–76, 80, 81, 86, 105, 111, 112, 192
meter, 17, 22, 52, 62, 78, 79, 86, 112, 120, 140, 141, 145, 146–49, 158–59, 163, 165, 169, 200, 215–17
metonym/metonymy, 12, 35, 45, 49, 54, 88, 105, 108, 116, 121, 126, 150, 151, 153, 159, 165, 179, 182, 189, 190, 195, 200, 207
Millner, Jesse, 145
Miłosz, Czesław, 51–52
Mnemosyne/mnemonic. *See* memory
Monk, Thelonius, 191
Moore, Marianne, 30
Morrison, Toni, 211
motive (magazine), 25
Muse(s), 4, 38, 47, 51, 53, 85, 131, 134, 137,

139, 142, 143, 151, 154, 159, 162, 164,
165, 194, 205, 207, 208

Nagy, Gregory, 13, 38, 142, 152, 154, 160,
167, 183–84, 194, 197, 207, 209, 221
Neoplatonism, 12, 93
Neruda, Pablo, 15, 16
Nerval, Gérard de, 139, 192, 197, 199–201
neurolinguists, 11, 62
Niebuhr, Reinhold, 25
Niedecker, Lorine, 142
nightingale, 65, 150–51, 152, 154
Noah, 69
Notley, Alice, 132
Nurkse, D., 145

obscurity, 17, 27, 28, 134, 177, 197, 201–3
ode, choral, 7, 52, 65, 79, 80, 127, 129,
130, 131–32, 137, 151, 154, 155, 161–65,
167, 186, 189, 198, 205–9, 210–11, 216.
See also song
Odysseus, 156–58, 170, 171, 184
Old English, 70, 179–82, 185, 187
Olson, Charles, 24, 97
Opie, Iona and Peter, 59
Oppen, George, 24
Oulipo, 61
Ovid, 167

Page, D. L., 210
Paley, Grace, 48
Paris (Trojan prince), 6
Parker, Charlie, 191
paronomasia, 2, 32, 35, 138
Parra, Nicanor, 18
Parshchikov, Alexei, 69, 97, 111
Pasternak, Boris, 8, 69, 73, 76, 82, 109,
120, 125–26
Patten, Glenn, 206–7
Pausanias, 137
Penelope, 151
Perec, Georges, 61
Pessoa, Fernando, 49
Phaiakians (Phaeacians), 14, 156, 157
phonetic figure, 2, 29, 30, 32, 58, 59, 61,

63, 64, 65, 66, 67, 70, 73, 75, 76, 80,
81, 82, 83, 85, 115, 118, 127, 135, 140,
141, 142, 146, 159, 164, 168, 184, 185,
215, 217
Pindar, 5, 12, 52, 70, 79, 130, 131, 132, 137,
140, 151–52, 154, 155, 161–67, 170, 177–
78, 182, 183, 186, 189, 194, 198, 200,
203, 205–9, 210–11, 214, 215, 218
Plath, Sylvia, 132
Plato/Platonism, 25, 26, 29, 31, 32, 97,
105, 134, 145
Plotinus, 105
Plutarch, 132
Poe, Edgar Allan, 7
poetic self, 108, 166, 167, 209–12
Pokorny, Julius, 14, 38
Ponge, Francis, 33
Pope, Alexander, 142, 169–70
Pound, Ezra, 5, 8, 15, 16, 23, 29, 30, 88,
89, 132, 148, 151, 153, 154, 155, 160, 171,
172, 174, 181, 201, 210, 216, 217
Powell, Jim, 100–101
Proto-Indo-European, 5, 14, 38, 52, 60,
148, 173
Pseudo-Dionysius the Areopagite,
93–94
Pushkin, Alexander, 75, 81, 85

Queneau, Raymond, 61
quotation. *See* citation

Race, William, 131, 206, 218
Racine, Jean, 31, 201
recollection. *See* memory
remembrance. *See* memory
Rexroth, Kenneth, 15
rhapsode, 38, 61, 130, 131, 152
rhyme, 10, 58–86, 92, 112, 118–20, 127,
159, 161, 164, 169, 184, 200, 201; centrifugal, 10, 68, 78, 82, 119 (*see also*
centrifugal movement of thought);
centripetal, 68, 78; rhyming to death,
62
rhythm, 2, 26, 29, 48, 49, 52, 61, 66, 70,
84, 86, 122, 126, 132, 135, 136, 140, 141,